Getting Off the Radiator

[left] Mom in the late 1930s with her first car, a Model T named "Big Bertha." "Her friends would pile into the car, some even riding on the running boards, and they would drive all over town. Mom was the popular girl in town, having come from one of the more wealthy families."

[below] In March 2004 all of us flew to Arizona for Dad's 80th birthday. It was the first time in many years we'd all been together. Back: Brian, Paula, John, Michael; front: Beth, Ann, and I (Dorothy).

Getting Off the Radiator

A Story of Shame, Guilt, & Forgiveness

Dorothy Preston

SHANTI ARTS PUBLISHING
BRUNSWICK, MAINE

Getting Off the Radiator

A Story of Shame, Guilt, & Forgiveness

Published by Shanti Arts Publishing
Interior and cover design by Shanti Arts Designs

Shanti Arts LLC
193 Hillside Road
Brunswick, Maine 04011
shantiarts.com

Shanti Arts is committed to producing quality books that are engaging and memorable. We are proud to offer this book as part of that commitment. This book is a memoir, written from the author's present recollections of experiences that occurred over many years. She relied on personal memory as well as interviews with family and friends, excerpts from her father's memoirs, personal letters, and other research. The dialogue presented in this book is not intended to represent word-for-word transcripts; events and scenes are not precise representations. Rather, the author has tried to cast them in a way that evokes the feeling and meaning of what was said. In all instances, the essence of the conversation is accurate. The names and characteristics of some individuals have been changed, but only when doing so had no impact on the veracity and substance of the story. The author's writing is based on her understanding and interpretation of events that happened. Another person might remember and write it differently, but this author has tried to remain faithful to her own experience. Her motives are clean. Everything here is true, but it may not be entirely factual.

ISBN: 978-1-951651-86-2 (softcover)
ISBN: 978-1-951651-87-9 (ebook)

Library of Congress Control Number: 2021939475

To all the special mothers who touched my life:
Elizabeth Jane Paul (Preston) Franklin
Mary Napolitan
Doris Deliso
Elizabeth Zanetti
Angie Durkin
Isabel Spaziani
Carol Duchesneau

and to my brother John (1945-2021), "I hope you dance"

Tower in the Sky

Farewell to you and the youth I have spent with you.
It was but yesterday we met in a dream.
You have sung to me, in my aloneness,
and I of your longings, have built a
Tower in the sky.
But now our sleep has fled, and our dream is over
And it is no longer dawn!
The noontide is upon us and our half waking has turned to a fuller day,
and we must part.
If, in the twilight of memory, we should meet once more, we shall speak
again together, and you shall sing to me a deeper song!
And if our hands should meet in another dream,
we shall build another
Tower in the sky.

—Elizabeth Jane Paul Preston

Contents

Acknowledgments

Thank you to the many people who helped me through this process. To my siblings, thank you for putting up with myriad questions and interviews, and the pain that reliving this may have caused. You have always been there for me, through all the joys and all the sorrows. I love each and every one of you!

To "AnnMaria," who took on the "Mom" role and kept us all close. To Beth, my chum through it all, thanks for all our great adventures, may there be many more to come. To Paula, who always treated me like "her baby" even when she had her own. To my brother John, who passed during the writing of this book; may you dance in heaven with Mom, knowing how much we all love and miss you both. To Brian, whom I have grown so close to in my older age; happy flying to you and Ruth who both seem forever young! To Michael, my hero; thank you for always being there for me and for your adorable sense of humor!

To my children, Timothy and Heather, you have taught me the greatest lessons in life. You are my heart and my soul.

To my wonderful husband, Peter, who has put up with my "nose being buried in the computer" for upwards of three years. Thank you for your kind, loving support.

To all of my wonderful nieces and nephews who will carry on the Preston name and Mom's legacy.

To Kevin Phillips and Rhonda Spaziani, my best and dearest friends to this day; Kevin, you helped guide me and push me when I needed it most throughout my life; and Rhonda, my rock and confidant. We sure were Cowgirls, then...! I luff you, Mary! To Carole Duchesneau, Gina Zanetti, and those who wish to remain nameless—I love you all! To Teddy and Angie Durkin who helped glue me back together after Ray's death. To Bob Bopp, who resurfaced during the writing of this book and whose kind and helpful feedback was extremely appreciated. To Traci Sobocinski, whose guidance helped me find my voice and who drove me like a drill sergeant whenever I got lazy. To Mark Malatesta, whose amazing coaching and guidance I could not have done without. Thank you so much for your patience and help!

And very special thanks goes out to Carolyn Artin, my dear friend and editor extraordinaire, who generously volunteered her time to help with copy editing my manuscript more than once. Thank you, thank you, and thank you!!

And lastly to Mom, who taught me loyalty, how to love and how to forgive. I will love you forever!

[top] Mom and Dad in their happy years.

[top right] Mom and Dad in 1955; they look very much in love in Venezuela.

[bottom] Dad, Michael, John, Brian, Ann, and Mom return to the Buena Vista home in 1962 with the Christmas tree on the car roof.

Part I

SILK STOCKINGS

(The Early Years)

Mom and Dad bought the twenty-eight-room house on Buena Vista Plaza in 1960 before I was born for $20,000. "The number of rooms in our house was always a topic of conjecture. It really depended on what you actually counted as a room." Comparing this to the image below, it's clear that many renovations were done to the house from its earlier days. If those walls could talk . . .

This image of the house as it appeared in 1898 was in that year's Scientific American, Building Edition. *"The residence . . . is the home of Mr. Louis Frank Newman, of Springfield, Mass., and is known as 'Villa Bluff,' deriving its name from the bluff on which it is located, overlooking the Connecticut River, with broad views of the Berkshire range of hills." The house boasted cobblestone piazza and terraces, oak paneling, linen wall coverings, billiard room, dumb-waiter, a bathroom with a sky painted on the ceiling and the "Triumphal Procession of the Mermaid," on all four walls of the room, and was illuminated by 105 sixteen-candle electric light bulbs.*

CHAPTER ONE

So Long, Farewell

I'm not sure if the memories of when Dad left are real or just a compilation of stories combined with the vague memories of a child, but one thing is for sure: Dad abandoned Mom and all seven of us kids without a trace when I was three years old.

Mom refused to leave the twenty-eight-room mansion we lived in—I think because she believed it was a beacon for Dad to return to. But after several years had passed with no sign of Dad, Mom was forced to go on welfare and rent out rooms, and the mansion became infested with roaches, drug abusers, alcoholics, hippies, thieves—and even a murderer.

These early times before Dad left are woven together through a murky lens. I've pulled from old letters as well as my father's memoirs that he left for us later in life. Nevertheless, some things never leave you, and some things scar for life.

It's as though I'm watching from some faraway place, hovering above as the scenes slowly fade into view like a cartoon character drifting into a dream state.

It was sometime in March of 1964. My parents were already on another round of drinks, which was never a good idea. The melodic sounds of Jerry Vale played softly in the background. The dim light bounced reflections off the window onto the mottled gold wallpaper. Black velvet flocked images of minstrels perched beside their harps ran sequentially about the vast living room.

Dad was reading the paper in a crisp white shirt that was tucked tightly into his black pleated trousers. His long fingers lingered close to his drink. Sweat dripping from the glass had formed a pool of water on the carved octagonal table inlaid with ivory. The towering brass candlesticks threatened to topple from the mantle as Mom vigorously stoked the fire, spraying sparks onto the marble hearth, dangerously close to her white Persian rug.

The wide gray furry chair where Dad sat was a favorite spot for Beth and me to sit in side-by-side when Dad wasn't around. I loved to drape myself across it and write my name in the upholstery's nap with my bare feet. I could just reach with my toes and touch the tip of the large teardrop crystals hanging from the nearby lamp and watch them swing and reflect the light from the window.

My oldest brother, John, was sitting on the couch with his nose buried in a physics textbook. It seemed he was a permanent fixture on that couch. Even though he was a freshman in college at the University of Massachusetts, he hitchhiked home every weekend to study in the living room. His long, lean legs stretched out in front of him and almost touched the white marble table in the center. His tawny hair lay flat against his forehead as he furrowed his brow in deep concentration.

My brother Brian was probably down in the weight room pumping iron. Sometimes I'd watch John and Brian as they grunted and clanked the weight bar down on its stand. I never understood what they were doing since it didn't look like they were having any fun.

Beth and I were lying on our stomachs on the floor in our footy pajamas. I swung my feet trying to keep up with Beth as we colored in our Charlie Brown coloring books. I copied everything Beth did, even her lisp that she had long since conquered.

I could hear my older sisters, Ann and Paula, banging around in the kitchen. I knew they were making hot chocolate, and I was waiting in gleeful anticipation of the first sip of steaming milk and frothy marshmallows.

"Dick, I saw Joan Putnam today in the grocery store," Mom said. "They're having one of their posh parties tomorrow. What do you say we go hobnob with the rich and famous?" She turned away from her fire-tending duties with the same beaming smile that always got her what she wanted.

Joan and her husband, Bill, lived across the ravine from us, which was part of our backyard where we went sledding in the winter. It was a cavernous expanse that filled the void between our yard and the other yards along the dead-end street that paralleled Buena Vista Plaza where we lived. Bill Putnam was the founder of Springfield's first local television station, and he had his own editorial program before the nightly news.

"Why do you care about hobnobbing with those phonies?" Dad said as he raised his eyes briefly from the paper. He threw down the paper and grabbed his drink from the table. I could hear the ice tinkling in his glass as he swished the gold liquid and poured it down his throat.

"In all my forty years I have never felt so overwhelmed! Even the army wasn't this paralyzing," Dad said. "And you're bothering me with petty social events? Really, Elizabeth." He moved his hand across the receding hair that he'd carefully combed and starkly greased to his head.

"Do you have any idea how important my job was?" Dad continued. "And they had the audacity to fire me for not having a contract for one of my proposals. I still can't believe it," he said as he shook his hanging head. He went to the table and refilled his drink from a crystal decanter.

"Besides, do you want these neighbors to start rumors too? I've had about all I can take from elites sticking their noses in our business."

"But, Dick, these people are different than our Connecticut neighbors. Besides, you love a good party just as much as I do, and it will cheer you up! Maybe we can make some new connections."

Dad just sighed. He looked old and tired. "All right, Dear Heart. We can have John watch the kids while we're gone."

I looked up from coloring Peppermint Patty's hair with my green crayon in time to see John shoot Dad a look. But the look was gone as quickly as it had come, for fear Dad would reprimand him or whip out his belt.

Mom set the poker back in its holder and grabbed her drink from the coffee table with a satisfied grin.

"You girls go drink your hot chocolate and then I'll come up and tuck you into bed," she said. Mom always tucked us in. I don't ever remember a time when Dad tucked me in or kissed me goodnight. He always seemed too preoccupied with work to bother with Beth and me. John said he wasn't always like that, and he used to play and laugh with the boys before he got mean.

The next afternoon Beth and I were doing somersaults over the lavender velvet pouf in the center hall entryway beneath the crystal chandelier. I could never quite make it all the way over and usually toppled off before I even reached the large center button.

Just as I was coming to my feet, John bounded down the front hall stairs and swooped me up and threw me into the air. "Wheeeeee!" he yelled.

I liked how my stomach felt woozy like it stayed on the ground, the same feeling I got on the swing set outside, so I asked him to do it again, but he told me he needed to go talk to Mother, and walked into the kitchen.

I thought it was funny how John called Mom "Mother" when the rest of us just called her Ma or Mom. But then, John was always the most serious of all my brothers and sisters, probably because he was in college, I reasoned.

Mom was wearing a simple cotton house-dress and pink kitten heels as she bustled around the kitchen waiting on Ann, who sat quietly chewing her food at the table.

Dad was in a deep reverie as he sat eating his sandwich, a marked furrow between his brows. He was facing the wall of windows that looked out toward the ravine. The bare winter trees allowed us to see the Russos' brick mansion across the way, where our friend Anita lived. I could almost see Anita standing at the end of the path waving as she always did.

"Dick, I'm going upstairs to get ready for the party now," Mom announced as she took off her apron and tossed it onto the back of one of the kitchen chairs.

"It's only five o'clock, Elizabeth. Why do you need to get ready so early?" Dad said as he turned a cold stare on her. He got up and placed his plate on the shiny pink tile counter and accidentally knocked over a dirty glass.

"Dammit, why can't you kids do the chores that are assigned to you?" he said. "AnnMaria, go tell your sister Paula that it's her turn to do the dishes, and she needs to come down here immediately."

I was sitting quietly next to Beth, not wanting to be noticed by Dad since his temper seemed pretty bad these days. I knew I didn't want to get whacked with a hairbrush on the bare bottom like he did to Beth once, so I slid down in my chair and kicked Beth in the shin before getting up to go follow Mom.

As Beth and I ran up the stairs, my sister Paula was bounding down. At the second landing, she mounted the wooden banister and slid down the railing.

"I'm telling Mom," Beth threatened.

"Shut up you little brat and mind your business," Paula said as she jumped to the floor with a thud. By the time I mastered the side banister slide as a shortcut to the downstairs center hall, it'd been so overused that the rickety rail threatened to break from its balusters. For now I just resorted to the straddle method, using my hands as brakes before reaching the bottom newel post.

Mom's dressing room was a magical place with built-in dressers that were hidden behind lavender painted doors, a curvy dressing table with velvet curtains that matched the room's lavender and white flocked wallpaper, and three walk-in closets that were full of tailored dresses and suits—one for Dad, two for Mom.

Every night Mom wound her baby-fine blonde hair into tiny pin curls with crisscrossed bobby pins and then covered her head with a colorful babushka. In the morning she'd unpin, then brush and tease it into her signature swoop just above her forehead.

Beth and I dove beneath the dressing table and giggled excitedly as we waited for Mom's pink kitten heels to approach. At only five feet, two inches, Mom needed all the help she could get to stand as tall as Dad's shoulder.

Our moment had arrived, and Beth and I jumped out and lifted our arms. "Surprise!"

"Oh, girls, you scared me half to death," Mom said clutching her chest.

I never wondered if Mom was pretending every time I did this because she always acted surprised, even when Beth and I crawled across the living room floor thinking we'd gone the entire length undetected until we jumped up behind her chair.

After our surprise attack, Beth ran off, but I sat on the daybed so I could watch Mom get ready.

Mom carefully drew shapely silk stockings from her drawers, then went to her closet and pulled out two dresses. She made a funny face as she looked at them, holding each in front of her as she gazed at her sleek figure in the full-length mirror on the bathroom door.

"Whatchya think, Cha-Cha, do you like the red one or the black one?"

Mom would always tell the story of how I looked like a Latin dancer when I was a baby because I swiveled my bottom until my diaper fell down. I rolled my eyes every time I heard it, but now, so many years later, I'd give just about anything to hear that story one more time.

I voted for the red dress.

She chose just the right accessories, picking through the costume jewelry on her dressing table like she was choosing a piece of assorted chocolate. She'd pick it up, look it over, and put it back with a frown; the only thing that was missing was the pinch to see what was inside. Then she meticulously applied lipstick, with pursed lips as if blowing kisses into the mirror. Once she was done, we walked downstairs so she could present herself to Dad. I knew she was anticipating his admiring Wow! and when she didn't get it, her face and shoulders slumped like a deflated balloon. So I tugged on her dress and told her how pretty I thought she looked.

It's a scene that plays over and over in my head: my brother Michael destroying the houses Beth and I built from the wood blocks that Grandpa Bill had made for my brothers years before. Maybe the catastrophic sound of the tumbling blocks somehow collided with the memory of Dad leaving.

It was the morning after the party. *Looney Tunes* was playing on the television set in the corner, and Porky Pig was yelling out "Th-th-th-that's All Folks!" Beth and I were constructing one of our intricate Barbie houses on the floor just outside the playroom in the upstairs hall. Michael was lurking near the television set. His fringed eyes looked nothing like the glamorous ones that prompted Mom to call him Pansy Eyes—a name he despised. He might as well have been fluttering his hands like Snidely Whiplash with an evil grin pasted on his face.

Beth sat on the floor next to me with matted and stringy hair and ratty hand-me-down pajamas with holes in both knees. I could almost hear Mom yelling at her to pull her hair back. I want to see your forehead, she'd say. Mom was always fussing over our hair, and she'd make all us girls roll our straight hair into pin curls like hers the night before every holiday.

Beth urged me to go downstairs for some Cap'n Crunch cereal, and that's when we heard the tragic sound of blocks crashing to the floor. The look of horror on Beth's face mirrored my own as we made a frantic dash up the stairs.

"Whoops, I tripped!" Michael said. I was angry, but mostly sad when I saw Barbie lying under some blocks like she'd been crushed, so I swooped in to save her. In the background I heard Beth yelling at Michael about what a dumb stupid jerk he was. Michael just laughed and ran down the back stairs. I knew he was going to visit our dog Dudley, whom Dad never let into the front part of the house—that's where Michael always hung out.

Our house was sectioned off so that the back part of the house served as servants' quarters with narrow staircases running from the back hall on the first floor where Dudley was, and another that ran up to the apartment on the third floor. I always felt like I was entering another world when I went back there because of the dark wood. I preferred the white wood in the front with the big airy rooms, but there was one room in the back that had pretty pink floral wallpaper and a big mahogany bed with head and foot boards that Mom bought when they first got the house. Beth and I loved to play in that room, but sometimes I was afraid to walk out into the dark hall. We thought about taking our blocks in there to play, but decided it was too close to where Michael was hanging out, so we decided to rebuild in the forbidden side of the living room, thinking the two marble tables in front of the Monster would make a good base for our construction. The Monster was a white sofa with wooden dragons carved into the armrests. I don't remember, but they told me I'm the one who gave it its name; as a baby, I'd shriek in terror whenever I looked at the dragons whose mouths were eye level to me.

The plastic runner that ran to the side porch from the center hall was the delineation for No Man's Land. Dad made Mom cover both the Monster and the two gold Victorian chairs on that side of the room with plastic, rendering them completely unwelcoming to anyone who even thought about sitting in them.

The afternoon light streamed in from the window behind the Monster as I was balancing the last block onto the peak of my Barbie house when the sound of Mom and Dad shrieking in the upstairs hallway interrupted my concentration.

Beth just shrugged when I looked at her. We tried to drown out the sounds by humming. Ann put another forty-five on the tiny record player across the room. "Sugar Shack" started playing as she and Paula busied themselves pulling records from the round blue carrier that held all their favorites. I could hear them whispering something about little pitchers having big ears. It always made Beth mad when they said that, but I didn't know what it meant.

"Wanna go play outside?" Beth asked. I nodded meekly, and we abandoned our blocks in the living room, regardless of Michael or the possible penalties.

We pulled on our coats and snow pants, grabbed Beth's Fisher Price Tick-Tock Teaching Clock, and ran outside to sit in our favorite spot under the willow tree that was situated in the center of the plaza at the foot of our street. There were only six houses on our street, ours being the original that matched the pillars at the entryway.

Even in the winter, the sweeping willow boughs served as a magical dome of protection that always brought me peace. It was the same place where Mrs. Page, our neighbor, snapped a summer picture of Beth holding her clock with me by her side. That picture subsequently became a pastel painting and induced endless taunting from Michael with "I see London, I see France, I see Dorothy's underpants."

Beth wound up the Tick-Tock Clock so it played "Grandfather's Clock," and the face of the clock rotated around as it displayed various scenes. We sat in the snow listening to the music and watching our breath as it fogged around our faces. I made a snow angel with my legs as I kicked my red rubber boots in and out wondering why Mom and Dad were so mad at each other.

I leaned my head backward and looked up at the graceful tree. Once I heard John tell Brian how Dad made him cut a willow switch so Dad could use it to swat him—I think John forgot to do the dishes. Mom tried the same trick years later on some of us, but we all just laughed because we knew she'd never actually go through with it.

Mom's voice echoed through the winter afternoon, pulling me from my daydreaming as she called from the veranda for us to come inside.

Mom's face was swollen and red; I knew she'd been crying, but her eyes weren't welcoming and warm, so I quietly approached instead of running to her like I wanted.

Broad wooden columns lined the cobblestone wall on the veranda where she stood, which gave way to a rectangular flower garden. The veranda was about forty-seven feet long by fourteen feet wide with a sparkly red granolithic stone floor.

Soon Mom's favorite lilies of the valley would be popping their heads from the cold ground in the flower bed. I was never sure what was truly Mom's favorite flower, since she said the same of daffodils, lilacs, and magnolias.

At the far end of the veranda was a screened-in porch off the living room where we would sit in our creaky rockers on hot summer evenings or glide on the glider, listening intently to tales of when Mom and Dad were young and in love, or her tales of growing up in her small town. I can still smell the charcoal briquettes smoldering as Mom stood at the grill, flipping burgers and waving smoke from her face, a massive bowl of potato salad covered in plastic wrap waiting on the picnic table nearby.

"I want you girls to go get ready for your bath before dinner," Mom said as she tugged at her green woolen sweater. "I'll be up to check on you shortly." We'd never even gotten out of our jammies that day, but we did as we were told.

"I call the good side," Beth said as she dashed up the stairs.

I quickly responded, "That's no fair, I always get stuck on the stupid spout end. You think just 'cause you're older you can act like Ann and Paula."

Arching my back over the spout with my washcloth draped over my chest like it was a bathing suit, I lathered up a Mr. Bubble beard and spit bubbles across the tub at Beth. That sparked a splashing war, and before long we were whirring our hands around and around until we created a whirlpool wave that flooded the bathroom floor. That was when Ann walked in.

"What the hell are you little jerks doing?" she yelled as she grabbed the doorknob to keep from slipping in the water.

Since Ann was ten years old, she had more privileges, but she also had more duties, so Ann was sent to check on us instead of Mom.

I'd heard stories of how Mom assigned all kinds of duties to my older siblings. Like changing my diaper. Apparently, I would only let Ann change my diaper without a fuss, but since she wasn't as experienced, Brian would stand behind her and change me as Ann tucked her hands out of sight.

Mom still looked disheveled when I went down to the kitchen for dinner. Dad was not around, and nobody asked where he was. We'd heard them fighting and knew better than to say anything, so we sat and ate in virtual silence that night. Mom was seated at the head where Dad usually sat, picking despondently at her food.

At bedtime, I asked Mom if I could take Beth's Tick-Tock Clock to bed with me so I could go to sleep to the rhythmic music, which always calmed me down. I wound it up until it stopped and then wound it again until at last I fell asleep with the wooden clock cradled in my arms.

"Shhh, wake up, Cha-Cha," Mom whispered, as she gently shook me awake. Her musky scent evoked an almost palpable calm, until I noticed that all three of my older sisters were standing in my room wearing their winter coats. Ann, with her arms folded over her chest; Paula, shifting side-to-side with her hands in her pockets and her shoulders up to her ears; and Beth, clutching her favorite tattered pink rabbit.

I could feel Mom tugging at the toy clock I'd fallen asleep with. I just wanted to lie back down and twist the knob so the music would play again.

"We have to go, but we need to be quiet," Mom said as she pulled my blue woolen coat over my arms. Mom was wearing her black tailored coat with the red belt and the mother of pearl buttons closed right up to her neck.

My static hair stuck to my mouth like feathers. Mom's cold fingers brushed the soft wisps away as she hoisted me from my warm nest and clutched me tightly to her bosom. We made our way down the nursery hallway out to the center hall, my sisters trailing behind.

Shards of broken porcelain littered the floor. When I flash back to this scene, there are scattered white bits strewn about like someone dropped a bowl of popcorn.

I have no memory of ever kneeling at the altar, but have heard many stories from my siblings of how Dad made them all kneel for nightly prayers.

The statues from the altar were conspicuously absent. I felt a rush of air all the way to the pit of my stomach as I noticed my older brothers, Brian and Michael, standing at the foot of the third-floor stairway that was the delineation for the servant's quarters in the back part of the house. My oldest brother, John, had already gone back to college earlier that day. The ashen looks on my brothers' faces frightened me. *Where is Dad?*

"Come on, girls," Mom whispered as she herded us through the hallway like we were walking through a minefield. Statues crunched underfoot. I noticed the Mary and Jesus statue that always stood in the center of the altar was almost intact, with only a large chip missing from its base. It lay on its side next to the radiator. I wanted to reach for it and rub my fingers over Mary's bumpy blue robes, but Mom had other ideas.

"Hurry! Go quietly down the back stairs so we don't wake your father!"

The old wooden stairs creaked and moaned with every step we took. Mom's arms were tense around me as we made our descent. I tasted my salty tears as they streamed into my mouth.

Why are we running away?

We made our way through the snow to the driveway. Even with moonlight, the dark sky made it difficult to navigate the rutted path that ran to the plaza at the front of the house. Mom stumbled and grabbed a branch from the lilac bush to keep from falling with me in her arms.

"Mom, what is that?" Ann asked as she tugged on Mom's sleeve.

I heard Mom gasp, and I whipped my head around and caught a quick glimpse of what appeared to be a dark stain in the snow. "Don't look," Mom said as she forced my head back down on her shoulder. "Come on, everyone, we need to move!" Mom's breathing was heavy, and I could feel her heart racing as she pulled me even more tightly to her and herded her flock up the street.

The Napolitans' house stood at the top of our dead end street, and we were heading down their driveway made of the same sparkly pink granite as our veranda. The driveway wound to the back of their house, the same driveway where I would spend countless hours jump-roping and drawing hopscotch patterns with Luke Napolitan and skip down in gleeful anticipation of playing up in their third-floor billiard room and laying on the tiger rug with the green glassy eyes and fangy teeth. But this night only held a disconcerting terror for all of us.

Mrs. Napolitan greeted us like a command soldier.

"Come in, Elizabeth, I've been waiting for you. I have Alicia making up the beds upstairs," Mrs. Napolitan's blue eyes softened in sympathy as she let us in. "Bring the two girls to the upstairs bedroom where Alicia is. Joe is already in bed—he has to leave early in the morning. Paula, you can go up to Christine's room and stay with her."

Paula and Christine were both nine years old and were best friends. Mrs. Napolitan's formidable take-charge attitude was sometimes scary, but somehow I always knew she was like a giant marshmallow on the inside.

Sometimes Mrs. Napolitan would scream at Christine and Paula. Like the time they caught a skunk and wanted to keep it as a pet. Mrs. Napolitan let them keep it in the garage until it sprayed them and they were promptly dunked into a tomato bath.

The Napolitans also had homes in Washington, D.C. and Edgartown on Martha's Vineyard. I never knew Mr. Napolitan very well since he wasn't home much. I knew he had an important job, but it wasn't until years later that I learned he was an internationally known political consultant who worked on over one hundred campaigns, including helping spearhead President John F. Kennedy's 1960 presidential campaign.

Whenever I saw Mr. Napolitan—or any of my friend's fathers for that matter—my stomach turned inside out. Their deep, powerful voices reminded me of Burgermeister Meisterburger from *Santa Claus Is Comin' to Town* and told me that they had no time for silly children. This was the voice that was in my head for much of my young adult life—men were powerful and wanted nothing to do with the likes of me.

I have no recollection of being beaten by my father—I imagine I was much too young, but his imposing presence was always looming in some distant part of my mind.

Mrs. Napolitan ushered Brian, Michael, and Ann into the other room as though she were conducting a covert mission.

"You kids go sit in the summer room while we get things ready upstairs. I'll make you some hot cocoa when I come back down."

Mom took Beth and me up the elaborate mahogany staircase that was illuminated by the moonlit sky through the stained-glass skylight.

Our house was big, but the Napolitan's was grander. Even now, many of my dreams take place in that house.

Alicia readied our rooms. Years later I would follow her around watching with delight as she made beds and dusted. That was when I decided I wanted to be a maid when I grew up. The other kids wanted to be doctors, or lawyers, or princesses. But I told my first-grade teacher that I wanted to be a maid because I loved how Alicia made beds so meticulously you could bounce a quarter from the springy fabric.

I could hear Mom in the next room talking to Mrs. Napolitan. Beth sat on the pink-and-blue-striped chair in the corner, hugging her knees and her stuffed rabbit with her coat tucked under her footy pajamas as if she were in a cocoon.

Beth was closest to me in age by two and a half years, and we did just about everything together. Beth's eyes got squinty when she laughed, so you could hardly see them, and she had a funny little dimple just below her nose and above her mouth. Mom called them her "Chinese upside-down eyes" and "cockeyed dimple." But Beth's eyes weren't smiling this night. She looked as confused as I felt.

Mom's cries echoed down the hallway. And then cut—the lights go out—no memory, no stories can fill in this blank. Like a needle dragging across a record—then fast-forward—Dad is gone and out of our lives.

We found out later that Dad had stumbled outside after cutting his head, presumably while trashing the statues from the altar, leaving a trail of blood on the stair landing and in the snow.

I have no memory of Dad's actual leaving.

Beth's most prominent memory is of seeing footsteps in the snow and Dad's car gone from the driveway.

I picture Beth standing at the window in Mom's room overlooking the plaza, a tiny tear trickling down her smooth cheek as she gazes in a trance at the tracks in the snow.

We didn't know it then, but it would be another twelve years before we would see our father again.

[top left] Mom and the girls pose at Easter with Mom's blow-up bunny. I'm in front of Mom at the very bottom of the picture.

[bottom left] John and Brian are in the back; Paula, Michael, and Ann are in the middle; Beth, Mom, and I are in front next to Mom's favorite cherub lamp; Christmas 1965.

[right] Mom poses for pictures to send to Dad to try to get him to come back.

CHAPTER TWO

Desperate Measures

The details trickled in over the years as to why Dad left. Mom always told us he had a nervous breakdown after he lost his high-profile job with the Hamilton Standard's division of United Aircraft.

Mom always bragged about Dad's IQ being off the charts. I wondered where my IQ was on the charts. I wasn't even sure I made the charts.

Dad wanted to pass along some of his history, so he wrote some notes to us later in life. From them I learned that Hamilton Standard had just gotten the moonsuit contract from the National Aeronautics and Space Administration (NASA), and Dad had been a manager of the Biosciences and Technology Department. He was working on an experimental study to improve man's capability to live in extreme environments such as space that was called the Cyborg Study.

I think Dad was mighty impressed with himself. "I even had Dick Allen, a senior staff member of the Hoover Institution, reporting to me!!!" He noted with all three exclamation points.

Dad said losing that job was the biggest blow of his life. Reading that in Dad's notes wrenched my guts, but by then I had long since come to terms with him abandoning us.

Mom protected the image of Dad for as long as she could muster. She always told us he was the love of her life. She believed for years that he would come back someday. The ugly stories didn't start to come out until much later when Mom began to lose herself. Like how Dad cheated on her with his brother's wife. The name "Joan" was always spoken as though Mom were spitting tacks.

I knew Dad was offered a job in California, but the facts surrounding it were as clear as a breath blown window on a cold day. I never knew whether Dad wanted us all to traipse off to California with him and Mom refused to go, or if he was just leaving us. All I knew was that it was the catalyst for the night the statues came off the altar. I knew Mom wasn't completely innocent in all of it, but my protective armor was engaged for most of my formative years when it came to Mom.

In his memoirs, Dad glossed over the time when he left us. He conveniently dismissed his actions, blaming it on the prescribed drug he was given for depression and stating that the memories were "too painful to write about." I wanted to spit at the pages when I read those words. (Okay, so maybe I hadn't come to terms with it.)

> I had two sets of demands, one at work to develop N.A.S.A. contracts to support my research, and the other to rehab and overhaul many of the elements in our new home that either didn't work or needed to be modified. I had to repair the furnace, strip paint off the wood walls, repair the elevator, and many other items. We also had to search out furniture that was affordable to start filling up the twenty or so rooms in the Springfield house, so it meant running out to every estate sale we could find on the weekends and watching the papers for ads! As you know, that was the beginning of extreme trauma for every one of us in the family, so I will not dwell on this part of history to any extent, other than on some highlights, regarding my career path. I can never forgive myself for my actions over the next years, and I hope God has, and you all, including your mother, have. I have confessed my behavior in those years, but I still cannot forgive myself. Just writing all this has put me through some very difficult memories.

I've spent most of my life trying to reconcile my emotions, throwing them into the air like pizza dough and whirling them around until it became so thin my fingers poked through.

I didn't want to know about Dad's career path. Why does he even think that matters? All I wanted to know was why he left us. But it is a question that remains unanswered.

I began interviewing Mom when I was in my early twenties, with the lofty idea of writing a book about this woman who I deemed fascinating and who had overcome so much. But those meager words etched in blue ballpoint remained in my spiral bound notebook only to disclose some early details about Mom scrawled over several pages. Later, Dad's memoir would help to fill in the blanks.

Elizabeth Jane Paul (Mom) was born in 1920 in the remote town of Browns Valley, Minnesota. Browns Valley, although small, was a quaint town of approximately 1,200 people. Mom's parents were William L. Paul and Dorothy Bliss Plant. Mom's father, Grandpa Bill was a well-respected banker in town.

Mom had three brothers, one of whom was her twin brother, John, who died at the age of thirteen of scarlet fever. Mom said she had no idea how serious his illness was and grew resentful that she had to wait on him. By the time he died, it was too late, and she never got the chance to tell him she was sorry. As a result, she drilled into our heads to "never let the sun go down on a quarrel." With seven of us, that was not always easy. But Mom's story struck a nerve in Beth, who for many years would never go to sleep mad, and there were many nights I took advantage of that.

Mom puffed up when she told me about her escapades with her first Model T car she named Bertha, telling the stories with a childlike wonder. Her friends would pile into the car, some even riding on the running boards, and they would drive all over town. Mom was a popular girl in town, having come from one of the more wealthy families.

Richard J. Preston (Dad) moved to Minneapolis for the tenth grade and was a grade behind actors James Arness and his brother Peter Graves. (Arness is best known for portraying Marshal Matt Dillon in the television series *Gunsmoke*, and Peter Graves is best known for his role as Jim Phelps in the television series *Mission: Impossible.*)

Dad wrote in his memoirs that he and Mom met in Browns Valley, Minnesota, in 1939, just after WWII began. Mom's older brother, James, introduced them when Dad was fifteen years old and Mom was nineteen. Dad was convinced that his grandmother, Clara Sprague Preston, arranged that introduction after she'd seen Mom walk by their furniture store in town.

"There's the perfect girl for you," she said. "Not Alfreda Weinkauf."

Dad said they were drawn together by their zest and love for life.

My father joined the Navy in January 1943 as a V-5 Aviation Cadet, and three days after he joined, he secretly married my mother in Mason City, Iowa. Dad told us years later that a V-5 Cadet was not supposed to be married, so once he reported his marriage, he was honorably discharged from the Navy. After that he enlisted in the Army. Of course Mom moved around with Dad and even drove staff cars as a job.

> After that I enlisted in the Army and went through basic training... Your mother joined me there for a few months, until I went into the Army Specialized Training Program and went to college for basic engineering in Brookings, South Dakota. Again, your mother joined me there, and we drove Big Bertha Buick down for transportation... Assigned to fly anti-submarine patrol as the radio operator on B-25s and B26s from Phoenix out over the Pacific, until the war was over... Your mother and two-month-old John joined me about two months before I was discharged on points on November 30, 1945.

Dad just missed being sent to Germany in the Signal Corps for the Battle of the Bulge. They took soldiers alphabetically and got to the middle of the P's. Subsequently, he was assigned to fly anti-submarine patrol as the radio operator until the war was over.

Although Mom and Dad struggled financially for many years, they lived a full life in those days. They tried many different business ventures, including a movie theater in Lime Springs, Iowa, in 1948, when Brian was only a year old. Mom told me they came up with the idea to do home movies around Lime Springs and showed them with the regular movie once a month. She told me how Dad got a local pilot to take him up to shoot movies from the air, and how they'd remodeled the theater only to have to file bankruptcy three months later after the Lime Springs area was hit with a polio epidemic.

In 1952 Dad took a job as a Nuclear Electronic Technician in Idaho Falls at $400 per month. He worked with many of the pioneers in the nuclear industry, including several of the physicists who had been involved in the Manhattan Project, which was specifically for the development of the atomic bomb. He continued to develop electronic equipment, which led to the first of his seven patents.

During my teen years, I likened Mom to a cross between Scarlett O'Hara from *Gone with the Wind* and Joan Crawford. I, her protégé, watched and learned. We had been through hell and back together, and here I was interviewing her like she was some glamorous Hollywood movie star, which she was for the first ten years of my life.

My fifteen-year-old self might have felt differently faced off against Mom in her faux leopard coat and wild hair, gauging how bad her daily hangover was by how she smelled. But somehow my twenty-something self had circled back to a place of love and forgiveness.

In the years before I was born, my family moved all over, including Minnesota; Iowa; Caracas, Venezuela; and Connecticut, before Mom finally found her dream home and we all settled in the twenty-plus room home on Buena Vista Plaza in Springfield, Massachusetts.

The Springfield house had a pulse of its own that beat to the rhythm of Mom, and eventually to me. It would morph not only into my playmate but somehow into an integral part of me that I could not let go of, haunting my dreams even still.

Even though the house had a butler's pantry, a dumbwaiter, and an elevator, long gone were any house staff by the time I was born. I had heard stories of our maid, Ina, who my parents hired after my mother broke her foot in Caracas while living there during one of my father's job relocations. I was told they brought Ina back with them when they fled the country during the Venezuelan *coup d'état* that took place in 1958; they moved back to the states and settled in Willimantic, Connecticut. Ina practically raised my sister Paula, who spoke only Spanish as a baby. By the time I was born seven years later, Ina was gone, right along with Paula's Spanish. Now we were the servants.

"Cha Cha, get my coffee, will ya?" Was a common morning mantra. I loved making Mom's coffee and watching the Cremora slowly melt into the hot mixture as it magically transformed to the color of my favorite stuffed bear, Sackie. I didn't mind running errands for Mom and my older siblings. It made me feel important, like I was special. I felt honored to run to Nagels pharmacy a few blocks down the street, clutching the two quarters Ann gave me to go fetch a pack of Marlboro cigarettes. Ann insists I couldn't say Marlboro correctly and instead called them "Marblubs."

After Dad left, everything changed and Mom was never the same. She tried everything to get Dad to return home.

Mom was forty-four years old when she asked my eleven-year-old sister, Ann, to take seductive photos of her; she had no one else to ask. I didn't witness the photo shoot, but I saw the resulting pictures many years later. She wore a jet-black bustier with fishnet stockings, and gold stiletto shoes. A glamorous faux ruby necklace dangled on her décolletage with earrings to match. The statement jewels looked like something a queen would wear. Her hair was curled and sprayed with copious amounts of hairspray, a tortoise and diamond tiara strategically placed atop her head. Her lips blazed with ruby red lipstick. One elbow rested on the bolster pillow beneath her head on the Monster while holding up a cigarette, wearing a seductive smile. I imagine the plotting of this photo shoot was quite elaborate right down to running to the store to buy cigarettes given she'd never smoked in her life, and at that point neither did any of my siblings.

The second shot was in the dining room that boasted of Mom's ostentatious taste. A Waterford crystal chandelier dangled above the massive dining table, red-and-black flocked walls abutting the white wainscoting below. Three-paned glass windows were hidden behind white satin Austrian balloon shades swathed by heavy red velvet drapes gathered in the center by a gold tassel that would outshine any admiral's. Mom was positioned on the red velvet, high-backed piece in the corner that we called the Queen chair. Her right leg was raised as she held it with her muscular arm. Once again, trying her best to look sleek and sexy in the hopes that she could win back our father. She wanted Dad to see exactly what he was missing.

Those first holidays after Dad left were the most desperate for Mom. She always prepared for our Thanksgiving feast a few days in advance.

She laid out bread to get stale for her stuffing all over the kitchen and the adjoining kitchen pantry.

Mom always stuffed the turkey and put it in the oven the night before, cooking it on low heat. The memory of waking to the smell of Mom's stuffed turkey fills my head with images of white linen tablecloths, Haviland china, and silver that I was forced to polish at every holiday once I was old enough.

A few days before Thanksgiving, Beth and I were busy playing king and queen in the dining room. Just as Beth had taken her royal seat on the queen chair, we heard Ann and Paula coming down the stairs.

"Hurry, the enemy approaches," Beth called out as we scurried into the little cabinets in the buffet to hide from them.

The buffet was adorned with Mom's silver dishes, and the drawers housed silverware engraved with Grandpa's initials, WLP. There was a mirror on top with a shelf above it that was held up in front by two spiraled columns.

I climbed into one of the smaller single cabinets, and Beth climbed into the center double cabinet, and we pulled the grated doors closed behind us.

"I can't believe we have to polish the stupid silver," Ann said. I could see her red pants and the bottom part of her white-and-black sweater as she moved around. "Hey, why weren't you in your bed this morning?" Ann asked Paula.

"I slept in Mom's bed last night. And you'll never guess who called again," Paula whispered.

"Let me guess—Dad?"

"Yup, it was sometime in the middle of the night, and I could hear him crying on the other end. He called her 'dear heart' so of course that got her going, and they were both carrying on. Then I heard some woman's voice talking in the background, which got Mom all riled up. I didn't sleep much after that, and she cried most of the night," Paula said.

Suddenly, I had an itch and I moved my foot and accidentally kicked the grate on the door.

"What are you little brats doing down there eavesdropping?" Paula yelled as she bent over to see us hiding in the cabinets. Beth busted out of her cabinet and scurried away, but I was not quick enough, so Ann leaned over and turned the little key in the door, locking me in. "There, that'll teach you to be nosy," she said as she held the key close to my face in front of the grate.

"How's it feel to be in a cage?" Paula laughed.

"I have to tinkle. Let me out!" But they just stood laughing at me until they saw a puddle emptying out of the cabinet. At that point they knew they would be in trouble, so they quickly unlocked the door and I scuttled out in a wet mess and ran crying to Mom.

This was a story Ann and Paula laughed themselves to tears recollecting for years. But I had the last laugh the day Ann moved that urine-stained piece of furniture into her own home years later.

After waking to the aroma of turkey on Thanksgiving morning, Beth and I ran downstairs to find Mom, whom we knew would be busy in the kitchen already. Ann and Paula were finishing up the last of the silver polishing in the butler's pantry, which connected the dining room to the kitchen beyond. They stood at the white porcelain butler's sink near the window and the glass-enclosed shelves, busy at their tasks. Beth slid open the wooden window that was once used by the kitchen staff to hand out plates of food and poked her head through.

"I'll take a scoop of stuffing to go, please," Beth would yell to Mom.

Mom was wearing a pink-and-white apron, which protected her red satin dress, her hair was perfectly curled, and she wore the same spectacular faux ruby necklace she wore in her boudoir picture for Dad. She looked like she was ready to go out to one of the parties that she and Dad had always attended. I wondered if she even slept last night, or if she spent the night stuffing the turkey and prettying up.

Mom pushed by us carrying a hot dish and placed it in the warming oven near the swinging door.

"Hurry up and finish that silver, girls. I want to take a Thanksgiving picture for your father as soon as I bring the turkey out." Instinctively I knew this was the driving factor in how much effort she'd put into the day. "Beth and Dorothy, you two go upstairs and get dressed. There will be plenty of stuffing for you later." Everyone else was already wearing their holiday clothes, so Beth and I went and put on our dresses too.

"Come on, kids, it's time for our picture," Mom said as she set up Dad's old Kodak Brownie on the tripod. Beth and I were playing under the dining table, whose ornate legs were carved to look like dragons that faced out at angles on either side with a space between that provided a perfect seat for each of us. The shelter from the overhanging tablecloth made an ideal fort, and the table was stretched to capacity for Thanksgiving dinner, so we had plenty of room.

I heard Mom tell John to carry the turkey out to the table as I flounced Barbie around, pretending she was going to see Ken for Thanksgiving dinner.

"Ann . . . Paul . . . Beth and Dorothy, come out from underneath the table." Mom could never say one of our names without saying someone else's first, but usually "Beth and Dorothy" just went together, and we'd answer with "What and Worthy," thinking we were very funny.

"I don't know why we have to send anything to Dad. I'm glad he's gone. He's a big stupid meanie and I hate him!" Beth said as she climbed out from our fort.

Mom immediately crouched down to Beth and grabbed her by the shoulders.

"Don't you ever say that, Beth. He loves you children. He was the love of my life," she said wistfully, as she stood up. "He's still the love of my life." I could see Mom fighting the tears that threatened to pour from her eyes.

"Is that why he left us, Mom?" Brian yelled from across the table.

"I don't want him to come back either," Ann chimed in.

And, with that, chaos broke out. I always felt like I was watching a movie in slow motion when my family started fighting. Like I could just fade away into a big comfy chair with a bowl of popcorn, and none of them would even know I was there. I liked being invisible.

I stood off to the side as my older siblings squabbled. Each spouted their own perceived injustices at the hands of my father until Mom stomped her foot loudly on the floor and banged her fist down on the dining table.

"Stop it now, all of you! I will not have you talking about your father like that. He loved you all, and he's very sick. He wasn't always mean, and you all know it. I won't have it, d'ya hear me? Now let's all sit so I can take this picture."

Mom was seated at the table with the turkey in front of her. She pulled Beth and me onto her lap. The resulting photo shows not one of us smiling. Even Mom only made a lame attempt to look happy. Anger showed on everyone's face but mine because all you could see of me was the top of my head and my right eye peering from behind the turkey.

We ate in silence. The three boys sat on the side of the table closest to the fireplace, and the four of us girls on the other side, with Mom in Dad's old seat at the head of the table.

Years later I found a note Mom had scratched on a piece of paper on which she mimicked my lisp. Since Dad was still calling then, she probably wrote it so she could recite it over the phone. "Dorothy independently carrying her plate and sitting in your place at the table—announces 'I'm in Daddy'th chair—Daddy'th nice so I'm in hith chair!' Beth, quietly and sadly sitting, asked why 'I miss Daddy!' 'What kind of car ith Daddythe? I want Daddy now. I want to kisth Daddy cause I like Daddy. I like Daddy better much than you! . . . When ith that sthupid Daddy coming home for Chrithmuth?'"

Holidays brought with them images of Mom sitting on the radiator in the dining room, Andy Williams's "Dear Heart" playing in the background so Mom could bash herself in the head with the pain it brought as she remembered when Dad called her that, her drink tinkling in the dark room as she gazed at the Christmas tree through the vast opening that spanned into the living room and engulfed the entire doorframe. I sometimes wonder if Mom and Dad ever sat there together drinking themselves into oblivion. This was Mom's perch every Christmas without fail.

◈

The phone calls from Dad grew more infrequent, and I could tell Mom was beginning to lose hope, but she did her best to hide it from us.

Mom loved the holidays, but her favorite was always Christmas. She always said that Christmas was all about anticipation, and our house was abuzz with lots of anticipation and decorations at Christmas time.

Mom and Dad started the tradition of going out to cut the biggest tree at the tree farm after they bought the big house in Springfield, and Mom was not going to change things now. It was our first Christmas without Dad, and Mom wanted us kids to feel like nothing had changed.

Before we left for our tree hunt, Mom asked my brother John to roll up the small Persian rug in the living room in preparation for the tree. The family story is that Mom purchased the two matching rugs using a diamond ring Beth found out in the yard one day. After having ignored Beth's pleas to pay attention to her "pretty shiny ring," it finally caught Mom's eye as it sparkled during Beth's bath one evening. I imagine Beth was none too happy to give it up to pay for a rug.

John carried the small rug into the coat room, where it stayed until the tree came down after the Epiphany, or "Little Christmas," as Mom called it. The Epiphany is the manifestation of Christ to the Gentiles and is celebrated on January 6. Mom was adamant that the tree stay up until after that, but often it would stay up even longer, so that not only did we get Christmas anticipation, but we also got another month of post-Christmas enjoyment.

Our Christmas trees were always enormous. You could barely see the station wagon underneath it as we drove it home, making our car look like a gigantic tree on wheels. I felt spine-tingling delight whenever I climbed into the car to go Christmas tree hunting, as though I were stepping into an enchanted tree fort. I'd peer from the window through the hanging boughs and watch the amazed looks on people's faces as we drove by, giggling with delight. I knew Mom was missing Dad as she drove us home with the big tree on the car, but she belted out Christmas carols the whole way home regardless.

My brothers would have friends over to help with getting the tree into the house. They'd tug, and pull, and push, and grunt, and the massive tree would stay stubbornly stuck in the doorway as Mom stood by rubbing her chin.

I ran around to the side door by the screened-in porch to get a better view as they tugged the tree in to the living room.

I could hear the commotion from the other side as Mom barked out orders.

"Maybe we can cut off a few boughs at the bottom," she'd say.

"What's this 'we' shit, Ma?" Michael snapped, rubbing the sweat from his brow and making an angry face at Brian. We ended up hacking off the top portion of the tree, which became a smaller second tree that we put in the corner of the dining room near the queen chair. Paula's eyes lit up when Mom told her decorating it could be her responsibility. She adopted the baby tree as her own, and it became her special thrill. Years later the task of decorating the "baby tree" was handed down to me. I tended it with care for years, wrapping lights and ornaments in a box marked with black magic marker: Dorothy's Tree.

Putting the tree up was another story. Mom grossly underestimated the height of the tree, her judgment fogged by the lure of sending Dad a picture of all of us in front of the tree so he could see what he was missing.

It would stand to reason that perhaps Mom should have chosen a smaller tree that didn't need to be cannibalized, but what's the fun in that? The big tree, or rather bush at this point, was tethered to the drapery rod that spanned the window in the "L-shaped" part of the living room that mirrored the three-paned windows directly across in the dining room. With four lines attached, the tree was like a Thanksgiving float at the Macy's Day parade.

With a growing number of friends—and then alcohol thrown into the mix—each year became more and more eventful. Like the time one of Brian's drunken friends emerged from the tree with a bird's nest in one hand and a bottle of wine in another, sap and pine needles covering his face—a story that was told over and over again through the years with added flair and exaggeration. I lost count of how many times the tree toppled, breaking countless decorations. This finally forced Michael or Brian to nail the stand to the floor, insisting that the Persian rug would cover the holes once it was back down.

Every year, neighbors and friends alike would gather to help erect the Preston Christmas tree. Even now, forty-plus years later, they still talk about the times we decorated our Christmas trees as epic events.

The smell of pine filled the house for weeks after we put up the tree. The crèche was front and center under the tree, with the baby Jesus, the three Wise Men, and all the animals. Christmas albums were stacked by the hi-fi, with the likes of Perry Como, Ella Fitzgerald, Steve Lawrence and Eydie Gormé, just to name a few.

Mom would wind the cut boughs around the stair rails, throw up mistletoe and stockings, and voila, our house was transformed into a magical Christmas wonderland.

Sometimes I'd crawl under the tree and pretend I was camping in the woods, which more often than not resulted in another broken ornament.

Mom always made Christmas Eve memorable. This year, she invited Father Boneventure, the neighborhood priest, his two sisters, Mary and Louise, and his brother Tony. They were all older than Mom and none were married, but they liked to imbibe in a "cup of cheer" during the holiday season.

Mom loved to entertain. She and Dad always had lavish parties when they lived in Mansfield, Connecticut, and I knew having people over now made her feel more normal. Mom made hot toddies for the grownups and eggnog for us kids. She put chestnuts, Brazil nuts, stuffed celery, and dates filled with peanut butter out on the tables in fancy crystal dishes with nutcrackers and picks perched beside them, and the scent of pecan sandies filled the air with their sugary aroma. Bing Crosby belted out "I'm Dreaming of a White Christmas," every light in the house on. We knew Santa was coming, and the excitement was palpable.

Gone were the plastic furniture covers and runner from the forbidden side of the living room. Dudley was released from his back-hall quarantine, and the only room he wasn't allowed in was the living room.

Dad had not allowed us to receive birthday gifts the year before he left, and not more than one Christmas gift because they couldn't afford it, so this year Mom wanted to spoil us, and with Grandpa Bill's help, she did just that. She always let us open one gift on Christmas Eve, and most of the time it was new pajamas. To some kids that might not be so exciting, but to Beth and me, it was like heaven. We ran upstairs to put on our new jammies then ran back downstairs and jumped in front of Mom and the neighbors to present ourselves.

"Surprise!" We'd yell out as though it were a huge deal.

"Girls, why don't you sing some Christmas carols for the neighbors?" Mom said proudly. Even in our shyness, we were happy to oblige since we loved singing carols.

Beth and I anticipated Christmas morning for weeks, and we'd hound Mom to tell us what presents she got for us.

"Ask me no secrets, I'll tell you no lies," she'd sing in her off-key voice, never caving. Sometimes we'd even sneak around trying to find where she'd hidden them, but she was always too clever, and we only once found one of our presents.

Mom only wrapped a few presents, and the rest remained unwrapped where Santa left them with our stockings that were always filled with animal crackers, ribbon candy, and an orange or banana.

On Christmas morning we were not allowed to go downstairs until Mom was up. We awoke at the crack of dawn like all other kids and begged her to go downstairs. "Mom, get up, we want to see what Santa brought us."

When she was finally up and dressed, she had us all gather at the top of the stairs. "You all wait here until I say you can come down," she instructed as she walked ahead of us. My older siblings didn't seem quite as excited as Beth and I were, and I couldn't understand why.

"Okay, kids, you can come down now!" We were already charging at "Okay."

Mom pointed us all to the appropriate chair or couch where Santa had left our presents. Beth's and mine were on either end of the Monster. Mom didn't have to tell me which one was mine—I spotted the Budding Beauty Vanity I had asked for and slowly walked over and lifted the lid. The tiny lipstick and the glass bottle of toilet water were peering up at me along with all the other items necessary for making oneself beautiful. The Tussy toilet water didn't smell like Mom's Tabu perfume, but I didn't care as I dabbed some just behind my ears, then pursed my lips like Mom always did to put on my lipstick.

"Hey, Cha-Cha, did you see what else Santa brought for you?" Mom said as she directed me to the Monster where the Mattel Yacker Larry the Lion sat proudly with his fuzzy golden mane. The tag that hung from his neck said, *I can talk!* I could hear the quiet purring sound as I slowly drew the string out. *Oh, I scared myself!* and *I'm ferocious, aren't I?* were the first things out of his mouth. His mouth and eyes moved when he talked. I looked over and saw Beth playing with Crackers the Parrot, who also talked and was bright green with colorful feathers made of felt and big bulging eyes.

Michael was pretending to be interested in Larry when suddenly he grabbed Larry from me.

"Ooooh, I think I scared myself," he mimicked as he burst into laughter.

"Give him back, Michael!" I cried.

"I wonder if Larry can fly," he said as he ran away and bounded up the stairs to the third floor. I began to chase him.

"Michael, give him back to me." I had gotten as far as the first landing when suddenly Larry the Lion came flying down from above. I looked up and saw Michael leaning over the third-floor railing at the top, the stained glass sky light just above his head illuminating Larry's flight. Larry landed just below where I was standing and tumbled to the bottom of the stairs. I ran quickly to his rescue and hugged him tightly. But when I pulled on his string, Larry no longer talked. His mouth still moved, but nothing came out. I was completely devastated, and I started to cry. I ran to Mom, who was getting the camera ready on the tripod again. She was all in white but for her ruby-red painted toenails exposed by strappy sandals below calf-length pants and red dangly ball earrings. A red-and-white Christmas corsage was strategically pinned to her lapel.

"Michael broke Larry the Lion, Mom," I sobbed. Just then Michael arrived back on the scene looking sheepish. I had already discovered that the only way Michael knew how to show us he loved us was through teasing, but I was still angry.

"I'm sorry, honey, I was just playing. I didn't think I would break him."

I glared at him through my tears and then turned back to Mom. "Can you fix him?"

"I'll try my best," Mom assured. But it turned out nobody could fix him, and Mom ended up buying me a new Larry sometime after Christmas.

Mom orchestrated another Dad-luring portrait that Christmas. The lot of us looked rumpled and bedraggled. Mom, the proverbial lily among the thorns.

My gift from Mom that Christmas was a blue satiny dress with a pink bow. I had never owned anything so beautiful. I ran to Mom and hugged her tightly then ran up to my room to try on the dress. I primped all day in front of my little vanity in my new dress, just like Mom did.

Mom watched us all with a wistful look as we buried ourselves in the magic of Christmas, managing to forget that something, or someone, was missing, but Mom never forgot. It was lost on me then that suddenly she had nobody to shower her with gifts as she was doing for us, but it never mattered to her since seeing her children happy was always her priority.

Later that evening, after dinner and all the festivities, we were all lounging in the living room except for Mom. She came in to put a record on the stereo and then quickly exited again with a solemn look on her face.

When I walked out to use the downstairs bathroom, I saw Mom perched on the long radiator in the dining room in the dark. She had made it through the day without breaking down, and now it was time to sit with herself in the dark corner of her mind.

Mom continued to take us all to Mass on Sundays. Kneeling at the altar in our upstairs hallway had become a thing of the past now that most of the statues were broken, missing a hand, or chipped like the statue of Mary and Jesus that would remain on the altar for the next thirty or so years, its chip a constant reminder of the night Dad went off the deep end.

I didn't know how to say the rosary yet, but I liked to hold the pretty blue glass beads and move my fingers over them like my brothers and sisters did.

We girls had to wear veils to church that we'd affix to our heads with a bobby pin. They reminded me of the lace doilies Grandma Dorothy made that Mom had strewn about the house. Mom's mother passed away after Ann was born, so I never met her. Whenever I'd complain about my name, I was barraged with comments from Mom about what a saint Grandma Dorothy was and that I should be honored to have such a beautiful name. But I still hated how everyone teased me and recited lines from *The Wizard of Oz*.

When we went to church, Mom said we only had to stay for the three main parts; I wasn't sure which parts those were, and I didn't really care. I preferred daydreaming or gazing at the statues and the pretty stained glass windows to listening to Father Choquette's monotone drone that put half the parishioners to sleep.

After I made my First Holy Communion and could receive the host, Father Choquette would curl his lip like he was snarling at me every time he placed the Eucharist on my tongue. I often wondered if I'd stepped in dog-doo.

Nobody was allowed to touch the host except the priest—not even to loosen it from the roof of your mouth after it invariably suctioned itself there—lest you turn to stone. Mom was appalled when the church changed the rules and let you take the host in your hands. I wondered if Father Choquette had something to do with that.

Mom refused to take Communion from anyone other than a priest. She would not acknowledge the laymen handing out Communion at the heads of different aisles and would bound across several pews just to get to the priest and stick out her tongue to receive the holy host, still refusing to ever take it in her hands. This practice was ingrained in me at an early age. I, too, could not bring myself to take Communion from anyone other than a priest on those rare occasions, like weddings or funerals, when I would take Communion, and it took many years before I could take it my hands. Sometimes Beth would nudge me and tell me that I couldn't take Communion since she knew I hadn't gone to confession, but I didn't care and would brazenly take it anyway, and I was never struck by a lightning bolt.

I was nervous the first time I had to go to confession, waiting in a line that was organized by our last names. I was thankful my name started with a "P" and not an "A" since I never liked being first for anything—unless it was to get ice cream. I watched each kid from my class exit the confessional with heads bowed and hands folded as they made their way back to the pew to say their penance as we were instructed. When I finally made my way to the front of the line, I tentatively entered the dark box. There was a faint orange glow streaming in from the top. I knelt on the tiny soft kneeler and nervously waited. I could hear the muffled voice of the priest speaking to the person on the other side. I wondered if their box was as dark as mine. I heard the shuffling sound of the door opening to reveal a mesh covering in front of the orange backlit face of Father Choquette.

"Bless me Father, for I have sinned . . . "

You are normally supposed to say how long it had been since your last confession, but since this was my first time, I'm not sure how I finished that sentence.

"I-I-stole a dime from my mother's pocketbook," I meekly pronounced. I really hadn't, but I had no idea what else to say. I'd been practicing this the entire time I stood in line. But that's not unusual. After all, Catholics and ex-Catholics alike can attest to having lied in the confessional. I kept my head bowed, as any contrite sinner would do, and waited for my penance.

"You will say three Hail Marys and ten Our Fathers. Now go in peace," he said as he waved his hand in the sign of the cross in front of the screen. The tiny door shushed closed and the other opened on the opposite side. As I exited the box, I could feel my face burning in shame, although I wasn't sure why—I'd done nothing wrong. Yvette Savoie was still in line along with a few others, but I avoided making eye contact and bowed my head. I knelt at my pew to say my penance. I would receive a similar penance many times over and I wondered if it was standard procedure. The guy who got six Hail Marys and maybe twenty Our Fathers would have to be a murderer or something. I thought maybe next time I'd tell Father Choquette I lied about lying.

Mom was caught off guard when the church reintroduced the tradition of shaking hands with each other as a sign of peace. She'd mysteriously get her hand caught in her coat pocket or would nervously dig into her purse pretending to be looking for something. Sometimes her hand would emerge with a dirty snot rag, and she would start to blow her nose and look around apologetically.

"Why on earth do I have to shake hands with people in Mass," Mom would spout after we dashed from church early.

"Mom, it is so embarrassing that you won't shake people's hands during the sign of peace. Your fiddling around is so obvious," Ann said as we descended the broad stone steps of the church.

"We never had to shake hands before. I don't know why they are making us do it now. That man standing next to me was sniffling, and I didn't want to catch his cold," Mom defended.

Michael was pulling Ann's hair as he walked behind her. I turned to see him whistling while looking up at the sky as if it wasn't him. Ann absently swatted his hand away in frustration. "Michael, stop being a brat."

Mom called Michael and Ann "Dutch twins" because they were close in age, and they were always bickering. Michael continued to taunt her as we walked to the car, and finally, Ann turned and started swatting at him with both hands in a mad fury as they both broke out into laughter.

My siblings' embarrassment over Mom's church antics was a sentiment I grew to acquire as well—until I didn't—until finally, the absurdity of it all and her nervous energy struck me as hysterical.

Mom continued taking holiday pictures and sending them to Dad. At Easter we'd pose in the living room next to Mom's favorite lamp—a crazy thing with a silver cherub hiding behind a golden strand of ivy. (Mom's key phrase when anyone was roughhousing was "not near my lamp.") We'd gather around Mom the queen, our pin-curled hair puffing from our Easter bonnets, and a giant plastic Easter bunny standing behind us, eating a carrot. Or she'd schlep us all out to stand in front of the blooming magnolia tree in the backyard.

No matter how hard Mom tried, Dad never showed his face. I'll never know how many pictures and letters she sent him during that time when she still knew where he was.

I found out years later about the physical abuse John and Brian suffered at Dad's hand, including an incident where Dad wielded a gun against Mom and John when they lived in the Connecticut house. Dad even fired shots, but John was never sure if he aimed at them or even meant to shoot them; he just said it was the most frightened he'd ever been in his entire life.

We were told that after Dad went to California, he fell into a deep depression. Ann was twelve the last time she spoke to Dad on the phone. She told me how Dad accused her of sounding just like her mother, and she responded with, "You think I sound just like Mom? Good, because I'm proud of that, so fuck you!" and slammed down the phone. Mom never said a word about her swearing. Ann just said she was beaming.

We learned later that Dad told Mom she was too pasty, and we heard those words flailed around throughout my entire life, especially after we found out that Dad had a preference for black women.

That was around the time that Mom ran off to California. Rumor had it that Mom either threatened Dad with a gun (probably the same one he used on her) or threatened to kill herself, which would seem more likely. Nevertheless, it was the incident that drove Dad into hiding for the next ten or so years. I found a copy of the restraining order Dad imposed on Mom years later when my friend Kevin and I were cleaning Mom's den.

I was never aware how much Mom was suffering because she kept her game face for quite a while. Besides, I was too caught up in my own adventures, like playing in the upstairs linen closet with Beth. We'd pretend the closet was our house, and from my third-floor perch on the top shelf, I'd swing my feet and let the light chain dangle in my face and then blow it away. Beth always got the first and second floors—yet another perk of being older.

Mom left to go on trips a bunch of times, no doubt in search of Dad after he disappeared without a trace. I never knew where she was going but would anticipate her return, knowing she had some prize packed away in her red monarch suitcase for Beth and me.

My older siblings were always in charge when Mom went away. One day John got tired of Beth and me clamoring for whees and hoisted us up onto the freezer to get us out of his hair. My stomach froze when John walked away and left us there, but I quickly decided I liked the view. The light in the center of the room over the table looked like four jack-o-lanterns, each in a different vibrant color and hanging at varying levels. The kitchen wallpaper looked like confetti with illustrations of people wearing sombreros on a dark blue background that matched the woodwork around the windows. All the rest of the woodwork was a honey-colored maple. I used to lie in bed and pretend I lived on the ceiling and that the world was upside down; now I could do the same from above.

When John finally came back to get us from the top of the freezer, he had a devilish glint in his eyes like he thought he just taught us a lesson. But he didn't know he'd just created a monster worse than the whee monster. Now Beth and I were clamoring for him to put us up on top of the freezer. It didn't take long for us to devise a way of getting back up on our own, which involved climbing onto the counter, stepping on the handle of the pantry door, and then somehow catapulting ourselves over to the freezer.

[top] Beth (on the right) and I sit under the willow tree with our favorite Tick-Tock Clock. Our neighbor, Mrs. Dorothy Page, later made a painting from this picture, which hangs to this day in Beth's house.

[bottom] I'm in my new dress at Christmas, sitting before my Budding Beauty Vanity.

CHAPTER THREE

Jilted

Being the only girl of four children, Mom was her Daddy's little girl, so when Dad stranded us without a dime, she ran to Grandpa for support. But even he couldn't get Mom to consider selling the Springfield house. It was like asking her to cut off her right arm. That was when Scarlett O'Hara first visited us: *Oh Fiddle-Dee-Dee, why, I could never sell Tara.*

Grandpa was not a millionaire, but he lived comfortably. He owned three sharecrop farms, one of which he sold in order to help us. He also gave Mom a credit card for Sears Roebuck so she could buy us clothing as needed. I liked wearing pretty dresses just like Mom, but Mom rarely used Grandpa's Sears card on me, with the exception of Christmastime. The first piece of clothing I remember getting that wasn't someone else's hand-me-down was my silky blue dress. I also remember fishing through a drawer full of colorful stockings that had already gone through Ann, Paula, and Beth, in a vain attempt to find a pair that weren't either full of holes or burred up with lint that could never be removed.

Then there was the time she bought me my first pair of white patent leather Mary Janes after she grew tired of seeing me wearing red sneakers—the only shoes I owned—with every dress. When we came back from the shoe store, I took out my new Mary Janes with swelling pride so I could show them off.

"Be careful, those might reflect your underwear," Michael laughed.

"Shut up Michael. You're stupid," I said and then took them to my room. I admired them as though they were a china doll. I polished them with the edge of my dress and then carefully packed them back into the pink-and-white shoe box. I even stuffed the toe and covered them with the white tissue paper, then lovingly slid them under my bed for safekeeping. I didn't have to share these with anyone.

Even with Grandpa's help, money was tight, so Mom was forced to take a job as a housekeeper for Papa Luca, a wealthy widower who owned a mansion in Longmeadow. He was also our friend Anita Russo's grandfather. Before moving to Longmeadow, Papa Luca was an industrialist and the developer of the Merritt Parkway, and he helped build the water system for the 1949 World's Fair on Long Island.

Usually I went to the Napolitan's when Mom went to work, but sometimes she'd bring me with her. I loved going to Papa Luca's house because there were always new things to explore in the grand mansion. Mom let me run all over the house while she was working.

"Go play, and be good," she'd say as she shooed me away.

Whenever we went to Papa Luca's, Mom preened and primped in front of the mirror, assessing and reassessing. She'd pull tissue from her bosom to blot her lipstick and then stuff it back, presumably for later use.

"How's my hair in the back, Cha-Cha?" she'd ask, then furiously shoo me away before lavishly spraying her head with hairspray.

"Go away, I don't want you breathing this," she'd warn. I'd watch from the doorway as the Aqua Net fog engulfed her form. Then she'd run, coughing and waving, from the room.

"Come on, Cha-Cha, Mrs. Napolitan gave Alicia the day off, so you're coming to work with me today."

I was happily roaming around upstairs at Papa Luca's—an entirely new fantasy land—wishing Beth could be exploring with me; expeditions like these were always more fun when shared. I knew I shouldn't be poking into closets, but something intrigued me. That was when I saw the lady in the closet.

I ran down the stairs as fast as I could, screaming about the lady in the closet. When I got to the breakfast nook, it was as though I'd walked through the doors of Narnia; the sun streaming in from the glass doors nearly blinded me and stopped me in my tracks. Papa Luca's round wired spectacles reflected the vibrant blue coffee cup on the table in front of him, and Mom sat across from him at the octagonal glass table, ankles crossed and crooked to one side, hands resting demurely in her lap—neither of them fazed by my terror. I half expected little blue birds to be draping ribbons as they gracefully flitted about the room.

"It's just a mannequin, honey," Mom said with a bashful laugh that sounded funny. Why is Mom acting so weird, like some kind of a movie star or something? I imagined her coyly covering her mouth with a titter as Papa Luca told a joke.

I wondered why she wasn't making beds like Alicia did at the Napolitan's.

"Run to the kitchen and grab a cookie, Cha. Papa Luca and I are talking," Mom said, giggling like a schoolgirl.

Several months later, Mom took me to work with her again. I loved that she seemed happier and back to her old self.

"Cha-Cha, get my purse for me. I can't find my lipstick anywhere." Occasionally, Mom would allow me to rummage through her purse. I'd dig through bobby pins and used tissues and pull out her lipstick and pretend to put it on, or sometimes dab perfume on my wrist when she wasn't looking. I loved the smell of her purse.

Mom and I arrived at Papa Luca's house around ten in the morning. Papa Luca stood at the door with a worried frown. "Come in, Elizabeth, I need to speak to you."

"You sound so serious, John. Is there something wrong?" Mom said, with a timid smile.

"Dorothy, you go off and play in the other room while your mother and I talk."

I did as I was told and ran into the room where the television set was. It wasn't on, so I walked around pretending I was in my own castle, using Barbie as my magic wand.

It wasn't long before Mom bustled in with a tear-stained puffy face and smudged lipstick.

"Come on, Dorothy, we have to go home now, and we won't be coming back." I was confused. I wanted to come back. I liked playing in the big old house and listening to Mom giggle.

We went outside without seeing Papa Luca and got into our car. Mom threw the stick on the column into drive and revved the gas as she sped down the long driveway. I knelt on the seat beside her so I could look back at the magnificent brick house with the fountain in the front yard. That was when I saw Papa Luca standing at the side door where we always entered, wearing his three-piece suit, overcoat, and top hat, like he was getting ready to leave. There was a solemn look on his face.

Once we were out of the driveway, Mom's shoulders slumped and her whole body shook as she clutched the steering wheel.

"I just can't believe he's going to marry that woman. I don't know what he sees in her. I thought he actually cared for me! What a fool," she said, dramatically emphasizing the word "fool." I knew Mom wasn't really talking to me. When she pounded the palm of her hand on the steering wheel, rainbows danced merrily around the car from sunlight hitting the two-carat diamond she always wore on her right ring finger, the same ring all four of us girls would swap every six months many years later.

I hated it when Mom cried because it made me sad too. How could I have known that she'd been targeting Papa Luca as a replacement for Dad?

Although the little girl in me likes to think Mom remained celibate after Dad left, the woman in me likes to think she had a passionate love affair with Papa Luca and was happy for a time. I imagine he could have loved her—and probably did—but he had to choose someone with less baggage and perhaps less scandal. And perhaps theirs was a story he could never tell, a story she would never tell, but a story that would perhaps bring a joyful smile to their lips in private moments of nostalgia.

Ann and Paula had both started dating and were constantly bickering over clothes.

"Stay out of my closet, Paula. I know you've been stealing my clothes," Ann said as she stuffed a spoonful of Rice Krispies into her mouth. I could hear popping noises from her bowl even over the roaring sound in my own head from the Cocoa Puffs I was chewing. *Here they go again!*

"I have nothing to wear for my date, Ann. Come on? Besides, you've already hemmed up most of your skirts so I can't wear them anymore. Let me borrow the purple one, p-p-please?"

Mom quietly watched with a satisfied look on her face as my sisters squabbled about miniskirts. She was thrilled to see two of her daughters going out with Russo boys, since they were one of the most prominent and wealthy families in the neighborhood.

John sat quietly eating his cereal in deep thought. Once the bickering stopped, he quietly told Mom that he'd quit his senior year of college and come help out if Mom would agree to sell the house and hand the purse strings over to him.

"Mother, you've got to stop acting like Scarlet O'Hara and give up the plantation. You know Grandpa can't help you forever."

"I will not sell this house, John! Your father and I put our hearts and souls into it, and I won't give up. I just won't." We all knew the hope that Dad would someday return was always in the back of Mom's mind. The house was her lighthouse and beacon for him to find his way home.

"But, Mother, you won't make it. Can't you see this is a sinking ship? You need to get rid of it. It's sucking the life out of you."

"I agree with John. I think it's time to sell, Mom," Brian chimed in.

I didn't want Mom to sell our house. I loved everything about it, so I was relieved she didn't comply.

John graduated from the University of Massachusetts with a degree in physics in 1967. He married his college girlfriend Phyllis a year later. Like Dad, he became a physicist and later got his Ph.D. While working on a grant for NATO in May 1992 in La Spezia, Italy, John co-wrote a book entitled *Ocean Reverberation* with Dale Ellis and H. G. Urban.

The book addressed the emerging trends in ocean reverberation research and had something to do with Scattering and High Frequency Measurements and Mechanisms—basically way over my head. We just knew that John couldn't talk about much of what he did, so we began calling him the spy.

Beth and I were the lost children of the family and were always concocting some new game as though we were living in our own world. One day we overturned our wooden picnic table on top of a log and pretended it was Noah's Ark, rocking back and forth with loud clunking sounds each time it hit the ground. We'd play jump rope and hopscotch on the veranda. If the sun hit it just right, it was like there were a million sparkly jewels glittering in the stone.

One day that summer I was playing outdoors with Beth. We were pretending that the stoops on either side of the front porch railings were our storefronts. "I'll take a dozen eggs," Beth said as she slapped down two of the long green rhododendron leaves that served as our money; the eggs were buds from one of the flower bushes.

Paula and Ann were riding their bikes around the plaza; I could hear the gravel and sand as they hit the one patch where they almost always skidded. Brian was out in the grass with a magnifying glass looking at bugs. Dad used to take my brothers camping, hiking, and fishing, which is when Brian developed his penchant for the outdoors. I was surprised to see him outside since he spent most of his time down in the weight room pumping up his already bulked-up form.

"Lita, I want you to take your sister up for her nap now," Mom hollered from her bedroom window as Paula whizzed by on her bike. "Lita" was Mom's pet name for Paula. She had pet names for all of us. John's was Jughead, Brian, Huckleberry; Michael, Pansy Eyes; Ann, AnnMaria Danmatia; Beth, Bitsy Beth (or as she later became known, Spit-fire); and mine was Cha-Cha.

"But Mom, I'm not tired! I don't want to take a nap. I'm not a baby anymore," I yelled as I craned my neck up toward her window.

Paula didn't want to stop playing to take me up to bed any more than I wanted to go, but Mom insisted.

The tin roof outside my window spanned the length of my room, Mom's bathroom, and one of the back rooms. My sisters used to climb down the trellis after sunning themselves on the roof to get out of doing chores.

From my window I could see Ann still riding her bike around the plaza, and I longed to be back at my store. "Paula, don't leave; I'm scared to be in here alone. There's a monster in that picture," I cried.

"There is no monster there, my baby. Besides, you always have your Guardian Angel watching over you so there is nothing to worry about," she said. Paula was only ten years old, but she always liked playing the role of mother. The concept of my guardian angel had been drilled into my head to the point that I always thought I was being watched and that a little angel always sat on my right shoulder.

"Do you want me to sing you to sleep?" Paula asked. I loved it when Paula sang to me. She began singing "Down in the Valley" while gently patting my hair as I drifted off to sleep.

If Beth and I weren't finding new adventures around the house, we were out gallivanting in the neighborhood. Nobody cared or paid attention as long as we were home by dinnertime. We saw movies at the Bing Theatre for a dollar, and sometimes we'd walk into Blake's Department Store and browse through the expensive clothes that Mom would never be able to afford. The new-clothes-smell filled my head and made me want to stay for hours. We'd mill around until they shooed us from the store. Some days we'd run to Western Beef at the foot of the hill to buy penny candy, taking hours to fill our tiny brown bags as we carefully selected each piece. Or we'd go to Buckey's Corner, twirl on the stools, and order fountain drinks. Mom regularly sent us to Crown Market to get three pounds of ground beef from the deli.

One day after buying a long skinny bag of puffy Cheetos at Snyder's Market at the end of Sumner Avenue, we decided to take a short cut and dodged behind the house that was on the corner of Sumner and Longhill Street. We sauntered through the yard, munching on our Cheetos when some man bolted out his door with a rifle in his arms aimed right at us.

"You get off my land, you trespassers, before I call the police," he growled. Beth and I froze for an instant—mid munch—then we bolted from the yard and didn't stop until we were home, Cheetos dropping like breadcrumbs from the bag.

Although none of those stores are there now, I can still remember the smells of each one of them as though it were yesterday. If you look hard enough, you can still see the Snyder's name etched on the abandoned storefront when you drive by.

I never trusted Michael after the time he told me he just wanted to feel how loose my tooth was and then yanked it out as soon as I let him feel it, a trick I might have fallen for more than once given Michael's penchant for being adorably convincing—a sentiment I can only say now looking back. So when he told me he wouldn't let go of my bicycle seat when he was teaching me to ride, I wasn't surprised when, as soon as the tires were rolling, I was on my own, and shortly thereafter, on the ground. I was always jealous that Beth had the pretty stingray bicycle with the sparkly banana seat and fancy streamers flying from the handlebars. My bike was someone's crappy hand-me-down that Michael spray-painted in the basement to try and make it look better—it didn't work. Instead, the splotchy green bike was just plain ugly and had no cool banana seat or streamers.

Other than Anita Russo, Beth and I mostly just had each other until the Petersons moved in next door, and Lizzy and Mary became our best friends. We'd put on acrobat shows in the back yard on our swing sets. We even planned a production of Rapunzel. I was Rapunzel, and the tiny triangular window above the second-floor landing was the tower from which I threw my rope hair. We pinned together blankets for our curtain that we'd throw from the second floor railing, and we'd invite the neighbors to come be our audience. Usually only Mom and Mrs. Peterson came and sat cheering us loudly with their cocktails in hand.

With Dad, and now John gone from the house, Mom quietly acquiesced as Brian started taking on the father role, and he and Ann would go at it with a vengeance. I remember vicious fights where things were thrown and hair was pulled until Mom would be forced to intervene. One time Ann threw a silver box and hit Brian square in the head, waking the angry beast inside him and making the rest of us run for our lives. I was afraid of Brian's temper, but I knew he got over things almost as quickly as his temper flared, and he'd apologize with sad puppy eyes that made you want to hug him—that is, until he started drinking.

I never remembered John or Michael getting mad or yelling, but then John managed to escape early on. Maybe Michael was more like me and preferred the shadows to the confrontational brash of my other siblings.

At that time, everyone seemed to be fighting more. Phrases like "I'm your elder," "You got out," "I got in," or "Cut it out," "Quit it," "Shut up," "Don't," "Stop it," and "No" were commonplace in those days. But the worst were Paula and Beth who were always at war in some form or other, shoving each other and pulling hair. Maybe it was because they were the middle children and somehow lost, or maybe they were just too much alike.

[above] Grandpa Bill's house where Mom grew up in Browns Valley, Minnesota.

[left] Grandpa Bill and Mom.

[below] Grandpa Bill on the veranda at the Buena Vista house.

CHAPTER FOUR

Minnesnowta

Beth and I were hanging from the back porch rails like we always did. Regardless of the pigeon poop that always seemed to be there, we'd hook our feet on the bottom rail and hold the top rail while dropping backward. The woozy sensation in my stomach was similar to the one I got when John gave us whees. I'd swing and dangle my long blonde hair, sometimes thwapping Beth in the face with it.

I liked how everything looked upside down. Even Beth's face looked funny as she dangled beside me, revealing a slight gap between her two front teeth. Sometimes I'd stick my fingernail beneath the peeling paint on the railing and flick it off.

"Hey, Blondies!" I heard along with the sound of jangling milk bottles.

"Hi, Hank," we both said in unison. Some people thought Beth and I were twins, but we'd always give each other that knowing look when anyone said it because we didn't think we looked anything alike. Nevertheless, sometimes Mom dressed us like twins, and we both hated it.

Hank delivered milk every week. I loved to lick the fresh cream from the cardboard stopper whenever Mom wasn't looking.

"Oh, good morning, Hank," Mom said, poking her head out the back door.

"Hello, Mrs. Preston. Listen, I hate to ask, but you're a bit behind on your milk money. Can I bother you to pay up that tab now?" Hank said.

"Oh my, would it be okay if I paid you next week, Hank?" Mom said, tilting her head with a coquettish smile glued to her face like she was Doris Day selling Happy Soap.

"Okay, Mrs. Preston. I'll see you next week then." I didn't know then that our days of delivered milk were numbered.

"Come on in, girls, I have an announcement to make," Mom said as she grabbed two of the glass milk bottles from the steel crate. "And grab those other bottles, will ya?"

Ann and Paula were at the kitchen table, and Michael was standing by the open refrigerator door, taking a swig of milk. I could hear Brian pounding away at the piano in the other room, playing the same monotonous tune he always played, head down, hair swinging like Schroeder from my Charlie

Brown coloring books. The only thing missing was Snoopy blissfully dancing on top with his head in the air.

"Michael Joseph Anthony, you stop drinking from that container right now! You're going to give everyone your germs," Mom shouted.

Michael grinned, wiped his mouth with the back of his sleeve, and put the milk back with a loud burp.

I wanted to go drink from the milk bottle like Michael did, but instead I sat in one of the wooden chairs next to Beth who had her chin on the table, kicking her feet wildly back and forth like she was on an invisible treadmill. It looked like fun so I joined in.

"We're going on a road trip, and I want you all to start getting your things together," Mom said.

"A road trip? And just where are we going?" Ann asked with a deep frown.

"We're going to drive out to Browns Valley to visit your Grandpa Bill," Mom said.

"I'm not going," said Michael as he sauntered out of the room.

"Mom, you don't even have a driver's license, and you're going to drive us out to Minnesota in your old jalopy?" Ann said.

"I want to go, Mom. I never met Grandpa," I said, thinking it would be fun to go on an adventure. I hoped we'd whoosh away in a big stretch limo like Richie Rich's.

"Me too," Beth chimed in. Beth was almost nine and I was six. We had never traveled before so we were excited.

Ann and Paula both rolled their eyes. "Do I have to go, Mom? Christine asked me to go with them to the Vineyard this summer," Paula said.

"Oh, really? When were you going to ask me? May I remind you that you're only thirteen years old, and you need to get my permission? You think you're so mature," Mom said, wagging her finger in Paula's face.

All the hub-bub came to a blaring crescendo as Brian pounded out the last note of his piano riff and sound and motion stopped. A dusty haze hung in the air and swirled as though dancing in the sunbeam streaming through the window.

The next thing I knew, Beth and I were packing our things into paper bags that we rolled closed and stuffed in the way back of Mom's white Ford Falcon station wagon along with pillows and blankets.

We left Brian and Michael home to watch the house. We will never know what shenanigans they were up to while we were gone, but Mom felt they were old enough to stay home, and besides, there was no room in the car for them anyway.

Mom was in the driver's seat with Ann by her side, and Paula was in the back seat with a cooler and various bags stuffed wherever they could fit. Beth and I were safely ensconced in the way back with our "luggage" surrounding us on all sides. Just as Mom was about to get in the car, she remembered something.

"Wait here, you girls. I have to get one more thing," she said as she ran back into the house. She was wearing a bright yellow cotton dress and white leather sandals. Her hair was flipped in its usual fashion in front and rolled into a French twist behind her head, held with bobby pins. She returned carrying a long machete, the one Dad used to cut brush when they were camping up in Maine years ago. She carefully stashed the tool under the front seat.

"Why are you bringing that, Mom?" Ann said.

"For protection, of course. Do you think I'm going to travel all the way out west with you girls with no protection?"

"Seriously, Mom? Do you really think you'll use that thing?" Ann said with a sarcastic frown.

Ann navigated the course from the passenger seat as we swept across eight states. Beth and I watched from the rear window as the scenery flipped like pages in a magazine. Sometimes I'd lay backwards with my head against the door so I could look at the sky or at the light posts that cast a shadowy frame over my face. I'd stare at the white lines that shot from the rear like a flame and pretended we were in a rocket. Or I'd whip up a poem with which to delight Mom.

Many years later I came across one such poem that Mom had saved with that summer's date scratched at the top. "Bunnies are funny, just like your cakes are yummy. When I eat anyone else's I get sick to my tummy."

Beth and I felt like we were in our own little world in the way back and out of reach. I'd watch with great interest as a fly that had unwittingly entered the car crashed into the windows and buzzed with fervor as though somehow he thought he could break free. Paula finally got sick of the fly and whacked him with a newspaper, leaving his squished remains on the window. Sometimes I'd squint and pretend it was something else, like what I did with puffy clouds that I'd turn into castles or animals.

I knew Paula was mad because she didn't get to go to the Vineyard with Christine, and she pouted most of the way. "One little, two little, three little Indians, four little, five little, six little Indians . . . ," I started to sing.

"Wait, I want to sing the roll-over song," Beth said.

"There were ten in the bed, and the little one said, 'Roll over! Roll over!' So they all rolled over, and one fell out. There were nine in the bed. And the little one said . . . "

"You two be quiet back there," Paula yelled.

Then Ann chimed in. "Ninety-nine bottles of beer on the wall, ninety-nine bottles of beer. Take one down and pass it around, ninety-eight bottles of beer on the wall . . . "

"You all are driving me nuts. I wish I were on the Vineyard right now," Paula said as she tucked her head down and covered her ears.

It was a long trip and Mom would stop at motels with pools at night so we could swim. Ann and Paula would yell about staying on their own sides of the bed every night. It seemed like they were always bickering.

Sometimes during the day Mom would stop at Stuckey's and let us traipse around the store. One time Mom bought me a balloon that was a blue mouse inside another clear balloon. I was overwhelmed by it and kept staring at it as I lay curled up in my fortress, until Beth got mad at me and popped it. I remember crying for hours afterward. I let the sun go down on a quarrel for many nights after that.

For reasons I can't fathom, that event was so traumatic for me that I even kept the guts of that balloon stored in my old broken ceramic bank for years. By the time I finally did part with it, it had practically melted into the sides of the bank.

Our trip was uneventful until somehow we ended up near the Canadian border. Although Mom did not have a good sense of direction, Ann is partly to blame since she was supposed to be navigating. Mom drove into a rotary when she realized she had no idea where we were.

"AnnMaria, which way do I go?" I could hear the tension in her voice. Ann was studying the map trying to figure it out when she looked up and noticed that Mom was still driving around the rotary.

"Hurry up, gosh-darn-it!" Mom sputtered as she continued to go around.

Suddenly, Ann burst into high-pitched hysterical laughter. "I can't see the map," she cried. "My eyes are all watery from laughing so hard." Ann always thought it was funny when Mom blustered because she was sometimes hard to take seriously.

Mom kept driving around and around the rotary. Beth and I were watching from behind as the same things went by several times, Mom in a panic and Ann hysterically laughing. We giggled as we listened to them bicker and laugh, until finally, Mom made a decision and exited the rotary.

When Mom was able to pull over, they discovered we were way off the route. "We're pretty close to Niagara Falls, Mom. Let's go see them! It might be a fun adventure!" Ann said as they studied the map.

Mom made the best of our predicament and agreed even though we weren't prepared to cross the Canadian Border given the set of circumstances by which we had started this journey.

"May I see your driver's license, ma'am?" the border patrol guard asked when we finally reached the crossing. We all knew Mom was unlicensed but she dug in her purse nonetheless.

"Oh... ummm, it's in here somewhere," she said as she pulled out dirty tissues and batted her baby blues at him intermittently. After much stalling and the excavating of various items from her handbag, the border guard finally rolled his eyes and peered in at the chaos inside the car and us four young girls.

"That's okay, ma'am, go on through."

"I don't understand why you don't just get a license, Mom. We've lived in Massachusetts for eight years now. Are you afraid you won't get one because you're a horrible driver?" Ann asked.

"I am not a horrible driver. And for your information, I drove staff cars when your father was in the army during World War II. Back then you didn't even have to have a license. And besides, I had a license in Connecticut."

"So get one again so you don't have to be afraid every time you see a cop," Ann scolded.

"Pish posh, I don't need a license. The government has no right to regulate who can drive and who can't," she said with a smug nod as she drove ahead. We all knew Mom was a bit of a rebel, but sometimes her stubborn nature got the better of her.

I remember the immense falls that spit dewy droplets at my face through the thick foggy air. The rushing water was mesmerizing, like nothing I had ever heard or seen. It was an adventure that none of us would ever forget.

Browns Valley was a quaint little town where everyone knew everyone. Mom was in her glory being back home and seeing old familiar faces at every turn. I loved how she regressed to a little girl around "Daddy." It seemed to me that she had Grandpa wrapped around her pinkie. I would later learn that Mom had most men wrapped around her pinkie. How apropos that Mom had a copy of the painting *Pinkie* by Thomas Lawrence hanging in her bedroom above the fireplace. Somehow I equated Mom's spirit with that girl in the painting. She was only twelve years old when it was commissioned in 1794. She stood defiantly upon a craggy ledge overlooking a coastline with fluffy clouds dancing on a violet-blue and yellow skyline. Her white gown billowed gracefully in the wind. The pink satin sash about her waist matched the bonnet atop her black curly locks, ribbons blowing carelessly in the wind. Her creamy skin was alight with rosy cheeks and dark penetrating eyes as she brazenly stared out at the viewer.

Grandpa was standing at his side door to greet us when we arrived. I never saw Grandpa in anything other than a three-piece suit complete with bow tie. Even when I came down early for breakfast, Grandpa was always there in his suit. I half wondered if he slept in it.

Grandpa's stately white house with the black shutters was situated high atop a grassy knoll among graceful pine trees and next door to the church. Mom told us how she loved the bells that rang every Sunday morning and how she and her best friend, Vincent, would sometimes go and pull on the bell ropes then run away before the priest caught them. Vincent grew up in the house on the other side of the church. Vincent leaned toward the priesthood at a young age. Although Mom never told us, I would not be surprised if there had been an adolescent flirtation between them at one point, but God appears to have won that battle. I wondered if Vincent ever had to chase kids away from his church bells.

We entered the house and walked into the living room. The sun danced through the pines outside the paned windows and illuminated the wood-paneled parlor. A floral sofa covered in plastic sat in one lonely corner of the room. A worn wood-and-leather rocker sat close to the grand piano in the middle of the room. I could smell the musky scent of the leather as I entered the room. From the hallway, Westminster chimes sang out from the grandfather clock. Its quarter and hourly notes would randomly sing in unison with the church bells next door.

"You girls want some cinnamon graham crackers?" Grandpa asked. He reminded me of Santa on his days off with his red bow tie and twill vest covering his jolly belly.

"Ann, I thought you said Grandpa was mean," I whispered when he went into the pantry.

"He used to be stricter when we were little. Consider yourself lucky!" Ann replied.

"Hey, Daddy, where did you move the skillet to? It's not in its usual spot," Mom said as she bustled about in the kitchen. It was funny to hear Mom call someone "Daddy," and I giggled as I watched her maneuver around her familiar old home. At one point, she slid by Grandpa and grazed his cheek with a loving kiss. His face beamed as he silently acknowledged it, both so happy to be in each other's presence. I knew Mom felt safe, which is why she'd brought us here in the first place. She needed to be in a safe place, even if only for a short time.

I awoke the next morning not knowing where I was. I sat up and looked around, and nobody was in the dark room. There was a fresh towel draped over the washbasin at the foot of the bed, and sunlight threatened to burst in through the shade. I briefly wondered why there was a sink in the bedroom; it was as though we had sprung back into another century. There was a pink etched-glass lantern with dangling crystals sitting on the bedside table. I wasn't sure if it was electric or if it ran on fuel, and I did not remember from the night before. I wondered whose room I was in. Was it Uncle James's room, or Mom's, or Uncle Herb's, or could it have been her twin's, John, who died so many years ago? I did not like that thought but nevertheless was captivated by the contents of the room as I glanced around. I made a mental note to ask Mom just whose room I was sleeping in before embarking on my search to find my missing family members.

"Mom?" I yelled. But there was no answer, and I didn't hear any noise in the house. I began to panic as I walked across the hall to Ann and Paula's room. I noticed the window was open, and I could see my sisters sitting on the roof just outside the window. Mom was outdoors yelling up at them.

"You girls get off the ruff this instant! Grandpa Bill will have an apoplectic fit if he sees you up there."

"What did you say, Mom? Should we get off the 'ruff'?" Paula said as she crinkled up her face in laughter. "I don't see a dog around here. Do you, Ann?"

I was poking my head out the window. "Why are you guys out here? Why didn't anyone wake me up?"

"Hey, Mom, Dorothy's up. Can she come out on the ruff with us? Gotta love that 'Minnesnowta' accent, right, Mom? Maybe we can write a 'poim' about it. What do you think, Paula?" Ann laughed, using the name Mom always used for her home state. Mom's midwestern accent seemed to have gotten stronger since arriving here.

"You girls cut that out, and tell Dorothy to come eat her breakfast with Beth."

I heard the slamming of the squeaky screen door as I strolled down the stairs. Grandpa was sitting in his favorite rocker smoking his pipe.

"Come sit on my lap, Dorothy," Grandpa said. "Did you know that you are named after your grandmother Dorothy?"

I nodded. I was looking at his eyes that were crinkled up in delight behind his spectacles as he rocked with me in his creaky old rocker.

"What was Grandma like?" I asked.

"She was a fine and wonderful woman. You carry that name proudly and honorably, do ya hear?"

Our visit didn't seem long enough, and Mom cried and hugged her daddy tightly when we said our goodbyes. I saw him hand her something as she slid into the car with us all jammed in and ready for our journey home.

"Thanks, Daddy, I'll call you when we get home," Mom said as she blew him a kiss and backed out of the driveway with tears in her eyes.

[top] Christmas 1964. "The lot of us looked rumpled and bedraggled." I'm on Ann's shoulders

[bottom left] Thanksgiving 1964. Back: Michael, Brian, John; front: I'm hiding behind the turkey next to Mom then Beth, Paula, and Ann.

[bottom right] I don't look too happy as I stand next to Luke Napolitan in my hand-me-down clothing. Is he trying to hold my hand?

Part II

POOIE

(A New Reality)

[top] This was taken before Beth and I were born, but it's the table under which in later years we stashed food we didn't like. I have this table in my home still.

[bottom left] This is Father Clement, holding me on his lap. I'm wearing one of many dresses Mom brought back from Venezuela.

[bottom right] Mom with her Mexican maracas and straw hat. Mom brought many South American treasures home after her and Dad's brief stint there; hence, her style became a mixture of Victorian, South American, and Asian décor—a sometimes startling combination.

CHAPTER FIVE

Government Cheese, Renters, and a Mexican Divorce

After we got home from Minnesota, things got more and more difficult, and as predicted, Grandpa's money ran out and Mom had to resort to collecting welfare.

We stood in welfare lines in the south end of Springfield waiting to claim the food they doled out. They were long lines, and Mom brought Beth and me along while she waited. I could tell Beth hated it and would hang her head as we stood in line. I just thought she wanted to get home so we could play, but I found out years later how ashamed she was that we had to stand in those lines. I imagine Mom, too, was dreaming of better days as we stood around with people in tattered and dirty clothing, some women with young children clinging to their legs like we were back in the Great Depression. I always wondered what kind of cheese we'd get this time. Maybe it would be wrapped with a pretty label instead of the ugly brown wrapper. And maybe they'd give us real milk instead of the powdered stuff that Mom mixed with water and tasted yucky. I missed Hank the milkman and the yummy, creamy milk he delivered.

They used to send welfare agents to our house for inspections. Those visits always sent Mom into a frenzy, but I wasn't sure why. She'd whirl around moving things and directing us to help her like we were changing props for our next act. I imagine the inspectors didn't visit many twenty-eight-room mansions.

I always say twenty-eight rooms, but the number of rooms in our house was always a topic of conjecture. It depended on what you actually counted as a room. In my mind, I counted everything, including hallways, since many of them occupied a large portion of the house, and we usually had them set up so we could use them for various activities. Twenty-eight was my number; I think Beth's might have been twenty-seven.

"Hurry up, girls, the welfare people are coming," Mom would bellow as she hauled one of the ornately carved Chinese chairs into a closet. Out went the king and queen chair. The brass Persian lamp was hidden behind the Chinese screen, and various other things were carried to the back hallway. Mom threw a tattered blanket over the Monster hoping to disguise it. She'd pile mail and newspapers atop the intricately carved Chinese bar that opened out into different compartments, reminding me of a Russian nesting doll.

The assessors would come in and look around. Mom would nudge Beth and me to speak up when she introduced us. She'd get so exasperated at our shyness and would spout later about how people were going to think she beat us. I always thought she was talking enough for all of us. We might have embarrassed Mom, but mostly I think she embarrassed us. Sometimes I wanted to run and hide, like when she'd tell us to say thank you or excuse me before we even had the chance. Sometimes I'd just close my eyes and wait for her to stop talking. I hated being made the center of attention. I didn't get why Mom seemed to love it. But she didn't like being the center of the welfare agent's attention. After several questions and a disapproving sneer, they'd leave, and Mom would plunk herself down on the pouf in exhausted relief.

"Okay, we can move everything back now." Beth and I just rolled our eyes.

"Are you kidding, Mom? Why do we have to do this? Why not just leave everything out back in case they come again?" Beth reasoned.

"Because I will not keep everything put away. Besides, if they come back, we can just move it again."

Aunt Teddy was Grandma Dorothy's sister who lived in Melrose, Massachusetts, so visits from her were fairly regular. When Aunt Teddy came to visit, she would always bring Beth and me booklets of paper dolls that we'd pull from the perforated edges and play with for hours on end. Beth and I loved these visits, but we were usually shy with new people, so the day Father Clement knocked on our door, we were reserved and polite. Vincent, now Father Vincent, put Mom in touch with Father Clement so she would have a local priest she could confide in. Father Clement was dressed all in black with a clerical collar and a black fedora.

"Good morning, young ladies, is your mother home?" he asked when Beth answered the door, me at her side. He tipped his hat as he greeted us to display his round bald head. His eyes twinkled when he smiled, reminding me of the merry Santa in the animagic *Santa Claus Is Coming to Town*. It didn't take long for us to warm to Father Clement. Unlike most grown-ups, he seemed genuinely interested in whatever new game Beth and I were concocting.

Father Clement loved taking us out for milkshakes, and we'd pile into his white Oldsmobile and drive to the Howard Johnson's at the foot of our hill. Just the thought of its bright orange and teal roofs, cupolas, and weather vanes stirs up nostalgia so deep it makes my stomach do flip-flops. I always thought George Jetson should be behind the counter serving up cones under the Simple Simon and the Pieman logo.

We'd sit at the counter on round turquoise stools twirling between sips of our vanilla shakes.

"Those are awful, awful big shakes," Father Clement proclaimed as he watched me stand on my footrest on tippy toes to reach my straw. After that they simply became known as "awful-awfuls," and Father Clement took us out for them every time he visited.

We didn't know Father Clement's job was to council Mom, but he grew as close to us as any real father. He'd come around on Sundays and holidays. Father Clement grew to love all of us kids, but I think he had a special place in his heart for Beth and me since we were the babies of our abandoned flock. We would sit on his lap and listen as he told funny stories about some of the other priests and about his travel adventures. I could've listened to his smooth dulcet voice all day. Visits from Father Clement and Aunt Teddy were like portable beams of sunlight that I'd look forward to with pure joy.

When Father Clement was relocated to New Jersey, we were all saddened and our visits became fewer and fewer. But he still sent us cards for our birthdays and included a ten-dollar bill in every one of them. Once I sent him a lucky penny I'd found and taped to the inside of a preprinted Christmas card I found in Mom's den. He sent it back to me many years later with this note:

14 December 1977

Dear Dorothy:

In 1965 a little girl first sang a Christmas Carol for me—and then presented me with the finest Christmas greeting I have ever received.

Because time is marching on and I don't want this precious Greeting to be lost, I am returning it to you for safe keeping. It was not only the nicest Christmas Greeting I have ever received—it contained what was perhaps the Little Girl's total Christmas Bank Account in 1965—so it's a precious thing. Please guard it.

Since the only way of knowing if this communiqué ever reaches you is by your acknowledging it—please, send me a note in the self-addressed, already stamped envelope.

Merry Christmas and have a BURGER AT MACKS.

Love,

Father Clement

Years later I asked Father Clement to officiate at my wedding. He responded with a beautiful note (always typed) saying that his health was not conducive to travel. Seven years after that, I received a letter informing me of Father Clement's passing, which still brings me to my knees when I read it.

> I found your name and address among the personal effects of Rev. Clement Buckley, C.P. It is my painful duty to announce that he passed to his reward on the morning of July 22, 1987. Father Clement died in the rectory... He was preparing to celebrate the 9 AM Mass when he collapsed. His death was sudden, and he went just the way he wanted to—with his boots on.

I wonder sometimes if our lives would have been different if he had never moved away.

Mom fought the war over the house. It had become her Tara, but government cheese was not enough to keep us fed and the albatross of a house heated. We desperately needed more money, so Mom decided to rent out rooms.

Peter and Tom were our first renters; they rented the two rooms in the back on the second floor. The back part of the third floor was part of the original servants' quarters that we just called the Apartment. Although it did not have a kitchen, it had two large rooms, a bathroom, a walk-in cedar closet, and the stairway to the attic. The outer room had a set of three paned windows that looked out over the ravine.

The Amusement Room was sandwiched between Brian and Michael's shared room and John's room in the front part of the third floor. I imagine it was originally called the billiard room, but years later it simply became known as the Party Room. The pecky-cypress-paneled room was twenty feet wide by thirty-six feet long, with four large windows overlooking the front yard. Mom had our next-door neighbor, Mrs. Page, paint a mural from an Uncle Remus children's book on one wall, which depicted a waterwheel scene with vibrant greens and blues. Brer Bear and Brer Rabbit might have been walking along the path, but our mural was painted without the characters. I imagine Mom wanted to mimic her first dream house in Idaho Falls that she always talked about. She told us that a Walt Disney cartoonist had painted the walls.

A salesman named Walter ended up renting my brother John's old room. Walter was a curmudgeonly older man with a dry sense of humor. He'd come home and roll Beth and me up in the rug in the center hall.

"There, now you're a tootsie roll," he'd say gruffly. Then he'd pick up the end of the rug and roll us out onto the floor. It was much like when I'd roll down the hill in the ravine, only squishier since Beth was in the rug with me. We loved that game, and like with John, we'd clamor for more until he grew tired of us. Walter loved to tell jokes. "Close your eyes. Dark, isn't it?" he'd say and cackle hysterically while Beth and I smirked. We liked Walter because he played with us, unlike some of the other renters. He and Mom occasionally sat in the living room, talking and laughing over cocktails.

One evening we were all sitting at the kitchen table getting ready for dinner. I was sitting on the hard wooden chair, kicking my legs that did not quite reach the floor. I could hear sizzling sounds from the frying pan as Mom moved about, throwing a dash of this and a "sploosh" of that into the pan like a mad scientist. It was the way Mom always cooked, never believing in the accuracy of a measuring cup. She was pulling her finger from her mouth after sampling directly from the pan when Walter waltzed through the back door. In the beginning Mom asked all the renters to use that entrance; it was a request that was not honored for long.

"Hello, Walter," Mom called out to him. "We're having pooie for dinner, and you're welcome to join us if you'd like."

"Pooie? Well, that sounds pretty appetizing. What exactly is 'pooie'?" he asked.

"Oh, it's my special concoction of rice and various other things from the kitchen," she replied. Pooie smelled different every time Mom made it. Many years later I concocted my own version of it that I called nada in the kitchen.

"I think I'm all set, Elizabeth," Walter said as he strolled up the back hall.

Mom had her back to us, facing the stove, when I noticed Ann and Paula scooping the red concoction into their napkins while furtively glancing up to make sure Mom wasn't looking. I poked my head under the table to see what was going on. They were placing the loaded napkins into the convenient pockets under the table. Paula gave me a stern look of warning, so I kept my mouth shut and covered my mouth to keep from laughing.

"What's so funny, Cha-Cha?" Mom asked.

"Nothing, Mom, the pooie just looks funny," I said.

Other nights I saw them handing food to our dog Yardley who replaced Dudley after he died. Yardley was lucky enough to not be delegated to the back hall.

Pooie was not Mom's finest meal, but then Mom was never a great cook. Sometimes she'd surprise us with some good things like slosh burgers—Mom's version of a sloppy joe—but it wasn't long before we were eating more and more TV dinners or even cereal for dinner.

I was moved to the day bed in Mom's dressing room when Mom decided to rent out my room. It was the first and only time she rented out one of the front rooms on the second floor. I didn't mind giving up my room because the person we rented it to was Celia.

Celia was a fifth-grade schoolteacher who needed a place to stay while she was preparing for her wedding. The first time I saw her was when Mom interviewed her in the living room. Her willowy brunette hair was tucked up into a bun on top of her head. Her elegant legs were wrapped in baby blue capris. I loved her smile and her slight overbite.

Once I woke up to a puppet that Celia had made for me the night before. I remember how magical it was. She placed it on one of Mom's silver candlesticks and left it by my bedside so I'd see it when I woke up. I carried it around with me until its pointy red hat and felt body were worn bare and his bright yellow fuzzy buttons were lost.

I was heartsick when Celia moved out, but that was when Mom shuffled all us girls around so Ann and Paula could have their own rooms. Since Ann was the oldest girl, she got my old room at the end of the nursery hall and shared Mom's bathroom, and the rest of us were on the opposite end of the horseshoe that made up the front second floor. Our suite consisted of the pink room that Beth and I shared, the glass-enclosed sitting room with French double doors that was now Paula's room, and the sea foam playroom complete with fireplace, walk-in closet, and built-in enclosed dressers that abutted the small bathroom.

When Walter moved out, Mr. Franklin moved in, and there was a veritable swinging door of crazy renters that came and went after that, and most of them never paid their rent.

Patrick Murphy rented the third floor apartment in the servant's quarters out back.

"Top of the morning to ya, Mrs. Preston," Patrick said as he entered the kitchen one bright sunny morning.

"Good morning, Patrick. You wouldn't happen to have your rent money, would you?" Mom said as she flipped an egg in the cast-iron frying pan.

"Ah, darlin', yer lookin' mighty fine this morning. What lovely blue eyes ya have. They remind me of the icy blue waters from me hometown in Dublin. 'Tis a mighty fine place and many fine lassies, but none quite as fine as yerself, Mrs. Preston, if ya don't mind me sayin' so. May I call you Elizabeth?" Patrick's fiery blue eyes were ablaze with delight as he smoothed back his jet-black hair.

"Of course you may," Mom said, blushing.

"Now what was that you were askin' me?" he said.

"Oh, never mind, I'll get it from you later," Mom said with a flourish of her hand as she busied herself in the kitchen.

"Methinks Mom is a bit twitterpated with the Irishman, don't you, me wee sister?" Ann whispered to Paula. I started to laugh, and Paula silenced me with a look.

"Shush, we're not talking to you."

I stuck out my tongue and wagged my fingers over my ears. I hated how mean they were to Beth and me sometimes.

My brother John said Patrick was probably the most charming person he'd ever met. He only stayed with us for a few months and only paid for the first week.

Ding-Dong answered the ad to fill Lucci's empty room. Nobody can remember his real name, but I'm told the nickname suited him since, as

Michael put it, he wasn't right in the head. My siblings loved to make fun of him, and he was the brunt of many jokes and stories later in life.

Then there was Lucci, whom John called the "cute little Latina" and said that she had some side jobs that weren't totally legal.

Paula loved Lucci and would spend hours up in the apartment visiting her. Lucci used to do Paula's hair up into intricate braids, telling her it was how all the young girls in the Dominican Republic wore their hair. One morning Paula went up to visit Lucci and found she had moved out. She just disappeared without a word, leaving Paula sad and alone. Once again, Mom was shafted on the rent, but somehow she did not seem fazed by it. Mom forgave everyone their transgressions regardless of what they had done; it drove all of us nuts that she let so many people walk all over her. But in hindsight, that charity is what made her who she was and is why we all stood by her through her own transgressions.

Mr. Franklin, or Harold as he soon became known, was one of the last of the sane renters. He was a traveling seed salesman for Northrup King with New England as his territory. Mom took up where she left off with Walter and began having cocktails in the living room with him. They'd sit with their clinking glasses, chatting and laughing. Mom's favorite swizzle stick was her finger, especially after she'd had a few cocktails.

"Do you need a stir, Harold?" she'd ask as she ceremoniously stuck her finger into his drink to swizzle the tonic around.

"Well, I guess I did!" he'd say with a jovial laugh.

I'll never forget the time Beth and I decided to try some of Mom's vodka. It was a big deal, and we poured it into a small orange cup and ran behind the Monster to try it so nobody would see us. Neither one of us liked it; in fact, I think I remember spitting it back into the cup. I could not for the life of me understand what Mom saw in that stuff.

Paula and Beth were still in grammar school when I started at St. Joseph's. I'd heard a lot of bad things about the nuns, so I was pretty scared as we all walked the half-mile to the city bus on my first day. As we got near the corner bus stop, we could see the green city bus approaching, and we knew it was too late.

"Hurry up and run for it!" Paula yelled as she grabbed my hand and started to run. I stumbled after her as fast as I could, but we arrived about a minute too late, and the bus rolled past without us.

"Paula, we're always late for the bus! I'm tired of running for it every day," Beth said as she crouched to catch her breath. "Now we have to wait for the next bus, and we're going to be tardy on our first day."

"If you didn't take so long getting ready, we would have been out the door earlier, so don't you dare blame me, you little brat," Paula responded.

Paula marched me down the long hallway to my first-grade classroom.

I spotted my teacher standing in the doorway. The towering statue of the Mother Mary stared me down from the end of the hall.

Sister Ann waddled over. A tuft of dirty-blond hair peeked out from beneath the habit that snugged her pinched red face so tightly it looked like she might burst. I wanted to run as soon as I saw her. I longed to be home with Mom, eating my cereal in the kitchen.

Later that day when we were doing phonics exercises, Sister Ann came around to check mine. She saw something was wrong and corrected me. When she came around the second time and saw yet another mistake, her face grew even redder.

"Why can't you get this right?" she said as she grabbed my ear and vigorously shook it in front of the entire class. I could feel my face burning as tears of pain and humiliation streamed down my face. I could hear Michael's taunts in my head. *Look, Dot's turning all red*, and he would laugh and point.

"And why aren't you wearing a uniform like the other girls?" Sister Ann reprimanded.

"I don't have one, Sister," I replied meekly. The uniforms that Paula and Beth wore had changed from a solid navy-blue jumper, to a red-and-green plaid jumper, so there were no hand-me-down uniforms.

Thus, I made my first trip to the Mother Superior's office. Sister Jacqueline was wedged behind her desk, writing furiously. She wore a full habit, revealing no hair. "Excuse me, Mother Superior. Sister Ann said I had to come see you because I don't have a uniform yet."

Sister Jacqueline assessed me with her steely gaze. I was wearing my fuchsia dress with gold clips that closed the fake pocket flaps on my chest. My stockings were tattered and covered in tiny lint burrs as usual. Sometimes I tried to pick them off and bundle them into a great ball. My shoes were Beth's old scuffed Buster Browns; I'd long since outgrown my Mary Janes.

"You're the youngest Preston girl, aren't you?" Sister Jacqueline asked.

"Yes, Mother Superior."

She sighed and shook her head. "Go back to your classroom. I will call your mother and handle this."

The following week I was called back to the principal's office. Sister Florence, the fourth-grade teacher, was standing in the room. Her reputation preceded her. Paula had already had her, and Beth was currently in her class. She was short and round, and everyone called her "Penguin" behind her back. Beth told us how she would yell in class and shake her ruler at them when she was angry, which was most of the time.

"Another Preston girl," she said as she too assessed me. "Come with me, and try on your new uniform." I followed her down the dark hallway. All the classroom doors were closed, but I could hear muffled voices as I passed. Each door had a half-window that allowed you to peer in and see the class. Students sat at attention with their hands folded in front of them. I craned my head as I turned the corner past the fourth-grade classroom, hoping to see Beth, but we were moving too quickly. Sister Florence stopped at the next room and motioned me in as though she were the Ghost of Christmas Past. I tentatively entered as she pulled a new uniform from a cardboard box. I thought it was ugly and was glad I'd avoided wearing it, even if for a short time.

"Put it on," Sister Florence commanded as she stood over me with her pudgy hands resting on her ample hips.

"Yes, Sister." I was horrified that I had to change in front of her in a room that appeared to be a storage room of sorts. But I dared not question her, so I shyly pulled off my dress.

"Sister, I don't have a blouse. I only have my undershirt," I stammered as I looked up at her in my faded dingy undershirt and ratty stockings, burning up with humiliation.

"Just try it on, and then you can put your dress back on. But you make sure you wear it to school tomorrow with a proper white blouse." Little did I know that I'd be back in this very room a few years later being asked to strip from my ratty stockings.

I ran to Mom when I got home. She was sitting in the living room having a cocktail with Mr. Franklin.

"I hate school! Why do I have to go? The nuns are mean and horrible. The only thing I like is Jamie," I cried.

"Jamie? Is that your boyfriend, Sunshine?" Mr. Franklin teased.

"Come here, Cha-Cha," Mom said as she drew me into her arms. "You have to go to school to learn, and you will learn to like it," she said as she kissed my head and patted my hair. "Now, go on upstairs and play until suppertime."

A couple weeks later, I snuck into Mom's bed early, hoping she would forget to get me up for school. I tiptoed across the hall into her dressing room, careful not to step on the squeaky floorboards. I turned the knob as gently as possible, quietly crawled across the floor, and slithered into her bed.

"What are you doing in here, Cha? Isn't it time for you to be getting ready for school?"

"I don't feel good. I think I have a fever," I lied. She rolled over and placed her forearm across my forehead to assess. I loved her smell.

"Okay, I'll let you stay home today," she said with a mildly amused look on her face that she tried to hide. "I'll make you some breakfast." As soon as she left to go downstairs, I scampered out of bed to flip the television on and then snuggled back into her bed.

Soon she arrived with my breakfast of scrambled eggs, cottage cheese, and applesauce on Grandma Dorothy's wooden tray.

My television line-up for these sanctioned school-skipping days would consist of *Leave It to Beaver, The Dick Van Dyke Show, Bewitched*, and *I Dream of Jeannie*, all of which brought me to other fantasy worlds. I wanted to jump into Mayfield and have June and Ward tend to me like a mother and father should. I wanted to wear cute outfits and capri pants like Mary Tyler Moore. I wanted to twitch my nose or nod my head with my arms crossed and appear in another place like Samantha on *Bewitched* and Jeannie, and I often tried.

Mom usually remained in the kitchen while I was up in her bed. I was never sure what she was doing down there.

Around lunch time, she would arrive with more food on a tray. "I brought you an egg salad sandwich, Cha-Cha," she would say with an unusual amount of exuberance. It would be a few years before I discovered why. She set the tray down and came over to feel my head. "You feel much cooler now," she said with a dry smile, her eyes not really fixed on me as she meandered off into the next room, leaving me in the glory that was Mom's bed instead of blushing in front of crotchety nuns.

I remember the Vietnam draft being a big deal that whipped up riots all over the place. Our riot started when Mom got her Mexican divorce in the mail from Dad. Around that same time, Brian was drafted, and it was right after quitting college to help Mom. Brian told me he wasn't even packed and out of his dorm when he received his draft notice. "Assholes had the nerve to send a draft notice to my dormitory," he told me years later.

Although Brian was drafted into the Army, he made the decision to join the Marines instead, basically a fuck you (his words) to the draft board and a decision he'd later regret.

The Mexican divorce arrived right after my brother John's wedding, and Mom went into a Tasmanian devil-style tizzy that sent her traipsing off to Costa Rica in search of Dad once again. I'm not sure what tipped her off to go to Costa Rica. I mostly remember the wooden ashtray Mom brought back inscribed with Costa Rica below a colorful beach hut. I also remember the night Beth and I were spooked from the house while Mom was gone.

Dusk was descending into darkness when Beth and I came home to an empty house after playing at Anita's house. We were playing records in the living room when we heard a ghoulish sound emanating throughout the house. I froze instantly, feeling the hair standing up on the back of my neck. We'd heard noises before, and Mom just said it was "Yahooty," but we had never heard anything like this. I was convinced there was an evil ghost in the house. We both froze for an instant. I bolted straight for the front door without a word. I remember being more scared than I'd ever been, so the thought of grabbing my coat was not even on my radar, regardless of the cold weather. When I looked back from the top of the street, I was shocked to see Beth still at the door trying to pull her coat free.

Without thinking we traipsed on auto-pilot to the safest place we knew—the Napolitan's. Beth and I stood shivering as we frantically knocked at their back door.

"My goodness, you girls are white as sheets," Mrs. Napolitan said. "Come in and tell me what happened." As we tried to explain, we could see that she and Christine were skeptically looking at each other.

"That's nonsense. You girls know there's no such thing as ghosts. Where's your mother?"

"She went to Costa Rica to find Dad," Beth said, shivering as she hugged herself, her stringy hair hanging in her face.

"Who's watching out for you?"

"Michael is," I said. "But we don't know where he is. Nobody was home when we got home from Anita's."

Mrs. Napolitan instructed us to go into the kitchen and make some hot cocoa. "I'm going to get to the bottom of this," she said as she shook her head and waddled away.

We ended up sleeping over that night. I never did know if there were harsh words spoken to Mom and Michael about their dereliction of duty.

Nobody believed us about the ghost, and we didn't find out until months later that the sound came from Yardley, who'd learned to howl, something we'd never heard him do before. I wondered if Yardley was lonely and was howling because he, too, felt abandoned.

Michael quit school right after he turned sixteen. I was delighted to find out that quitting was an option. Michael kept it a secret until Mom drove by and saw him hanging out on the street corner one afternoon when he was supposed to be in school. "I will not have my son hanging out on corners like some hoodlum," she told him. I'd heard Mom threaten Michael with the truant officer a thousand times to try to scare him into going to school; she later used the same threats on me once I started following in Michael's footsteps. I instinctively knew that her threats were idle. She'd have stood at the doorway with the might of a lioness protecting her cubs had anyone ever tried to take one of her babies away. That's why what happened next was no surprise.

Brian was stationed in Camp Lejeune in North Carolina and had been in the Marines about a year when he called Mom and begged her to get him out. He told me years later that his drill sergeant was an asshole, and he hated the food.

Mom pulled it off and was able to get Brian out after calling in favors to some influential people, including Clifford Benson, one of her childhood friends who was a Minnesota State Senator, and Papa Luca, who contacted a congressman he knew—maybe the guilt of jilting Mom led to that favor.

Since Dad was gone, Mom decided to claim Brian as head of household, and Brian was released shortly thereafter. I think Mom still believed that Dad would someday return, but it was the only way she could get Brian out of the service.

Once Brian was home, he and Michael began having wild parties every weekend. Brian was twenty-two and Michael was eighteen. Cars lined the plaza every weekend, and drunks came and went haphazardly and mingled with whatever crazy renters were living there.

I'd lie in bed and listen to the din of the music and footsteps above my head in the party room. Sometimes I'd hear loud voices as people came barreling down the stairs either fighting or loudly talking with overtones of shushing sounds.

I was afraid of the dark so I tied a red ribbon to the lock latch below the doorknob near my bed so I could swing the door open just enough to get a peek now and then. It was as though they were in a different world, and I was peering through my tiny looking glass. I didn't like that they were creeping into my house and turning everything ugly. I wanted my clean playhouse back. I wanted Mom back. It was as though she'd left us, and I didn't even recognize her anymore. There was a fear rising in me that I didn't recognize then, but even now, with a slight trigger, I can be taken back to that very moment and see through that child's eyes.

Maybe all the partying took Mom back to happier days when she and Dad had been in the center of lavish social events with influential people. Maybe she was pretending that instead of drunks falling down our stairs, they were sauntering around in classy sequined gowns and tuxedos.

Mom was forty-nine. She'd always carried herself in a dignified manner, but she started to care about her appearance less and less and began to put on weight. In her mind she was still sleek and svelte, even though she couldn't fit into the posh tailored clothes she once wore that now hung deserted in her closet and soon left their hangers to lay in heaps on the floor that grew almost as tall as me. I imagine Mom trying on dresses that no longer fit her and then tossing them aside in frustration.

Mom was still the queen of my world, but somewhere deep down I knew my queen was beginning to fade.

I discovered that Brian, Michael, and Ann always seemed to be out of cigarettes and were bumming them off each other. Sometimes I would catch Brian stealing one from Ann's pack as it lay on the table, and he'd hush me so I wouldn't say anything. That was when I decided to be the hero and began stealing cigarettes and hiding them so I could produce them for my siblings whenever they ran out. I liked the feeling it gave me to be the star of the show and earn their appreciation. But my plan backfired when they started creeping into my room at night and going through the drawers of my vanity where I'd been stashing the cigarettes.

"What are you doing?" I asked Brian the first time I caught him.

"I know you have cigarettes stashed, Dorothy. Where are they?" It appeared to be a desperate emergency. I jumped out of bed and dug into the back of my drawer and gave him one.

"Come on, I know you have more where that came from. Give them to me," he slurred. His eyes were bloodshot but still puppy-dog eyes. I just wanted to go back to sleep, so I handed him the only other two I had.

Ann shook me several nights later. "Hey, Corkles Pot, wake up! I need you to pull my boots off. I can't get them off," she giggled through her hiccups.

"What? Why are you are waking me up to pull off your stupid boots?" I said in a daze. "Why are you acting all weird?" I tried to sit up straight to get a look at her.

"Come on, I can't get them off, and Paula refused to help me," she giggled as she plunked her boot up onto my pink-and-green striped bedspread. She had to use both hands as though she were picking up a heavy log. "And while you're at it, give me one of those 'Marblubs' you stole from me."

"Shut up, I know how to say it now," I said as I yanked on one of her brown leather cowboy boots.

"Will you guys be quiet! I'm trying to sleep," Beth barked from her bed.

These antics were becoming stale, so one morning I made a decision.

"I will not be stashing cigarettes for you guys anymore. I'm sick of getting woken up every night, so you can just stop looking," I announced as I placed three cigarettes on the kitchen table where Brian and Ann happened to be sitting. "These are the last ones I have, so have at 'em. And, Ann, find someone else to pull off your stupid boots in the middle of the night!" They looked at me for just one second and then dove at the cigarettes. I don't know who came out on top.

Between the cigarette poaching and Brian's early morning vanity rituals in front of my mirror, I was not getting much sleep. Sleep I desperately needed to make it through a school day. I surmised that during one of Brian's cigarette raids, he discovered that the two outer vanity mirrors were on hinges, allowing him to get a full view of his amazing self. I'd often wake up and catch him in my room, combing his hair in the mirror. But only after he'd swiped all of my trinkets out of the way. I was frustrated and wanted him to find another mirror which he ultimately did after Mom yelled at him to stop waking us up.

Not long after the parties began, we were told that Lizzy and Mary Peterson could no longer play with us. Beth and I were devastated to lose our friends.

"Are you serious, Mom? Why can't we play with them?" Beth whined after Mom told us the bad news.

"Mrs. Peterson said we're living in a den of iniquity," Mom said. "That phony witch," she added with a huff. "Like she's holier than thou!"

"What does that even mean? It's just not fair, and I hate her," Beth said as she ran to her room and slammed the door loudly behind her.

Mom was always throwing around some version of Bible quotes like "Judge not, lest ye be judged," or "There but for the grace of God go I," or "Don't look a gift horse in the mouth." We were thankful we could still play with Anita. Both the Russos and the Napolitans always welcomed us into their homes and never ostracized us.

Mary and Lizzie's older brother Kevin bravely started coming over to our house even though his sisters were banished. At first, he would come over at night and help me put up Christmas lights around the veranda. I remember stepping around the pillars on top of the stonewall, hanging on for dear life as we passed the string of lights back and forth to twist them around. Kevin was always incognito so his mother wouldn't know it was him. He'd borrow Mom's old wig (I don't know why she owned one), and then he'd put on Dad's old green army coat that was three times too big for him. I sometimes wonder if Mrs. Peterson knew he was coming over to help and just turned a blind eye.

One day Kevin arrived with some news.

"Mrs. Preston, my mother just told me that Mrs. Putnam knocked on our door asking her to sign a petition to have your children taken away," he proclaimed.

Mom stood up from the mess she was cleaning up on the floor and placed her hands on her hips. "She did WHAT?" she said with a quaver in her voice.

"She told me that she refused to sign because nobody should have their children taken from them. She also told me that Mr. Putnam is going to do an editorial about your family tomorrow night," Kevin said calmly, like he was delivering news about a cloudy day in New England. His blue eyes blazed as he twisted the hair at the nape of his neck, and he walked over to the kitchen table and plunked his lanky body into the wooden chair.

Mom was outraged and sputtered and fumed, but there was nothing she could do.

We sat around the television set like we did when Neil Armstrong and Buzz Aldrin set foot on the moon, only this time it was a different kind of tension and suspense. This time we knew we were about to be torn apart on local television with possibly hundreds of viewers.

Mom always had a flair for dramatics, and she was in full swing—almost literally. I thought she was going to throw the pink princess phone by her bedside at the television screen. Then she started shaking and crying into her hands hysterically. I don't remember which of my siblings tried to console her. I don't even think I fully understood everything that was said. I just remember the gist.

After a failed attempt to get my hands on the transcript, I asked each of my siblings if they could remember what Mr. Putnam actually said, and each of them told me that the other could tell it best. Brian told me Mr. Putnam said things like: *There's a family living on and abusing the welfare system while they are living in an elaborate home . . . With the help of an influential congressman, one son got out of the Marines on a hardship . . . I will bet you ten dollars to two stale donuts that he'll be a welfare beneficiary too . . . There are parties and riff-raff going in and out, and the truancy among the children is rampant . . . This is a home where the children should be taken from their mother, who clearly has no control over them.* Brian remembered the ten dollars to two stale donuts part best, and I could tell it pissed him off. Although our name was never mentioned, it was clear to anyone who knew us who Mr. Putnam was talking about.

Brian told me that Papa Luca was so angry that his name was inadvertently mentioned for his part in getting Brian out of the service that he forced Mr. Putnam to recant. That was the only part he recanted or apologized for, and we quickly became the blight of the neighborhood.

Somehow, the threat of being taken away from Mom became real. I had always dreamed of having a normal life with a father like Anita Russo or the Petersons had. I often fantasized what my room would look like. I even fled from reality by joining the Scholastic Book Club and devouring every book I could get my hands on. I especially loved the ones with introverted girls like me who enjoyed adventure and escapism. But now the thought of leaving Mom—of leaving home—was unconscionable.

Mrs. Putnam's petition failed and so did her sanctimonious attitude when her husband left her for one of the news anchors he'd been having an affair with.

Every time I saw Putnam's face on television, I wanted to spit at him. I reverted to calling him "Putnam" since I lost all respect for the man.

One summer day Mr. Franklin and Mom were in their usual spots in the living room when I sauntered in. "So how's your boyfriend Jamie?" Mr. Franklin asked.

"Mr. Franklin, I like Patrick now!" I answered.

"You are so fickle, Cha-Cha," Mom chimed in.

"Hey, Elizabeth, can I just have the kids call me Harold?" he asked.

"Of course, Hafey, that will be fine,"

"Hey, Mr. . . I mean . . . Harold, Mom must like you since she gave you a nickname!" I said as I sat down.

"Cha-Cha, you and Bethy run along and go play outside now, ya hear," Mom said, waving me away.

We went out to the swing set near Mrs. Page's house.

"Hey, Beth," I shouted, as I kicked my legs out in front of me to launch myself from my swing. "Let's see if we can climb to the top of the pillars!" I got up and ran toward the stone gazebo. The roof of the gazebo had been destroyed in a hurricane years before we bought the house, and the only things remaining were three stone benches, the dog house, and the pillars that once held up the roof. About eighteen inches of re-bar protruded from the tops of the pillars. The dog house, a replica of the big house, was sandwiched between two of the pillars.

After John put us on top of the freezer that day, we discovered that we liked to climb. Somehow it took me to a place where only I could be, and nobody could touch me.

From the stone benches, we hoisted ourselves up onto the roof of the dog house and then managed to shimmy up to the top of the pillars and sat with the post between our legs.

"I'm the king of the world!" I pronounced from my pillar as I raised my arm.

"No, I'm the king. You're the queen," Beth proclaimed.

"You always have to be better—you're such a jerk!" I said, sticking my tongue out at her.

We were interrupted by Mom yelling for us as she clanged the dinner bell that hung outside the back door.

Mom looked funny when we arrived at the kitchen. Her hair was mussed up, and her white shirt had a stain just above her left breast.

"Harold is moving out," she announced as she placed potato chips on top of a tuna casserole with a grimace. I knew either Yardley or the table pouch would be getting fed under the table tonight.

"Why?" Beth asked but seemed bored.

"His territory has changed, and he's moving to Harrisburg," she said as she swished down the remaining contents of her glass.

"Harrisburg? Where the heck is that?" I asked.

"Pennsylvania," she said, a withdrawn look on her face. Another of my favorite renters leaving, I thought, with a downcast look.

"But I don't want him to go, Mom. I like him, and he always brings us taffy," I said. I knew Mom was sad, too, but I was more concerned about myself right then. Why do they keep leaving us just when I get used to them?

After Harold left, Mom joined a group called Parents Without Partners. And it wasn't long after that when one of those partners came calling.

Beth and I were out riding our bikes around the plaza one afternoon when a shiny red Jaguar pulled in and parked in front of our house. A tall tanned man with salt-and-pepper hair emerged from the vehicle. He wore pressed and pleated black trousers with a white short-sleeved polo shirt and Ray-Ban sunglasses.

"Hello there girls! You must be Beth and Dorothy? Say, are you girls twins?" He had a velvety smooth voice that could have lulled me to sleep.

"Who are you?" Beth said suspiciously as she straddled her bike on the tip of its yellow banana seat. I was busy staring at the chrome ornament on the hood of his car that looked like it was about to take a giant leap. I held my splotchy green spray-painted bicycle beside me as I tipped my head to look under the Jaguar, wondering how it was attached.

"My name is Joe," he said. "Is your mother home?"

"You sound just like that guy from all the scary movies. What's his name?" Beth said as she rubbed her chin. "Vincent Price, that's it! I'll go get my mother."

Many suitors were suddenly courting Mom. Now that she was a single woman, she used her charms on whomever she could to win favors.

"Mom, why are these guys coming around lately?" I asked one afternoon.

"They are just friends, Cha, what's it to ya?" Although I loved the idea of an idyllic life with two loving parents like on *Leave It to Beaver* or *The Brady Bunch*, I wasn't quite sure I was ready to get attached to a new father figure.

"I don't want a new father," I said, grimacing.

"Me neither," Beth chimed in as she scanned the contents of the refrigerator.

"Well, nobody said anything about a new father, so get that right out of your heads. Besides, you will only ever have one father."

Rocco was Mom's car mechanic who later sold her a lemon that we called the Bomb. He'd arrive at the house in his greasy one-piece jumper to pick up her car, take it back to his shop, and then deliver it back to her later—nothing like service—but there was always a price to pay. Beth and I were very hard on all these men who were not our father—or Harold, whom we liked best of all.

Norman Barden was another suitor Mom met through her new club. I didn't like the sound of his gruff voice or the way his square head looked like a wiry Brillo pad.

"Yeah, this is Norman. Is your mother there?" He reminded me of an angry militant bootcamp commander whenever he called and barked out orders for us to go retrieve our mother. I would sarcastically salute and then stick out my tongue, knowing he couldn't see me.

"Mom, it's Barden," I yelled up from the phone booth, making sure I held the phone close enough so he could hear. I wanted him to know that I disliked him just as much as he seemed to dislike us.

"I don't like that guy," I told Mom later. "He's mean and ugly."

"Judge not, lest ye be judged," she said as she applied her lipstick.

"I'm not judging him, Mom. He's just stupid. He's always barking orders at us whenever he calls, and I don't like him," I said.

"Yeah, Mom. I like the guy with the Vincent Price voice much better," Beth said. "But why do any of them have to come here?"

"I'm with Beth. Why don't you just go out with Joe? He's so much better than stupid Barden or Rocco," I said.

"Joe's a namby-pamby mama's boy. And he still lives at home with his mother at fifty years old," Mom replied.

"Then why go out with any of them?" I pleaded.

"Don't you like having friends? And don't you think I might too? I have nobody since your father left, so stop being so selfish," she said as she stomped out of the room.

Charlie showed up at our door one rainy afternoon. He was originally from Louisiana and was in the area on a big job installing carpet.

"Yeah, I'm answering the ad in the paper for a room for rent," he said, rubbing his scruffy beard. Mom never turned anyone away as long as there were empty rooms. The apartment happened to be empty at the time, so he took it.

"Mind if I keep my fish tanks here?" he said as he continued to vigorously scratch his wiry gray hair. His dirty green khaki pants hung loosely off his generous form. His yellow shirt revealed blotchy underarm stains that reeked even from ten feet away.

"Mom, that guy stinks," I said later. "Does he have to live here?"

"I don't think you understand that I need all the help I can get just to put food on the table and keep this place warm in the winter," she rationalized.

Charlie ended up hiring Michael and Brian to help him on the job and taught them how to sew carpet, and kick carpet, and just about everything you always wanted to know about carpet. Carpet laying became Michael's business and would carry him through life

One day Charlie walked into the kitchen when Beth, Paula, and I were sitting at the table snacking. He pulled up a chair and plunked himself down.

"Mornin'," he said as he drew Mom's newspaper near to him. "What are you kids doing with your day today?" He briefly looked up from the paper as though he were part of the family. Then he took a pen and a scrap of rumpled paper out of his pocket and put it down on the table. "Make a mark," he said as he shoved the paper in front of me.

"What do you mean?" I said.

"I mean make a mark, anything. I'll turn it into a picture."

I made a squiggly line on the page, and he quickly sketched a man with a hat.

"Wow, that's pretty good," Beth said.

"Now make a real mark," he said as he pounded the paper and shoved it at Beth. Beth made an intricate swirly mark on the paper, and Charlie quickly turned it into a house with trees and swirly flowers beside it. We continued in this fashion and discovered that there was nothing we could draw that he couldn't turn into a picture. He laughed as he got up to leave.

Mom sent me to tell Charlie he had a phone call one afternoon. The light from the glass door above lit the narrow stairway that led to the upstairs apartment. The glass on the door made a loud tinny sound when I knocked. Charlie answered the door, and I relayed my message. I looked around and saw that all four walls were lined with myriad fish tanks holding fish of all colors and sizes. I had never seen anything like it.

"Can I look?" I asked.

"Why sure," he said as he moved toward one of the tanks. "Look at this one, these are my faves—Siamese fightin' fish from Thailand." I watched as they swam gracefully around the tank displaying their long and elaborately colored fins.

"Go ahead and poke around. I'm going to get my phone call," he said as he left.

The smell in the room did not go unnoticed, but my fascination with the fish drove me to stay longer and look around. Garbage was strewn everywhere. There was an open pizza box with half-eaten crusts, and crushed cigarette butts had been tossed in the corner near the window. I wondered how long it was since Mom had seen the condition of the room or if she would even care. I spent some time enjoying the fish exhibit before my nose couldn't take it any longer.

Charlie let me come and visit the fish many times after that. Despite my reservations, I liked him. Mom let him cut glass in the basement, and he built his own fish tanks. By the time we started seeing cockroaches in the kitchen, it was too late. Mom always called them Charlie's cockroaches, and Charlie left us long before the cockroaches did.

[top left] Brian was 40 or 41 when this was taken. This professional photo was later made into a giant painting on canvas that was passed around the family over the years so we could always keep Brian close.

[top right] I'm sitting with a couple of friends, one of whom is wearing Mom's wig. This was taken before the velvet-flocked wallpaper above our heads began to peel.

[bottom left] My seventh-grade year at Saint Joseph's with my chum Diane. We had finally graduated from jumpers to skirts.

[bottom right] Ann, Paula, Brian, and Beverly. Brian and Beverly married and moved into our third floor, but the romance didn't last very long.

CHAPTER SIX

Changing Tides

I don't remember when Michael started calling Mom Liz, but it made Mom angry.

"Michael Joseph Anthony, I am your mother! I demand that you stop calling me Liz," she'd sputter and fume. But that only sparked him to say it more, until at some point it just became habit. We all knew it wasn't out of disrespect—he just loved to tease and get reactions. Like when he'd pin Beth and me down when we were little and tickle us till we cried or peed our pants; or how he'd smear peanut butter in Ann's hair and run away with her chasing, ultimately ending in a food fight and both of them covered in peanut butter and jelly, or flour, or whatever was in reach until Mom came in and broke it up.

When Michael came home with his daughter Lisa, I was eight years old. I never knew what was going on, I just remember a lot of whispering. Lisa was the first baby I'd ever held. Ann would bounce her like a ball on her lap, but I was afraid she'd break if I even moved. Michael told me later that Lisa was born under an alias since she was being prepped for adoption. Michael didn't want her to be adopted, so he concocted a plan with his friends Ray and Barry to kidnap the baby. Luckily, Joanne finally agreed to marry him, and Michael moved out of the house shortly after Lisa was born.

Brian was always pulling into the driveway with one beautiful woman or another. But the one I remember best was Squeaky. Squeaky's auburn hair was piled high atop her head in beehive fashion. She stood smiling with a blank stare in her white leather boots, yellow mini skirt, and tight white shirt that left little to the imagination.

"Hi, everyone, this is Puff," she said in a shrill piercing voice, illustrating immediately how she got her name. She held out a large fluffy purple key chain in her outstretched hand that was apparently "Puff." Brian laughed like a schoolboy.

"Isn't she cute? Come on Squeak, I'll show you my room," he said as he led her up the stairs. Mom didn't think she was so cute when she arrived with her pet boa constrictor on her next visit.

I remember well the day Brian arrived home with Beverly and announced they were getting married. We were all shocked, but Beverly seemed to make Brian happy, although all beautiful women made Brian happy.

They were married in Beverly's back yard, which seemed fitting to her hippie / flower child personality. Brian was the second of my siblings to be married by a Justice of the Peace, and Mom was none too pleased about that.

On their wedding day, Mom strolled over to Beverly, who was wearing a simple garden dress with baby's breath adorning her brown hair that was parted in the middle and fell softly to her mid-back.

"Welcome to the family, dear," Mom said. "Did you know that Brian is my lucky seven? Seven pounds, seven ounces, and born November twenty-seventh at seven P.M. We always called him Huckleberry because he loved every kind of critter there is," she said, patting Brian's back proudly. Brian blushed like a little boy as Mom was extolling his virtues.

"Isn't she great, Mom? I just love her," he said as he hugged Beverly close to him. I liked Beverly too. She had a friendly smile and was always kind to me.

After Charlie moved out, Brian and Beverly moved in and took over the entire third floor. At some point they began fighting, and before long Beverly packed her bags, leaving Brian to the assigned duties that Mom had bestowed upon him of disciplining us. Their bliss lasted short of a year.

Some mornings Mom woke up chipper and would barge into my room. *Seven-thirty, your face is dirty*, she'd say as she snapped my shade open all the way to the top.

"Mom, can I stay home today, please?" I pleaded.

"No, you need to go to school today. I know you aren't sick. Now get up."

Mom never paid attention to how we were dressed when we left for school, other than to make us wear those ugly red rubber slip-ons over our shoes when it rained. We would ditch them in the bushes as soon as we were out of sight because we were so embarrassed to be seen in them. But even more embarrassing was when Sister Florence, my fourth-grade teacher, pulled me out of class one autumn afternoon.

"Come with me," she instructed as she waddled ahead. I could see she was heading to the same storage room where she took me to try on my uniform in the first grade, and I began to cringe. I had no idea why she was singling me out, and I could feel my face burning once again as I walked behind her in shame.

"Now come in here, and put these stockings on," she said, handing me a brand new package of pantyhose. I never had a pair of sheer stockings like Mom's before, so part of me was excited when I saw them.

"You want me to put them on right here?" I asked tentatively, not sure how harshly she would respond.

"Yes. Now do it," she commanded. I looked up sheepishly and drew down my torn and lint-covered blue tights. She took them from me and tossed them briskly into a nearby trashcan as she nodded at me to proceed.

I hated that I always felt tattered and dirty. Why couldn't I have a normal family like Anita and some of my other friends? I was more than sure that their teachers never made them change in front of them in a cold storage room. My resentment was finally starting to rear its ugly head. I imagined that my classmates were in on the conspiracy and that they could see me through some hidden camera and were watching and laughing at me. I half expected—no, hoped—that Allen Funt would jump out and tell me that I was on *Candid Camera*, as I burned in embarrassment.

I hated school more than ever now and would do anything to not go, including spending an entire day hiding under Paula's bed after Brian got the call instead of Mom that I wasn't in school. I remember hearing Brian answer the phone, which was when I skittered under the bed in the next room before he burst in.

"Dorothy, where are you, you little bitch?" he snarled. Then he stomped into Paula's room where I was shaking like a leaf underneath the bed and praying that he would not find me. I could hear his heaving breath as he stood there for what seemed like an eternity with his feet visible at the foot of the bed. Finally, he left. But I stayed hidden in that very spot all day long like a frightened kitten, just waiting for Mom to come home and save me. I contemplated what I would say as I counted the wooden slats of the box spring and blew dust bunnies away from my face. I knew Mom would defend and protect me from Brian regardless.

I told that story to Brian years later and he felt contrite and sorry that he'd ever scared me to that degree.

Paula had just started the ninth grade at Forest Park Junior High. Like Michael, she decided not to continue with the nuns and opted for public school instead.

"Get out of my chair, you little brat," Paula said to Beth as she came into Mom's room where we were watching television one morning.

"You got out, and I got in," Beth said in a snide tone.

"I am your elder, and I was sitting there first, so move it—now!" Paula commanded as she shoved Beth.

"You're such a stupid jerk," Beth said as she pushed Paula back even harder. And thus began an ugly fight as they slapped each other and pulled each other's hair. I always seemed to take the role of audience, watching the chaos that was our life from a safe distance. But this time I ran to the top of the stairs and yelled down to Mom.

"Mom, Paula and Beth are fighting again."

Paula met Gary while visiting Christine in the Vineyard.

One day Paula and Gary were draped on Beth's twin bed as I was busy gluing yellow yarn that was supposed to be my hair to the shoe-shaped drawing I was working on. I noticed Paula and Gary smooching on the other bed beside me.

"You guys kiss like movie stars," I said.

"Four feet on the floor, and keep that door open," Mom yelled as she passed by my room. Mom only allowed it because it was out in the open, and I was there to chaperone.

After that, all of their letters were signed with "SWAHK" which, of course, meant Sealed with a Hollywood Kiss.

It seemed we were all falling apart. Now that Paula was dating, she never seemed to be around, and Ann was about to leave for college.

I was watching Road Runner outsmart Wile E. Coyote as he had a thousand times and wondering why he never learns. As I was contemplating this, Ann strolled over to the television set and turned it off. I watched the subtle glow from the tube in back gradually fade.

"Hey, what are you doing? I was watching that." I said as my drowsy mind caught up to real time.

"I need to talk to you, honey. You know I am getting ready to go away to college, and I have to tell you something because you are old enough to know now," Ann said as she nervously wrung her hands. "Mom is an alcoholic."

"What does that mean?" I asked.

"It means that she drinks too much, and sometimes she can't control herself."

"I don't get it. What are you saying?" I just couldn't grasp the seriousness of what she was telling me. I could hear the phone ringing somewhere off in the distance as I sat looking at the pretty wallpaper above Ann's head. I imagined it was a magical garden, and I wanted to jump into the scene and walk through the mossy gate over to the warm cozy cottage beyond.

"Dorothy, did you hear me? You need to be strong after I go. Can you do that?"

I wasn't ready for this. I wanted to cover my ears and sing to drown her out. I knew Mom had changed. It was as though by acknowledging it, I too would somehow change.

My mind was reeling. I remembered how silly Mom always seemed later in the day after she'd spent the day in the kitchen when I was home sick. I thought of how we were ostracized from our friends after Putnam's editorial and how dirty our house had become with scary prehistoric cockroaches that gave me nightmares. I thought about the strangers that roamed around with smelly beer cans and cigarette butts that'd wind up drowning in the can's remains.

I missed the Mom who laughed at all my silly childish games and who cheered us on at all of our made-up plays; the Mom who taught me how to make potato salad (one of the few things she could make well); the Mom who made up silly names for things like "plappying" the burgers; the one who mistakenly brushed her teeth with Desitin, mistaking it for toothpaste, and sprayed her hair with Arrid Extra Dry instead of Aqua Net because she was thinking of something else; the fashionable Mom whose flair for style was stunning and whose zest for life was even more so; the

Mom who wore silk stockings and blew kisses to herself in the mirror with ruby red lips.

Somehow none of the crazy had registered as abnormal until now. Beth and I had been living in a bubble inside our life-sized playhouse.

"It's okay, honey," Ann said as she lovingly took me into her arms and kissed my head.

By September, Ann had left for Lasalle Junior College. There was a part of me that left with her, my reasonable, loving sister who loved to laugh and tease almost as much as Michael did. I cried as she walked out the door, knowing she would never live under the same roof with us again.

Paula told Mom she was pregnant shortly after Ann left. Paula was only sixteen years old, but Mom felt she had no other choice but to allow her to marry Gary. Like with Michael's big secret, I was not privy to the conflict that went on behind closed doors when Mom found out.

With everyone bustling around the house to prepare for Paula's upcoming wedding in February, Mom shipped me off to Michael and Joanne's for New Year's Eve. That was the night I got drunk for the first time and witnessed more than I should have at age ten.

Michael let me have a beer that night. I remember it was bitter at first, and I didn't like the smell, but after a couple sips it wasn't so bad, and I decided I liked it much better than Mom's vodka. With Michael and Joanne distracted by their party, I took advantage of it and sucked down a few more beers—maybe it was just one more beer; I'm not sure. Or maybe I was sucking down the remains of the cans abandoned in the kitchen. My head was dizzy so I went to lay on top of Ranny the dog. He felt softer and smelled better than Yardley. Ranny let me lay on him until someone pulled me off and led me to the couch in the other room. My next memory was of waking to voices. At first I thought it was Paula. I think I even called out her name. But when I rolled over there were two naked people frolicking on the floor. I'm not sure how long I watched before Michael came in and angrily made them leave. I remember being intrigued, which prompted questions to Mom the next day. That was when I found myself in Mom's dressing room listening to her stammer and stumble over words like precious, and flower, and sanctity of marriage. I learned more when Anita and Beth and I found an old *Playboy* that Mom had confiscated from Brian. Anita tried to explain sex to me by sticking out one finger and poking it into her other circled hand, the idea of which I thought was disgusting.

Mom felt more comfortable explaining my menstrual cycle. She didn't want me to think I was dying like Ann did when she first got hers.

It was February 1972 when Paula and Gary were married. It was also the day before my eleventh birthday and a few days before President Nixon made his epic trip to China. Much to Mom's delight, they were married at Saint Joseph's Church. The reception was held at our house in the three front rooms. Mom was heavier than she'd ever been, but she looked beautiful in her gold lamé dress, watching her first daughter get married.

Paula and Gary moved to the Vineyard right after they were married. Paula didn't have a baby until over a year later. We all knew Gary was her ticket out.

Everything changed so fast. Like the crack of a whip, all my siblings were gone except Brian and Beth.

I started noticing everything Mom did, and I started to hate her for ruining our lives. There were still glimpses of the old Mom, like when we'd bake in the kitchen and make rhubarb pies together and whip up massive batches of potato salad. She taught me about boiling the potatoes in their jackets, making peeling them much easier. The kitchen became a bustling Mecca with clouds of flour rising into the air, butter and apple peels strewn about the table, rubber spatulas, and hand beaters. Sometimes Mom and I would have contests to see who could get the longest peel from an apple.

Other times were when we went to visit Paula in the Vineyard. I remember going to the Vineyard with just Mom many times. I'm not sure why Beth didn't join us, but it might have had something to do with how she and Paula always fought. Those were magical times when I got Mom all to myself. We'd pile into her maroon Lincoln Continental with the suicide doors and then stop for lunch before boarding the ferry in Woods Hole. The smell of the ocean air mingled with the wafting odor of fried fish. Seagulls soared and screeched above our heads when we got out of the car. We sat at a quiet corner booth by a window that looked out on a marsh where a pair of blue herons frolicked in the tall grass. I ate a burger, and Mom got fish and chips, and we laughed and talked like normal people.

Mom never wanted to sit inside on the ferry, so we always stood out on the deck and leaned over the rail so we could watch the ocean curl up like someone stuck a beater into a vat of milk. Mom's blonde hair would blow in the wind under her kerchief as she held onto the back of it, seemingly in some kind of ocean trance. I wondered if she was thinking about Dad. I loved her so intensely then that I wanted to cry.

The rumbling of the steamboat engine was lulling, as seagulls swarmed in circles, hoping for some stray pieces of bread; their piercing screams reminded me of Russos' summer cottage in Groton Long Point that smelled of mothballs. That was the time Paula found an injured seagull and wanted to nurse it back to health. Mom wouldn't let her touch it since she feared it carried germs, but we watched the seagulls with delight for the two weeks we were there. The injured seagull's mate never left her side, and Paula named the pair Henry and Henrietta.

When we arrived at Oak Bluffs, Paula was there to pick us up. She drove us past the gingerbread houses that Mom loved so much. She admired the intricate and brightly colored homes from the car window with the delight of a young child peering into a dollhouse.

Mom cooked dinners while we were there, and she never had a drink. We laughed and talked and romped in the waves at South Beach, which were exactly as Mom had claimed—the biggest waves she'd ever seen.

I made a lot of trips to the Vineyard after Paula moved there because at ten years old, Gary's sister Kathy was my new best friend. Mom would drop me at the bus station in Springfield, and I'd get off in Woods Hole, feeling very grown up. Sometimes I'd even take my bike and ride around the island with Kathy, or visit Gay Head with its breathtaking cliffs. Back then you could walk on the cliffs and snitch pieces of clay souvenirs, some of which I still have.

Later that summer we went to visit Grandpa Bill in Browns Valley again. This time Harold joined us.

I never saw Mom bring a man home to her bed, but I knew she was still stringing along the men that had proposed to her, and Harold was one of them.

All us kids liked Harold best of all. I would rather have poked my eyes out than to take any trip with the likes of Barden or Rocco, so we were happy to have Harold along.

Harold drove while Mom and Ann shared navigating duties; maybe with two of them we'd steer clear from the Canadian border.

"You two girls are going to sit in the back seat, and Paula and Gary can ride in the way back," Mom announced.

"That's not fair. Why can't me and Beth have the way back?" I whined.

"Beth and I," she corrected.

"But Mom, that's our spot. They just want to play kissy-face back there like they always do," I said.

"Shut up, you spoiled little brat," Paula said as she made a cozy spot for them in the way back. I folded my arms across my chest, slunk down in my seat, and pouted.

"Dorothy, get over it, and stop your pouting," Ann yelled from the front seat.

Since I couldn't stretch out in the back and sleep, I began slumping in my seat and laying my head on my pillow up against the cooler that was wedged between Beth and me.

We were in Elgin, Illinois, when we stopped for gas and a bathroom break. "I'm going to the bathroom," I said to Ann as I hopped out of the car. When I walked back to the car, it was gone.

"Gone? How could that be? They couldn't possibly have left without me. This has to be some kind of joke that Gary dreamed up," I thought. I walked around back, but there was no sign of them. When I saw the look on the gas station attendant's face, I knew it was no prank. Now I didn't feel so cool in my Coca-Cola pants as I sat anxiously waiting for them to return. The candy bar the nervous gas station attendant gave me stuck in my throat, fighting the lump that was already there. I bravely waited until at last they pulled into the lot, and I burst into tears like a three-year-old and ran for the car.

I was told that Harold had driven for several miles before anyone even noticed I was gone, and Mom only found out because I didn't answer when she asked what kind of sandwich I wanted.

"You're such a jerk, Ann," I said as I slapped her from the back seat. "I told you I was going to the bathroom."

"I'm so sorry, honey. I just forgot," she said on the brink of laughter.

"Why do you always think someone else's tragedies are so funny? Like when you laughed at Mom when she fell off the radiator. Why is that funny to you?" I yelled. Now Ann couldn't contain herself and was not trying to hold in her laughter any longer.

"How could you not think that was funny? You saw how she fell back like she was a stiff board!" she said.

"You are demented," I said. At least I got a Coke and a candy bar out of the deal.

Mom and Harold still went out of their way to find a hotel with a pool every night. They'd sit poolside with their tinkling drinks as they watched us with delight. Beth and I would do handstands, legs kicking wildly outside the water, trying to stay straight; Mom would never tell whose was best. We'd have tea parties sitting cross legged at the bottom of the pool—pinkies flared, cheeks bloated, hair swaying in slow motion like seaweed in the waves—until one of us gave in and pushed bug-eyed to the top for air. Our fingers wrinkled and felt like sandpaper, but we didn't care. It was only when our lips turned purple that Mom made us get out, and we'd stand shivering with a white Holiday Inn towel draped and snugged tightly around our shoulders.

"Hafey, will you mix me another?" Mom would ask, as she gave him a bewitching glance. She knew Harold would do just about anything for her, and she took full advantage of that.

Browns Valley was quaint as ever. This time we visited Bob and Ruth Clifford's cottage on Lake Traverse. Ruth was Mom's best friend when they were in grade school. Mom loved to tell us about how she could step over the river at its tip and into South Dakota. She taught us a few phrases from the local Indian Tribe that I still remember, but couldn't begin to spell. And Grandpa gave me one of his Indian arrow heads from his collection that I still have today.

I loved seeing Mom revert to her spirited youth when we were there. I wanted to stay and leave the cockroaches to the renters.

It was our last visit to Browns Valley before Grandpa died later that year.

Beth and I were coloring at the dining table preparing for our Halloween decorating fest, like we did every year, when Mom broke the news.

Orange and black construction paper was strewn about the table, and several already made jack-o-lanterns stood lined up and waiting to be hung beside the pictures of ghosts peeking from behind trees with speech bubbles that said "Boo."

I remember Mom sitting at the table, tears streaming down her face and telling us that he's with God now. But that didn't make me feel any better. I didn't know how to feel, and I don't even remember if I cried. I had learned to love Grandpa even though I only visited him twice. He always sent personalized letters on Wm. L. Paul stationery that he pounded out on his old typewriter that always seemed to raise the r's. Grandpa told me in a letter once that I wrote more letters than anyone else in the family.

Mom flew out to Browns Valley with Ann to attend the funeral and help to settle his things.

Since Mom had already used up all of her inheritance, she only got a few of Grandpa's things, including his favorite creaky wooden rocking chair with the leather seat. She put that chair in her room at the foot of her bed. Whenever I looked at it, it took me back to a time when Grandpa rocked me on his lap on our first trip to Browns Valley. Sometimes I'd find Mom slowly rocking and looking wistfully off into the distance. I knew she was reliving memories of her special daddy, a bittersweet nostalgia different from the pain on her face when she stared at the Christmas tree from the radiator. It broke my heart.

Mom, Beth, and I went to visit Harold in Harrisburg many times after our Browns Valley excursion. I always thought Harold's apartment was like a hotel—neat and clean. Beth and I would run to the room that was reserved for us and jump on the bed with its shiny green bedspread, just as we always did at hotels. Harold's sheets always matched the spreads until Mom bought him safari sheets with wild-colored animals on them. Since his taste was fairly conservative, I'm guessing the safari sheets were a bit of a stretch for him, but since Mom loved them, he loved them. I still have one flat sheet tucked away in an old trunk in my basement. For the life of me, I cannot ever get rid of it.

I loved having Mom to myself without the distractions of the house around us. I used to create fake newspapers with silly stories to entertain Mom and Harold. Mom's eyes would light up as she read them, and it fed my fire to do whatever I could to hold her attention.

Sometimes Mom and Harold would pack Beth and me up and head to Misquamicut Beach in Rhode Island. Mom would go have drinks with Harold in his adjoining room while Beth and I bounced on the beds or swam in the pool. Sometimes our rooms had Murphy beds, which provided hours of fun and playtime for us as we closed each other up into the wall. But most of my fun was spent out at the beach, playing in the waves and getting burned so badly my skin would bubble. Beth always thought I was gross when I'd pop the blisters and peel my skin like a grape then ball it up like a rubber ball. We'd lather Noxema all over us at night and walk around like zombies so we wouldn't get it on our nightgowns.

Summers were always too short though, and I knew that soon I'd have to go back to the nuns, the cockroaches, and the dreary renters.

[top left] I'm sitting on one of the trash picks that Kevin and I scored and lugged up to the third-floor party room.

[top right] Donning a couple of Mom's coats, my friend Rhonda and I pose in front of the main stairway.

[bottom left] Michael caught me at the door as I tried to sneak in under the radar with my snorkel jacket on.

[bottom right] Gina in the third-floor party room, standing in front of the Uncle Remus wall mural that Mrs. Page painted.

Part III

SALAD FACE

(Never a Dull Moment)

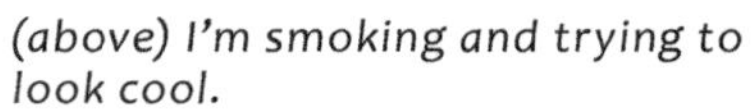

(above) I'm smoking and trying to look cool.

(above right) Barry, Gretchen, and Brian.

(right) Arthur, our renter who held the second mortgage to our house.

(below) I'm passing a joint to Beth.

CHAPTER SEVEN

Miss Havisham's Mansion

With things declining around the house, Kevin Peterson started coming over more often to help out with various projects, and I was always his sidekick.

We had already painted the old servants' kitchen off the regular kitchen—black, much to Mom's dismay. In our defense, it was the only paint we could find in the basement. We also cleaned out the closets in Mom's dressing room several times, but they always seemed to morph back into heaps of clothing. I remember jumping onto the pile of clothes like it was a pile of leaves. When I was younger, Kevin's sister Lizzy and I played dress-up with many of the old ball dresses Mom had.

Some of Mom's old ball dresses even served as costumes for our plays. One of the closets nearest to her room was full almost to the ceiling with a heap of worn clothing. The doorknob and the latch were broken, so the closet was always locked, but the skeleton key hung crookedly in the lock like someone once bent it trying to pry it open. I discovered later that it was Mom's secret vodka-hiding closet, which explains why she never liked us going in there and why she had a similar fit when we tried to clean it.

Kevin and I even tried to get the elevator running once and thought we had succeeded until Kevin got stuck inside. After that, we left it alone. That might have been the same day that a moth flew into my ear, and Kevin decided to suck it out with the vacuum cleaner—thankfully, Paula stopped him.

One day we decided to tackle Mom's den, which was Dad's old lair. It looked for all the world like a room in Miss Havisham's decrepit mansion—complete with cobwebs. Six windows spanned the outside wall at the front of the house surrounded by wood paneling. The inside wall had a fireplace abutting my room. (Beth had swiftly moved into Paula's old room, and she called it her "treehouse," leaving me the pink room all to myself.) The once lustrous and shimmery green couch had an old broken chair and some cardboard boxes on it. Hanging above the couch was a portrait of Dad that was painted when he was in his early thirties. His beady brown eyes stared off to one side, and his hair was already beginning to recede. It depicted a gentler and kinder face than the one I remembered.

Mom treated the space between the doors that adjoined my room and the den like a closet and stacked old newspapers and other crap inside. I knew Kevin and I had our work cut out for us. He stood twirling his hair at the nape of his neck before barking out orders.

"Dorothy, go get a bunch of those green trash bags so we can throw all this shit away."

Kevin dove right in. I stood looking at the faded yellowing wintry scene that was attached to the wall above the mantel when Kevin emerged from the closet with a letter in his hand. The green trash bag at his feet was already almost full, but I don't remember actually helping him fill it. He had already read me the restraining order from when Mom went after Dad in California with a gun, so I must have been walking around the room with my head in the clouds, like I so often found myself doing.

"Look what I found," he said. I braced myself as he began reading.

June 10, 1966

Dick:

This is a BEGGING PLEA FOR YOUR MERCY to extend us—YOUR FAMILY. You have written Jerry Sandler & myself I could have everything—BOTH houses & all contents—that all you wanted. Was Freedom & to be left Alone. I am prepared to grant you that. But to insure our children's future; & to make the present even livable again, I DESPERATELY need the money from the sale of the Connecticut house to apply to the mortgage on this house; refinance this, lower my monthly payments and be able to resourcefully & adequately care for the needs of our children. We cannot afford "real estate" investment—in the form of "TRUST" or long term "investment"- to build up equity. It is all a "house of cards"--ruination faces us ALL, unless you HELP salvage the pieces, by just "signing off" and allowing us to try to begin anew on firm and sound basis. It is not for me I beg, but for YOUR children. What good is "Trust Fund"—IF we all lose everything & have to move to the "North End"?! And I have been "officlally" ordered to sell Conn. house & refinance or face definite Foreclosure! HATE ME all you will--but why hurt our –"innocent seven"?

I do not know, or care to know the world in which you live--I only know the "world of our children"! The most important thing in Life! Each life has its great moment—its dearest desires—its fulfillment! John is home with Phyllis, stupefied, "twitterpated" with love & happiness; Brian is Intensely pursuing life with the same zest with which he formerly "stalked butterflies"—a

"Huckleberry Girl-Watcher", yet so seriously interested in the U of M's programs etc; Ann, excitedly attends and anticipates her First Dance tonight—giggles & dreams, & pretty "Magpie", all wrapped into one; Mike in his heartbreak & failure & even worse, his Pretended Indifference—taking all his undemonstrativeness out in crushing affection on "Dudley—Lita" asked on her first date, oh SO "officially" by Clement Russo for tomorrow night to a movie---she's all shocked with amazement he'd ask her, and so wistful-eyed, it hurts (just don't ever let anyone ELSE break her heart as you have); Beth—still SO sad and TRAGIC & misplaced, I have "nightmares of sorrow" over her—yet how ethereally beautiful & Dresden she is; Dorothy, finally forgotten you, ALMOST, so sharp & precocious it gladdens the heart;—oh yes, Dick all these Precious Treasures God Gifted US with, comprise MY LIFE; Not your life—you are freed of them; I want NEVER to be free of them—no matter what the Burdens, the heartbreak, or the problems-- they are my only pulsating heartbeat to LIFE-my children FOREVER! I must add the financial burden & your terrible accusations & their sorrows to all MY SOLE Responsibility. Oh I can handle money—but our babies—the IMPORTANT THINGS that "money-Filthy money" Can NEVER buy- that, I can handle much MORE--& that is what counts, Dick. Human love and all its sweet sweet burden are Mine, & mine alone. Please, and I Crawl, as you so dearly want to make me do—FREE US to live life as best we can. Stop telling Tulio all your nebulous accusations; untrue & unfair-what does it gain you? I do NOT ask anything more of you, Dick, except to let us—ALL 8 of us, LIVE, & LIVE Freely & Happily as best we can we without YOU—the Head of our Family! We are trying so hard—please stop knocking us—just HELP us cement together the Broken Pieces! To build our future without you & to try to start anew, OUT OF DEBT—the Conn. house, our "Bridge to Security", to rebuild this—OUR HOME, of our Heart & Love—present & future. I can make it with our children & God's help! But, still I BEG YOU to GIVE just this little bit to US to build our new life upon—Please, won't you give that much?

You are FREE & EMANCIPATED from US FOREVER—I make no more demands upon you except our children's safekeeping, cherished with Paternal & monetary fairness, just for THEIR survival; Not Mine! We will be a happy and loving "Eight"—& You, can be a Free & Roaming man, as you so DESIRE! Is it really asking TOO MUCH!

Elizabeth

Kevin was sitting beside me with his arm around me as I sat hunched and wracked with sobs that seemed to pour from the depths of my being.

Mom had pegged each one of us. She was always a drama queen, but it finally dawned on me that just maybe she had good reason. I was pulled from my reverie by the sound of Mom's screeching.

"What are you doing in here? You have no right! You stop that now! Those are my important papers. You can't throw my things out!" Mom's voice had risen to a high-pitched shriek as she grabbed the green trash bag and began to tear through it. She whipped out paper after paper. Even yellowed old newspaper articles that had been hastily torn out and folded in fourths were waved about as treasures. "I was saving this! It had a recipe I wanted in it! I can't believe you thought you could do this!" Tears were streaming down her face, and her eyes were wild with rage. I knew I was in trouble, and I slunk back behind Kevin, letting him do all the talking.

"Mrs. Preston, why do you need all this junk?" he said. "How can you even live like this? This room is just a big junk pile, and we're only trying to help."

"I don't want your help! You have no right, and I won't have it!" Mom continued to rummage through the trash bag, pulling out everything that we had just thrown away, so we decided it was time for another project. I don't know what happened to the letter that day, but it did wind up back in our hands years later.

"The gift shop is open," Kevin said as he walked into my room.

"And just what is that supposed to mean?" I asked.

"Dorothy, you are almost as bad as your mother. Look at all the crap you have in your room." I looked around. My bed was fastidiously made—I liked to sit on my pillow and slide in so I could sleep within a tight cocoon. I looked at my myriad trinkets displayed on every surface—my tiny Siamese kitten figurines, my jewelry box that opened with a ballerina twirling to the tune of Swan Lake, and the lace doily that Grandmother Dorothy had made. A cluster of homemade candles sat on the left side of the yellow painted vanity that used to hold up the old forts Beth and I built with blankets that were pinned together. Also on display were various tchotchkes, including my green ceramic bank that looked like a house. Beth had dropped it a few months back, so the top was perched precariously in place and never glued back. I liked it that way because I could keep my secret stuff in there without having to extract it through the hole on the bottom.

"What's so bad about this? It's not even close to as bad as her disgusting room. For the life of me I can't fathom how she can even stand sleeping in there!" I said.

Mom's room was a disgusting mess of papers, dirty dishes with caked-on food that had been sitting for who knows how long, snot rags, and tumbleweeds of dog hair, with clothes strewn about on every beautiful piece of furniture. Pinkie looked down in disdain at the degradation.

◈

I could always count on Kevin to keep me busy, even when I didn't want to be. I remember a day when I was daydreaming out in the yard that had become a waist-high hayfield—another spot where I could be invisible. Sometimes I felt more at home in the plush green grass with the sunlight shining down on my face than I did in the house that stood next to me.

I wanted to pluck one of the wispy cotton ball clouds from the sky and eat it. I could almost taste the sugary cotton candy as it dissolved in my mouth. The lazy sounds of summer swirled through my head and drowned out the echoes of the fighting that had become so rampant inside the house. The sun was shining on my face, and I could hear the drone of an airplane's propeller as it whirred above. Off in the distance, cicadas rang out their piercing buzz. I felt sleepy and drunk from this background music as I lay under the massive buttonwood tree that served as my umbrella, waving and rustling its leaves as if in unison with the rest of the universe. I remembered Michael telling me how Mrs. Consiglio brought some twigs over and told him to plant them near the tree so they would eventually fill in the gap between our homes. "Michael, this is the tree of the Holy Rosary," she told him. I was taken from my reverie when I heard someone swishing through the grass beyond.

"I know you're out here, Dorothy. I saw you come out," Kevin said as he waded through the yard like he was in the jungle. I half expected him to be carrying a machete and wearing a white safari hat. "You guys look like white trash living like this. Go get the mower. We're gonna chop the hell outta this mess."

Kevin watched in his wig as I pulled the mower from where it had been abandoned against the foundation. I started to lunge at the grass with it. The mower stalled about every five feet, and I had to keep pulling on the starter. Just as I had gotten it chugging for the umpteenth time, I looked up to see Mom's car barreling into the yard straight through the tall grass. I stood there in disbelief as she cut the engine next to the tree and the rusty old swing set where I had been laying.

"Did he follow me?" Mom said as she opened the car door with a loud thunk and got out.

"Mrs. Preston, are you crazy? What the hell are you doing?" Kevin said. "You could have killed your daughter!"

"There was a cop behind me, and I was afraid he was going to pull me over," Mom said as she staggered closer to us.

"Well maybe if you weren't driving the Bomb and got your license you wouldn't have to worry," I said. The Bomb was a circa 1956 Dodge Dart. It was shit brown with one pink fender and push button transmission—an acquisition from Rocco, her car mechanic boyfriend. I think Rocco was finally catching on that Mom wasn't really interested in him. I could picture him plotting retaliation as he picked out the lousiest car on his lot to present to Mom, who thought it was a great bargain at the low price of $300, and she couldn't say no. I don't know if Mom was more scared about driving drunk or about driving without a license. Maybe Mom had been watching too many cop shows or maybe she had a few too many screwdrivers at the Plush Poodle that day. She stood looking me up and down as though she'd just eaten liverwurst. I had my hands stuffed deeply into the pockets of my farmer jeans.

"I don't know why you insist on wearing those ugly pants that make you look like a boy," she sneered as she staggered toward the house. I wanted to comment on her lovely polyester stained attire, but I bit my tongue.

I just wanted everyone to leave me alone. I wanted to go back to my comfy place in the grass where no one could touch me.

It took several days to finish cutting the grass, and by that time it was time to start all over again.

Mom started ordering take-out a lot, but most times we just scavenged in the kitchen for food.

"What do you all want on your pizza?" Mom yelled out to us one evening.

I only liked plain pizza, but when the pizza arrived later it was covered in onions and peppers and mushrooms. I snarled at them when I opened the box and refused to eat it. I thought it smelled almost as bad as it looked.

"Just pick them off and eat it, you fastidious bitch!" Brian barked. I didn't know what fastidious meant, but I knew Brian was insulting me, so I stormed out of the room without any pizza.

After Beverly left, Brian moved to the back apartment where Charlie used to live, freeing up the party room for us.

Brian didn't tease or play with us like John and Michael did; he was too consumed with weight lifting and sunning himself. Regardless, most of my friends had crushes on Brian and would get all googley-eyed whenever he was around showing off his bulky form beneath his cut-off shorts and exposed ripped mid-section. Brian's hair gleamed almost as brightly as the sun he worshiped. But lately he was always mad. I remember him yelling in Beth's face one day when he had her pinned to the floor. I don't remember why; I just remember seeing the veins in his neck poking out and his red face tight and angry. I steered clear of him as much as I could.

That Thanksgiving, everyone came home but John. We awoke to the usual scent of the Thanksgiving turkey that had been cooking all night.

When I went to my seat, I noticed that Mom had been sampling more than the stuffing that morning.

She began carving the turkey, but she got frustrated with the knife and started pulling at the bird with her hands. Becoming enraged with the slippery meat, she slapped slabs of turkey and gobs of stuffing onto the plates, sneering as though the turkey had done something horrible to her. She was in her own world and took no notice of our shocked faces and whispers.

Her face was greasy like she'd been gnawing at a turkey leg in the kitchen. Her hair was a mess, and she wore the same baby blue pants and red-and-white polyester shirt she always seemed to be wearing. "Ann, she has 'salad face,'" Paula whispered, as she nudged Ann.

"What the heck is salad face?" I whispered back.

"That is salad face," Paula said as she pointed at Mom and mimicked the sneering face she was wearing.

"I don't get it, why salad face?" Beth asked.

"Because it's the look she always has on her face when she's drunk and eating her salads. We know it well."

I wanted to leave the table and go lay in bed and daydream about a different life. I hated Mom.

Mom had made a pistachio nut pie for dessert.

"What the hell is this?" Michael said as he pulled a large piece of plastic resembling a shredded rubber spatula from his mouth and then burst into a fit of laughter. "Hey, Liz, did you forget to take the spatula out before you hit blend?"

"Goldarn it, Michael, I wish you'd stop calling me Liz," Mom slurred. More pieces of the spatula showed up on a few more plates before it was dumped into the trash, and the spatula pie went down in Preston family history as one of Mom's finest dishes.

After dinner we girls would always clean up in the kitchen as we sang Christmas carols at the top of our lungs. I loved how the acoustics in the kitchen made us all sound like we were on stage. Mom appeared later in her usual place on the radiator, even though the Christmas tree wasn't even up yet.

We met Rachel and Wendy through Anita, and the lot of us, including Kevin, hung out all the time. Our weekends and evenings consisted of stealing the Bomb and taking it out for joy rides. With Kevin as our driver, we sped out to Rock-a-Dundee Road to scare ourselves as we re-told popular urban legends about murders and hauntings that supposedly took place there.

Sometimes we would walk up Longhill Street toward Anita's house and duck into the neighbors' yards when cars would stop and jeer at us. We partied in the Napolitans' summerhouse on the far end of their yard, drinking cans of Genesee Cream Ale, or Colt 45, and changed the words to "American Pie" to say, "and good ol' boys were drinking Colt 45, singin' this'll be the day I get high." Or we hung out at the tree house that Kevin's older brothers built out in the woods behind their house and sang "Jeremiah Was a Bullfrog" at the tops of our voices.

The Circle Gang was a group of boys that hung out at the grassy circle in the center of the neighborhood across the street. Beth and I were subject to their derision and commentary on many occasions when we walked by their turf on our way home from school or from Crown Market.

"Preston, you cheap bitch." The comment came from Stevie the paperboy. Stevie used to come collecting at our door every week.

"Collecting a qua-ta," he'd say, with an irritating swagger. He had grown used to us never paying on time, or tipping. In our defense, we were not privy to the tradition of tipping your paperboy. Stevie the paperboy would recant those words many years later when he was trying to lure me into his bed.

I was torn between wanting their attention and dreading what they might say. Nevertheless, I plodded by day after day, inviting any remark, like that day they yelled out chicken legs. In my thwarted mind, I translated that to fat legs.

I always thought I was fat even though I wasn't. I never liked much about myself—my overly elongated face, my too straight baby-fine hair. The only thing I liked was the color and the fun nicknames it engendered like Blondie and Sunshine. My hawk-like nose, which was similar to Brian's, generated comments that I looked like Glenn Close later in life; I was never sure if that was a compliment, and besides, I didn't like being associated with her infamous role of playing an obsessive stalking madwoman.

Once the Circle Gang members got wind of the fact that the Preston Manor was a party house, our doorbell rang all the time. One particularly chilly evening, Beth opened the door to about six familiar members of the Circle Gang.

"Hey, can we come in and party?" Mikey said as he peered at Beth with piercing green eyes and a gleaming white smile, as though he just walked off of a toothpaste commercial. Beth stood there for a moment, uncertain whether she wanted to allow them into our home when Anita breezed over.

"Oh, Bethy, I hope you don't mind that I asked these guys to come over tonight!" She flashed the tiny dimple on the side of her mouth. Beth looked sideways at her and then back at Mikey.

"Why not?" she said, "Come on in," as she swung the door open. "You could've at least asked ahead of time, Anita," Beth whispered, as they followed the boys into the living room.

The Circle Boys started coming over every weekend. It was never the same set of boys at first, so I anxiously waited for the ringing of our doorbell to see what cute boys would show up. I'd sit in the living room and shyly smile, not knowing what to say. I would never eat in front of a boy for fear I'd look stupid or would smear something on my face.

Like with Brian and Michael, Mom allowed us to have parties regardless of the fact that we were all under age. I'm not sure if she knew all that was going on under her roof or not.

I was eleven when I got my first real kiss involving tongue.

"Hey, wanna come see my bike?" Scott asked. He was Kevin's age, so he was several years older than me, but I was mesmerized by his stunning good looks. He was almost a twin to Beth's new crush, Mikey.

I remember having had a few beers that night—a habit I'd grown accustomed to since my New Year's Eve escapade at Michael's house. Scott led me out to the hedges that split our yard from the Napolitan's; I didn't care why his bike was there, I just blindly followed him. It didn't take long before he pulled me into his arms and started kissing me. I felt awkward and didn't know what to do, but I followed his lead as he vigorously rolled his tongue around in my mouth. He smelled like Dentyne gum, beer, and cigarettes—a combination that was somehow enticing. I wanted desperately to feel his curly black hair. He was taller than me so I had to reach up to touch it. I don't remember how long we stood there kissing. I might have floated back to the house. Somehow, Kevin got wind of what happened and relentlessly teased me.

"Dorothy, wanna go see my bike?" he'd say, as his body shook awkwardly with laughter.

I decided that smooching with boys was my favorite thing to do. Even though I'd had a lifetime of watching a pro, it would be a long time before I learned the art of flirting like Mom did.

Alcohol somehow gave me the courage I never had. In the school playground I hung out with the B crowd and never felt as pretty or as fashionable as Michele Talbot and Yvette Savoie. I'd slink in the corner, sneaking a cigarette, thinking I looked cool with my long scraggly hair parted in the middle and brashy blue eye shadow. I'd brag about how I'd gotten drunk that weekend, thinking everyone would be impressed. One of the boys from my sixth-grade class asked me to go out with him, which I thought was almost as good as getting someone's high school ring. I remember breaking the antenna from someone's car on Cherryvale Avenue once so my new boyfriend would see just how sassy I could be. I brazenly egged Crown Market with Anita, Rachel, and Wendy, after which the cops chased us. These were acts I'd never even thought of doing had I not been drinking. The guilt over those cruel acts haunts me still.

My body belied my brave facade through my rampant underarm perspiration problem, which was even worse than my blushing problem. I'd keep my arms plastered at my sides—only making matters worse—so no one would see the wet stains. Whenever I smooched with a boy, I was petrified that he'd feel my sweaty pits. Sometimes I'd just go change my shirt and lie about wanting to be more comfortable.

Ann came home for Easter that year, and we were standing in the kitchen coloring eggs. Ann was still smarting over the fact that Anita's brother had broken off their engagement, although it might have smarted Mom even more since she was desperate for one of us to marry into the Russo family. Since Paula and Mark had also broken up, there was one last hope, and that was Peter, who was my age.

I hovered over the newspapered kitchen table, holding my egg in the octagonal wire over my bowl of dye, when Arthur swished into the room.

Mom was like a magnet for lost souls, like someone walking into a pound, freeing all the poor animals, and then letting them follow her home. That's most likely how Arthur came to us.

Arthur was a merchant marine who'd rented out one of the back bedrooms. He wore his hair in military fashion and always wore grimy dark green army pants that looked like they belonged to an African pygmy.

"Whad you girls doin' in here," he said, sounding as though he had a handful of marbles in his mouth. "Let me show you something. I'll show you how to color eggs," Arthur said. "Elidabet, go get me some onions," he said to Mom as he rolled up his dirty sleeves, wiped his hands across his buzzed hair, then rubbed them together like a gleeful little boy. He busied himself poking around the kitchen, trying to find a pot to boil water. As he bent over, he revealed a flash of "plumber's crack" that none of us were happy to have witnessed.

Arthur boiled some onions and then fished them from the water as he pontificated. "You people need to learn the value of money. I still have the first dollar I ever earned right here in my wallet," he said as he patted his back pocket. He then grabbed a couple of the bright white eggs from the table and plunked them into the onion water. After several minutes, he pulled out the brown eggs with a satisfied smile.

"You see, you girls don't need that fancy coloring stuff."

"Uhhh, I think you can buy brown eggs at the grocery store, Arthur," Ann said, as we all burst into fits of laughter.

Michael walked in at the tail end of Arthur's production and burst into laughter as Arthur proudly pulled the brown egg from the water. "What a stupid cheap Polack," Michael said, shaking his head as he left the room.

"You people are stoopid!" Arthur said as he batted the air with his hand and left the room.

Although you wouldn't know it to look at him, Arthur was actually quite wealthy, and he knew a good deal when he saw one, so when he found out that Mom was in financial trouble, he ended up financing a second mortgage on the house. This was not without the caveat that he could come and go as he pleased and make whatever improvements he wanted to his investment. He'd tell Mom she owed him dividends and would throw the word around like some slack-jawed hee-haw from the deep South. It'd come out sounding something like "dib-i-dens."

Arthur would putter around the house, muttering to himself and barking orders at us. I steered clear of him as much as I could.

When Arthur brought home three shiny silver industrial-sized fire extinguishers—one for each floor—it was a temptation we couldn't resist, especially Michael. We'd stealthily hunt each other down, whether inside or out, as though we were in combat. It wasn't unusual to round a corner and get doused by a blast of water at any given time. Mom was at her wits' end.

One day Michael and his friend Barry were out on the back porch, leaning against the pillars, each with a can of Bud in their hands. Barry was Ray and Michael's old friend from their car-thieving "hoodlum" days after they'd all quit school.

The summer breeze was wafting through the unscreened open window in the kitchen. I could hear their muffled conversation, but was more interested in seizing this perfect opportunity. I knew dousing Barry wasn't a good idea given his hot temper, but like Eve and the poisonous apple, I just couldn't resist, wanting desperately to get back at Michael since I'd mostly been on the receiving end of our war games.

I approached my prey like Cato pouncing on Inspector Clouseau in the *Pink Panther* movies. Setting the can inside the black soapstone sink and resting the hose between my fingers set on the windowsill, I squeezed the handles and blasted them like I was dousing a roaring fire, laughing like a mad scientist until Arthur walked in and caught me.

"Dorty, what the hell do you think you're doin'? Those are not toys. You stoopid kids. You kids are so stoopid. Gimme that now," he sputtered, as he grabbed the fire extinguisher from me. Just then, I noticed Barry, infuriated and sopping wet, coming after me from the porch, so I ran as fast as I could to some hideaway on the third floor. Knowing I had to steer clear of Barry, I stayed there for the rest of the day.

Mom put up with Arthur because she had no choice, toying with him as she did all the other men in her life like a cat with a mouse. Arthur ended up proposing to Mom, bringing her tally to a whopping five. I'm pretty sure she never entertained the thought of marrying any of them, but she refused to let on lest she reveal that she was only using them to get the things she needed. I knew nobody would ever compare to Dad and that she would carry that flame forever in her heart as he was the only true love of her life. Despite the fact that none of us knew where Dad was, he danced in the corners of all our minds.

I woke up to a quiet house one Saturday morning, and I ventured down to the kitchen, taking my usual shortcut via the rickety banister.

As I jumped to the floor, I noticed the lighting was odd. Usually the sun streamed brightly through the windows from the living room and crept into the hall, but not this morning. As I tentatively approached the living room, I noticed a dish tub in the center of the room under the chandelier. The curtains were all drawn and the floor was littered with passed out drunks, including Brian who was on the yellow couch near the fireplace, snorts emanating from his gaping mouth. It reminded me of the time when Brian passed out in that very spot, and Barry stuck a potato chip in his mouth and Brian chewed it. We all thought it was hysterical since we thought he was out cold.

There were beer bottles and dirty ashtrays scattered about the room. Gray stains and cigarette burns on the once pristine Persian rug. The black velvet minstrels on the wallpaper now stood disheveled beside their harps, and some of the paper was peeling and torn. I stepped on a stray potato chip as I entered the room and cringed as I heard it crunch beneath my foot, hoping it wasn't a dead cockroach.

I looked up and saw remnants of singed baggies tied to the bottom part of the crystal chandelier that Mary Peterson had broken years before while jumping rope. I'd heard a lot of partying the night before since the living room was right below my room, but I could not fathom what had happened. I shivered and shook my head as I crept from the room to go get my cereal, then took it upstairs to eat, away from the foulness and degradation.

I learned later that this was Brian's latest party trick to affect a psychedelic light show. They'd tie a bunch of Baggies end-to-end, attach one end to the chandelier and light the other end on fire so molten plastic would drip down into a bucket of water beneath. Then they would lie on the floor and trip out to pyrotechnics.

It seemed stupid, but I wanted to see what all the hype was, so one night when Mom was out at the Plush Poodle, we tried it.

I was draped over the furry chair, drinking a Schlitz, my legs dangling over the side. Kevin, Wendy, and Beth were all perched on the couch, and Rachel and Anita were sitting cross-legged on the floor, smoking cigarettes with a grimy silver ashtray beside them that someone stole from a Holiday Inn.

After we gathered our tools, we turned off the lights, lit the baggies on fire, and lay on the floor beneath them.

I gazed wide-eyed up at the shadows on the ceiling that were wildly dancing and refracting light from the chandelier. The baggies made a loud "zzzzzip, zzzip" sound as they dripped into the pan. I felt like we were watching fireworks.

"Oooh, that is so cool," Rachel said.

"Wow, look at that one," Wendy added. All at once we had the grand finale as the last of the baggies dripped and zipped and sizzled into the pan with a final splash. We turned on the lights and noticed the chandelier was dark and dirty.

"I think it was already like that," Beth said, contemplating whether Mom would notice. It occurred to me that I would be the one to clean it next anyway, since I had already cleaned all three chandeliers at least twice, and nobody else seemed to care. I loved how they gleamed when they were clean, and Mom would always sing my praises afterward. The first time I cleaned them was when I helped Grandmother Elizabeth, Dad's mother, who'd come out to visit her grandchildren years after Dad had left. It was the first and only time I ever saw her.

[top left] A typical party scene at the manor, showing the decline of Mom's once beautiful house after all our decadent parties.

[top right] Sister Jane, the nun who would measure the length of our skirts.

[bottom left] Ray holding me up after he found me wandering the street. Not my finest moment.

[bottom right] Ray and Beth on the small balcony that overlooked Ray's six-foot-tall pot plant in the backyard.

CHAPTER EIGHT

Drunk Leading the Drunk

I met Gina on the city bus one day coming home from school. She got on two stops after me, wearing a blue plaid uniform, so I knew she went to Mount Carmel, the other Catholic school, down the street from St. Joseph's. She seemed to always be happy.

"Hey, Carole, how ya doin'?" she asked the pretty dark-haired girl who was sitting next to me, new to my school and a grade ahead of me. I had never spoken to Carole before that day, but we all began to chat on the ride home, and I found out that the two of them had attended Sumner Avenue Grammar School together.

Carole had penetrating eyes and a boisterous laugh that made heads turn from the seats in front of us and made me feel embarrassed because she was so loud. Carole got off the bus first, and a few stops later I pulled the string above my head to indicate to the driver that the next stop was mine.

"This is your stop too?" Gina said brightly. "Hey, how about we walk together? You got a dime I can borrow?" It was pouring rain, so when we got off the bus we ducked into Buckey's Corner so Gina could buy a candy bar. She tore open the wrapper of the Caravelle bar, and handed me half. "There, now I only owe you a nickel," she said with a giggle. A wisp of her frizzy hair got caught in her mouth along with the caramel that stretched from the candy bar in her hand, and she brushed it away with the back of her other hand.

"Okay, time to brave the weather," she said as she dashed from the store, stuffing the rest of the candy bar into her mouth. I loved her easygoing, confident spirit and was instantly enamored of her.

The rain was pelting down, and by the time we got to the end of Beechwood Avenue, it seemed as if we were walking through a river, so we took off our shoes and socks and used our slickers to cover our books. We were soaked to the bone by the time we reached the Circle Gang turf, which was when I found out that Gina was Stevie the paperboy's sister.

The Forest Park neighborhood where we lived housed the vast majority of Springfield's affluent Irish-Catholic families and, as in Gina's case,

Italian-Catholics. Most of the homes were Victorian mansions tightly knit around quiet curvy streets with little traffic. It was almost as though you'd stepped into Mr. Roger's neighborhood.

We stomped through puddles in our bare feet, gave up trying to stay dry, laughing merrily until we noticed the worms. Hundreds of worms swarmed around our feet. Now taking our shoes off didn't seem like such a good idea. I could hear Mom's voice warning me of the germy sidewalks where people spit. I thought it was funny since Mom was almost always barefoot, explaining her constant state of dirty black feet.

Gina and I grabbed each other's shoulders screaming and laughing as we tippy-toed around the worms as best we could until we were on the other side of the circle, where we went our separate ways.

"See ya tomorrow, Dorth, I'm running the rest of the way home!"

I ran home in my bare feet, getting pelted by the muddy water as I splashed through puddles. I dared not look down lest I discover I was stepping on more worms. I knew I had made a lifelong friend on that rainy day running through the worms.

I still had to sneak smoking cigarettes at home, but since Mom allowed Beth and our friends to smoke openly, it was easy enough for me to hand off my cigarette, like the day I handed Anita my cigarette after Mom barged into my room. I didn't realize she already had one, but she nonchalantly took mine and held the two cigarettes between her index and middle fingers.

"How are you today, Mrs. Preston?" Anita said, conversing with Mom while waving the cigarettes around. Mom didn't seem to notice that Anita was holding two cigarettes as they chatted and laughed. All our friends seemed to like Mom, and I couldn't understand why. I just wanted her to go away so I could smoke my cigarette. Maybe it was because she let them drink and smoke in her presence.

Gina and Carole started hanging around more and more. Gina didn't much care for the Circle Boys since her brother was a part of the gang; besides, she had her eye on the Zamboni driver at Cyr Arena in Forest Park.

Carole was as large as life with a dazzling white smile and deep dimples. She started calling me Doitalyboid, just another nickname to add to the long list my siblings had already given me. Paula thought it would be funny to throw a bunch of them together and came up with Bald-headed Maggot that does the Cha-Cha.

Like everyone else, Carole had a huge crush on Brian. The first time she saw him she grabbed my arm like a little girl who'd just seen the ice cream truck go by.

"Oh my God, Doit, who is that hunk?" Carole said as she dug her nails into my arm.

I'm not sure where we got our booze from, but there always seemed to be something to drink around the house. The Circle Boys always brought stuff with them, and sometimes Mom would even buy for us. I was never sure if she knew how much I was drinking.

If no one was around to buy for us, we'd hang out down at the packie on Fort Pleasant Ave. Carole would bravely approach strangers.

"Hey, Mister, can you get us a bottle of Tango?" she'd ask. After we scored our bottle, we would go out back and drink it or go back to Carole's basement where we were allowed to smoke.

That summer Beth and I went to visit Ann who'd moved to Mystic, Connecticut, after her first year of college. That's when we met Resa and her younger sister Rhonda.

I was as fickle with my girlfriends as I was with all the boys I'd been smooching. Anita, Rachel, Wendy, and Kevin had become more like family members, but I couldn't decide whether Kathy, Gina, Carole, or Rhonda—who'd started visiting on a regular basis—was my best friend.

One weekend when Rhonda was visiting, she and Carole and I were hanging out in my bathroom where we'd go to smoke when it was too cold outside.

Carole was lounging in the tub with a cigarette between her fingers blowing smoke rings above her head. That was when one of us came up with the idea to camp out in the bathroom.

When we went down to dinner later, we told Mom our plan. I was relieved to see that it was one of her good days when she didn't have Salad Face.

"You girls are just silly. Why on earth would you want to sleep in the bathroom?" she said as she shook her head. Michael's friend Ray, who'd become like another family member, happened to be sitting nearby and told us he'd come read us a bedtime story later. We didn't think much of it until he actually showed up with one of Ann's early childhood education books from college that she'd left behind.

Ray was always smiling and giggling like a big kid. He poked his curly dark head into the bathroom and then carefully climbed over us and into the empty bathtub. We were all in our jammies and bathrobes, with blankets and pillows on the floor as Ray cleared his throat and began to read: "Where did I come from . . . "

I chuckled to myself that it might have been a good source for Mom when she struggled to tell me about the facts of life a few years back.

For Christmas that year, Harold gave me a number ten can of ketchup, canned green beans, and a case of Stroh's beer. He always thought it was funny how much I loved all of these things (not necessarily together), and although I was underage, Mom allowed him to purchase the beer for me. Stroh's was not sold in New England. I'd tried it on one of our visits to

Prairie Du Rocher, Illinois, where Harold grew up, so I was very excited and couldn't wait to share my "exotic beer" with Carole and Gina. When they came over later, we snuck into the coatroom by the front door to drink it. I don't know why we felt the need to sneak since it was openly given to me as a gift, but we did. We decided to make the coatroom our little clubhouse for drinking beer. The coatroom was a long narrow corridor with various hooks and closets and a cubicle at the end where the mailbox was, which was convenient for smoking cigarettes since we could just blow the smoke out the mail slot.

Christmas night had become the time for neighbors to visit, especially old friends who'd already moved away and were home for the holidays. We kept our Christmas mornings for family, but after gifts and dinner, our doorbell was always ringing with people, like Christine Napolitan, stopping by to say hello.

After the Christmas hubbub was over and Harold had gone back to Harrisburg, Mom went back to her old patterns of heading out for the closest gin-joint every evening.

The Circle Boys had already rang the doorbell one Saturday. Beth was probably smooching somewhere with Mikey, Anita with Tommy, Rachel with Brian—who knows—all I know is that I was smooching with Timmy Parker.

Timmy was one of the neighborhood delinquents who taunted and teased whenever we'd walk by on our way home from school. I'm reminded of the old pigtail in the inkwell scenario and think perhaps he teased because he liked me, but one day he pushed too far, and Beth was unable to contain herself.

"Preston skank!" he yelled from his porch.

With a curved mouth akin to Sylvester Stallone and slanty blue eyes, he craned his head and spit—adding insult to injury.

Beth was like a bull, I could practically see the smoke puffing from her red face when she dropped her books, balled her fists and stormed over to Timmy. They began to tussle on the ground. I watched from a safe distance, not wanting any part of it.

"If you speak to us like that again, I'll kick your ass." Beth said through clenched teeth and pushed away.

Now this "Preston skank" is the object of Timmy's interest. Why am I so drawn to his punk, bad-boy attitude? We were smooching up a storm on the couch in the upper hall when I heard Arthur yelling from downstairs.

"Elidabet, Elidabet, you need to come down here and make these boys go home. Beth and Dorothy, where are you?" he yelled.

Fearing the sanctimonious Arthur would find us, I pulled away, but Timmy drew me back. His luscious lips were still wet from our kisses, and his lazy eyes were half closed. He'd just starting creeping his hand under my sweater—I could still feel the lingering tingle from his touch.

I reluctantly emerged from my love nest and walked down the stairs. Arthur was carrying one of the Chinese Chairs across the room and furiously placed it back in the center hall where it belonged. Tripping behind him was Stevie the paperboy.

"I found this boy out in the yard trying to steal your mother's valuable chair. What were you thinking, letting these people into your house?" he fumed.

"I wazn't stealing nothin'," Stevie slurred as he stumbled toward the door.

"That's right, you get out of here before I call the cops on you, you thief," Arthur yelled. I imagined that Stevie thought he was getting compensation for all those tips we never gave him.

"Where's your mother? You girls shouldn't be left unsupervised with these boys. What's the matter with you?" Arthur blustered and fumed. I rolled my eyes and listened, knowing if I resisted he'd make my life miserable.

"Are you girls so stupid that you don't realize these boys only want a warm place to party? They don't care about you."

Arthur may have had a point, but I was much too interested in getting back to the task at hand—Timmy.

The J. Geils Band was playing at the Springfield Civic Center. Weekends melted into each other through my drunken fog, but I remember smooching with Timmy under the strobe lights—*Hard Drivin' Man* jamming in the background, head swimming. He got up and before I knew what happened, someone else was in his place—Tony? Billy? I don't know, but he pulled me to him and took up where Timmy left off. I was angry that Timmy seemingly orchestrated the swap. My head was reeling. Is this a trick? But somehow I didn't care.

The next day I was ashamed and embarrassed, playing it over and over in my head. Why did they do that? But more importantly, why did I let it happen? I liked Timmy more than I cared to admit. I didn't see much of Timmy after that, except for maybe when Michael almost beat him up one night during a party. It wasn't long before I had a new crush—alcohol has a funny way of making you forget things, like shame.

I never heard from Timmy again, but at the time of this writing, as if on cue, I received a friend request on Facebook, prompting a catch-up session with Timmy over the phone. He didn't remember things the way I did, my drama being bigger than life—but apparently only to me. I was incredulous and could not believe I'd just spoken to my childhood sweetheart and nemesis after so many years. I floated for days as the words Timmy Fucking Parker slid from my tongue at unexpected intervals, like I had no control, eliciting emotions that I could neither understand nor define.

I grabbed a Schlitz from the six-pack Kevin brought over that was sitting on the round table with the black painted peace sign on top. Kevin and I trash-picked the table from a house on Cherryvale Avenue, and lugged it across the street and up three flights of stairs to the party room.

Bobby was sitting across from me on a brown wicker chair with orange cushions—another good trash-pick. His curly brown hair framed his face and bounced as he laughed at Kevin's jokes. I loved his adorable smile, which was almost as wide as his face. I'd love to kiss him, I mused. Only I couldn't muster the courage to talk to him and could only smile shyly when he looked my way. I knew my burning face was red, which only made matters worse. I wondered if he could see the stains from my sopping pits as I clenched my arms tighter to my sides.

Later Bobby asked me to go for a walk. The beer made me brave, so I agreed, and he led me to the gazebo out back. It was a cool evening, and the moon was illuminating his face as he pushed me against the pillar and kissed me. I fancied myself Katharine Hepburn from one of those late night black-and-white films I loved so much. Demurely throwing my head back, calf raised ever so slightly. Bobby's tongue probed deeply into my mouth as he twirled it around and around. I wondered if all the Circle Boys took the same kissing lessons. My head was spinning. I felt a tingling between my legs that I'd never felt before. He pushed his hand up my shirt and cupped my newly developing breasts with his warm hand. I was self-conscious about them, so I quickly pushed his hand away.

The next day I walked around reliving my night of smooching with Bobby. I could not get him out of my mind. Steak knife in hand, I mindlessly etched the epic date, September 28, 1973, into the side of our kitchen table, the inside door of the bathroom cabinet, the side of the peace sign table, whose remaining space would occupy ensuing dates. There it was, etched for eternity, or so I thought.

I found out shortly afterward that Bobby was going out with someone else. I was devastated. Her name was Martha; I hated her.

One night, there was a high school dance at Holy Name. I was not yet in high school, but I wanted to go since I'd heard Martha would be there.

Wendy was the first after Kevin to get her license, plus she went to Holy Name. Wendy was carefree and whimsical like a summer breeze, so I knew it wouldn't be hard to convince her to let me tag along. I didn't tell her that Mom said I couldn't go, figuring she wouldn't even know I was gone.

"Come on, Dorothy, jump in," Wendy said, pushing up her thick glasses as she sat in the driver's seat of her new car. I was feeling mighty proud that I'd been able to finagle my way into a high school dance, and I'd already had a few beers, or was it brandy?

I felt out of place standing near the back wall glaring at Martha in my drunken stupor. She had no idea I had designs on her new boyfriend. Finally, she approached and started chatting as though she hadn't noticed me glowering at her. To my surprise, she was sweet and nice, and before long I didn't hate her anymore.

I don't know how long I'd been there when I saw Mom storming toward me in a drunken rage. "Martha, please save me! Hide me from my mother. She's coming right now," I slurred as I darted toward the ladies' room to hide. I tugged my new best friend along with me. Of course Mom saw me and quickly caught me by the arm. I remember thinking how strong she was as she dragged me out of the ladies' room.

"I am not going with you," I resisted.

"Oh, yes, you are! How dare you defy me after I specifically said you couldn't come here tonight?" She said as she roughly led me to the side door. It was like some teen movie, where all the shocked attendants stood to the side covering their mouths in silent pity—not wanting to be associated with the prevailing drama.

Drunk leading the drunk, I thought, as Mom shoved me into the passenger seat of the Bomb and sped away.

It didn't take long for some of the Circle Gang's girlfriends to discover that we were stepping on their turf, and Beth's new love, Mikey, was considered their turf. One day, as Beth and I were walking home, we saw chalk writing on the ground: *Preston sucks dead dog's dicks.*

"What total assholes," Beth screeched. "This had to be Dee-Dee, that bitch!" She scuffed at the chalk, tears cutting a path through her beet-red face.

Beth never believed she was beautiful. Instead, she always thought she was an ugly duckling and completely lacked self-esteem, as did I, but that was no surprise after Mom drummed it onto our heads not to "fish for compliments" whenever we asked her if we looked pretty like her.

I knew Beth took it personally when Lizzy and Mary were banned from playing with us, and she became a bundle of pent-up emotions and anger. I imagine most of her rage stemmed from Dad—starting with that first bare-bottom spanking—but much of it came from the indignation for what Mom was putting us through by hanging on to the house, and the wars that had erupted between the two of them after everyone left. Beth never knew what to do with her anger—her needle teetering between 199 and 210 degrees—always ready to blow. Mom called her "spit-fire" for good reason, but sometimes I wish I had half her fire. Maybe then I wouldn't have let so many boys take advantage of me.

Ray, Beth, and I were sitting on the balcony outside my bedroom window one afternoon. Most of our balconies had no doors with the exception of one, so we had to climb out my window to get to it. From there, if you looked up you could see another balcony that had no access and was simply a decorative balcony with an identical one on the opposite side of the house.

The massive oak beside the gazebo was in its full glory as the green leaves waved and danced in the wind and created tiny shadows on the gravel beneath our feet where an old storm window was left abandoned.

Beth was sitting on the ledge with her face toward the sun, gazing out to some faraway place as Ray was seemingly observing her, and I, in turn was studying Ray's hand with the ugly green tattoo that said Born to Raise Hell just below his knuckles.

"Why'd you put that tattoo on your hand?" I asked.

"Why do you think? Bwa-ha-ha!" he answered as he pushed his bulbous nose right next to mine. His hair like a halo was wildly splayed out in every direction as he crossed his blue eyes to look like a mad man.

That was the day we decided to climb up to the top of our roof. I'm pretty sure it was Ray that instigated it since he instigated most of our crazy adventures, and since Beth and I still loved to climb and be up high, it didn't take much convincing.

We scoured the basement and found a ladder that we hoisted through the window and leaned against the house to climb up. I was scared at first, but the roof tiles were scratchy so our feet clung to them. I went from my hands and knees, slowly rising up to almost standing as I skittered to the peak of the house. Once I was safely straddled over the rooftop, the butterflies in my stomach began to calm down, and I was able to relax and enjoy the beautiful view.

There was an article in *Scientific American, Building Edition* (February 1898), that my brother John had discovered years earlier that referred to our house as Villa Bluff, deriving its name from the bluff on which it is located, overlooking the Connecticut River with broad views of the Berkshire range of hills. Sadly, most of the trees were overgrown by then, but from up there, you could see what inspired that description.

"Look at me, I'm Monkey Man," Ray said, pounding his chest. I knew Mom would've killed us if she'd seen us out there, but luckily, she was most likely poised barside at the Plush Poodle.

Ray liked to stun and amaze us with his daring zest for life, like the time he flung himself over the side balcony—the one with the door—where we liked to hang out smoking, drinking, and sunning ourselves. Ray was growing a pot plant in the service yard below that had grown to six feet.

"I'm gonna go check on my plant," he said, leaping from the rail. In an instant he was on the ground. "Come on down," he yelled from below. I liked being fearless like Ray, so I tentatively flung my leg over the edge, and with the help of Ray who was standing on the rooftop of the doorway below, I scampered down. I was never so scared in my life as I was while I hung there, but at the same time, it was exhilarating. Beth and I tried it a few times more, both climbing up and down, but it never got easier.

Later that summer a pack of us were partying up on the third floor. Mom had gone out earlier, and we thought she was gone for the evening when unexpectedly the doors flew open and in walked Mom. She was not alone. Stumbling behind her was a tall woman with short bleached blonde hair. She held her head high as though she were Grace Kelly entering a movie scene. If it weren't for her age, I might have thought she was eight months pregnant.

"Beth and Dorothy, you better not be smoking marijuana up here. I smell that funny stuff."

"Aww, come on, Ma, sit down and join the party. I'm the only one smoking," Ray lied.

"Yes, Mrs. Preston, come and party with us," Anita chimed in.

"Who's your new friend?" Ray asked.

"This is Beverly," Mom said as she conspiratorially grabbed Beverly's arm. "Come on Bev, let's join the party. These are my beautiful daughters Beth and Dorothy," she added as she waved her arm in our general direction.

"Well, it's nice to finally meet you gih-ls. I've heh-d so much about you," Beverly said in an affected English accent, trying hard not to slur. I was not far off in my movie star assessment.

Beverly stumbled and swallowed a burp as she made her way to the mangled wicker chair in the corner, another trash pick Kevin and I found. The chair threatened to collapse as Beverly plunked her ample body down.

"Hand me that marijuana cigarette. I wanna try a puff," Mom said as she poked at Ray's arm.

I felt my stomach turn. I wanted to vomit. I pulled my feet to my chest and hugged them as if it would make me disappear.

"Oh, Cha-Cha, don't look so holier-than-thou," Mom said with a wicked sneer. I knew she wanted to embarrass me in front of my friends; she reveled in this shit.

I noticed Kevin glaring at Mom from across the room. He probably felt the same agonizing embarrassment I felt. The other Circle Boys were seemingly engaged in their own conversation until Mom took the joint—you'd have thought E. F. Hutton walked into the room.

Mom made a big show, dramatically bringing the joint to her lips and holding the smoke in her mouth before sputtering and coughing it out.

"Elizabeth, you look pu-fectly ridiculous. What are you trying to prove anyway?" Beverly said as she swallowed another burp.

I don't remember much beyond that moment, but I do remember that Kevin didn't come over for a while after that night. Years later I recovered this letter from Mom's belongings.

Dear Mrs. Preston,

The reason I am writing this letter is because if I tried to tell it to your face you would think of some excuse to leave the room. Everybody in the goddam neighborhood uses you and it is beyond your control to stop it, you'll never be able to stop it. Everybody knows they can brown nose you and you'll break down and let them do what they want. I can't stand seeing you being taken advantage of more every time I come over. Why the hell do you think all the parents around here disapprove of their kids coming over your house? The die is cast as far as parents trusting you goes. Unfortunately, people don't give other people another chance, a bad reputation is hard to get rid of. I've tried so hard to help you but you don't want help from me, Ray or anyone else. Your poor kids are so miserable. Most of their (so called) friends use them so badly for the house. That goddam house is ruining you and your kids all because of your goddam stubborn attitude about selling it.

If you really loved your kids you would get out of this goddam neighborhood in to a new house. One that your kids wouldn't have to be embarrassed of all the time. How the hell do you think they like being outcasts? Beth and Dorothy are two of the most mature and responsible kids I ever met. Do you think they like to see their mother slowly dying in front of them? You can't last much longer constantly having the goddam worry of where's the next mortgage payment coming from?????

They are growing up with perverts living in the same house with them. I realize that you love that house but if you would sell and move you would make things easier for the kids and yourself. You're not happy now, your kids have no privacy in their own house. Are you married to that goddam place? You're going to have to sell the house after Beth and Dorothy leave home which is not that far off. If you sold now you could at least give Beth and Dorothy a few good happy memories of their teenage years. Wouldn't you like to be accepted by your neighbors socially? It's not as if you are leaving people that are your best friends.

Meet new people, and get a fresh start. If you really cared about your two kids you would move. I know you have hard times but that is no excuse for the condition your life is in now. Act like a mature person and weigh both sides and you'll realize I am right.

Thanks for all the good times I had at your house but I won't be coming over any more. Maybe once in a while. I'll help you move.

Show this to your kids. I think they will agree with me. I am only doing this for your own good. I can't stand seeing how you get used more every day.

Beth and Dorothy, I hope I can still be friends with you. Please do not show this to anyone but you three.

Thanks for everything,

Kevin

Although Kevin asked Mom to let Beth and me read it, I have no recollection of having seen it at the time.

When I graduated to the seventh grade, we girls were allowed to remove the tops of our jumpers. That was when Sister Jane started calling impromptu raids. We'd line up like prisoners and were told to kneel on the floor so as to measure the length of our skirts—it being forbidden to have a skirt more than an inch from the floor when kneeling. We'd shift on our knees and tug and pull, unrolling our skirts from its more fashionable state of mini.

I always felt like these drills were targeted at me, but then I was especially paranoid. Or was I?

Sister Jane would gruffly pull me aside and vigorously wipe at my blue eye shadow with a stiff brown paper towel while I winced and tried to pull away.

Sister Jane scared me even more than Brian, and she made it clear she despised me. She'd regularly pull me aside to rummage through my purse, ostensibly looking for cigarettes.

"You come with me," she'd point and say, with cold hard eyes. It was as though the grim reaper himself was pointing at me. She'd scornfully rifle through everything, including personal notes that were tucked away in my wallet. How could someone who is supposed to be working for God, engaged in the works of mercy and other ministries, be so innately evil? I have nightmares of this evil woman still.

"And what is this supposed to mean?" she'd ask as she grabbed my arm roughly.

"What do you mean, Sister?" Tears flowed onto my white blouse. I was so angry with myself for letting her see me cry.

"This note refers to your white picket fence. What does that mean?"

Denise, who was in eighth grade, had written the note. We passed notes to each other about boys all the time. I couldn't fathom why Sister Jane thought there might be something evil about a white picket fence. We only meant that we would live happily ever after. I despised her for making me feel so small. I wanted to run away and never come back. I didn't know I'd get my wish.

My classmate Jerry must have gotten wind that I was one of the "cool" girls in class. At least that's what I liked to believe the reason was for him asking me to score some pot for him. Since I knew I could get it from Ray, who was a dealer, I was only too happy to help—that is, until I heard the call from the intercom one day.

"Dorothy Preston, please come to the principal's office immediately."

Sister Norma was the new Mother Superior. I arrived at her office to see Jerry standing there looking rather sheepish. Sister Norma glared at me. I knew instantly what this was about.

"Where did you get this?" she asked as she produced the nickel bag I had just helped Jerry procure. I was shocked that he was stupid enough to have brought it to school and wondered just how he got caught with it.

I was now in the hot seat with Jerry standing behind me as Sister Norma drilled us both. As she asked him questions, I sat and waved my hand from behind the desk so Sister Norma couldn't see, either back and forth for "no" or up and down for "yes." Jerry did not get my sign language, or he just chose to ignore it as he buried me with blame. I didn't know how I had become the bad guy. I didn't even smoke pot—at least not yet.

That June we received a letter in the mail from the school stating that I was not welcome back for my final year at St. Joseph's. We knew that Jerry's wealthy family had political connections, so he was able to finish school. Mom was furious and tried to fight it, but she had used up most of her favors. I imagined Sister Jane dispassionately looking off in the distance as she slowly wiped her hands, ridding herself of the debris that was the last of the Preston clan.

I was through with evil nuns, so, following in Michael and Paula's footsteps, I shuffled off to Forest Park Jr. High School for my eighth grade year. They had just begun busing in kids from other districts, bringing a whole new set of problems for this shy pasty Catholic girl.

I hated my new school more than my last one. I tried to keep a low profile after some boy, for no reason, kicked me in the ass while I was walking down the hall.

I was slow to make friends and began skipping school even more than before. I gave up hiding under beds and began hiding behind stairways during class or smoking in the girls' room and staying there during class. I even ran off into the woods during my tennis class once—racket and all.

When I did attend class, I would slink into a seat in the back of the room, hoping nobody would notice me. But whenever I was called on, it seemed the entire class moved as one to turn and look at me. It was as though a wave was swallowing me up. I could always feel my face burning, and I hated that I had no control over it. Some of the kids taunted me about my red face.

Many years later, in college, I learned to take a seat in front of the class, thereby eliminating the need for the room to turn to see who was talking.

In the fall of 1974, Kevin left for college. He was the first of our group to leave home.

Beth switched to a new high school, only she opted for another Catholic school. Since we couldn't afford the tuition, Father Clement intervened on her behalf, and she was accepted on a tuition waiver after he sent this letter.

Dear Father Lafleur,

RE: ELIZABETH JANE PAUL PRESTON

I am writing to ask you to use the good graces of your pastoral office to have ELIZABETH JANE PAUL PRESTON accepted as a HARDSHIP case at Notre Dame High School.

This family lacks total financial ability to pay even a small part of the regular tuition at Notre Dame—but this is a girl who needs and sincerely desires the influences of Notre Dame.

Young Elizabeth Preston has been the innocent victim of a broken marriage and the traumatic upheaval in a home deeply affected by a father who abandoned all of them more than ten years ago.

I have an inkling that Mrs. Preston's undue haste and short fuse has not contributed to the best of relationships with the Fathers whose knowledge and experience have not always been heeded and followed—and I look on this, Father, as an added reason for my appealing to a brother priest on behalf of a girl whom I have known since her babyhood, whom I personally rate highly, and whom I hope will not be further hurt beyond that which she has already suffered. I see much at Notre Dame that can heal a lot of wounds in this child's life.

Praying that you will find it possible to help this deserving girl, I am,

Sincerely in Christ,

Clement Buckley, C.P.

Beth was sixteen when she brought her new friend Lynn home. Since I'd always hung out with Beth and the rest of our crew of friends that were her age, I thought nothing of tagging along.

Lynn's gravelly voice belied her lilting soprano singing voice, which I could listen to for hours. She was the first person I knew that had her own guitar and could sing. To me it was breathtaking.

I liked Lynn's badass attitude. She was much less refined than Beth, and besides, Lynn didn't mind me being around, unlike Beth, who for some reason changed her tune. Maybe she was protecting me from becoming like Mom.

One day Lynn scored an oversized nickel bag from school, and she and Beth were excited to go try it in the back yard. I tagged along despite the sharp look I got from Beth on our way out.

We stood in the tall grass that was as overgrown as ever. Lynn took the first hit from the fat joint. Her throat creaked, and her face turned red as she held in the smoke.

"This is good shit," she said as she exhaled a gray cloud of smoke. (They found out later that this good shit was oregano.) I figured if I was going to get kicked out of school for pot, I might as well try it.

One day Ray brought a brick of pot into the house and I gleefully offered to help him break it up. We started on the peace table in the party room, but it was too small, so I got the idea to use my old round saucer sled, and I ran to the basement to find it. I was careful not to look at the scary furnace that I'd been afraid of my entire life because it looked like a fiery monster awaiting its next victim. I slunk by the wooden dumbwaiter and stepped over a rusty bicycle pump. I was furiously brushing cobwebs from my face when I spotted the sled. It was the same sled that launched me over the three bumps in the ravine where we sledded every winter. I'd fly through the air and land with a thump at the bottom or twirl and sail into a pricker bush whose burrs I'd pick from my mittens for days.

I grabbed the sled and ran to the top of the stairs. But when I got there, the door slammed with a loud rattle. Then the light went out. I froze in panic until the light went back on, and I saw Michael's face pressed to the glass. He turned the light on and off to enhance the spooky effect.

"Michael, let me out," I screamed as I banged on the door with the sled tucked under my arm. He kept at it for a while making faces in the window and not saying a word, until he finally got tired of the game and let me out.

"And just what are you doing with that t'ing in the middle of the summer?" he asked pointing at the sled.

"Nothing. I'm just helping Ray with something. What are you doing here, anyway? You're such a stupid brat, Michael," I said as I pushed past him.

Ray was holding up a scale clipped to a baggie when I walked back in, nickel and dime bags spread by his side. I quickly got to work and practiced my rolling skills. I could roll a perfect joint with only one paper, unlike everyone else who I'd seen licking and sticking two zig-zag's together.

I proudly held up a joint and showed it to Ray.

"Wow, impressive! Now, light that up," he said with a laugh.

"Don't you dare smoke that, Dorothy! You're too young," Beth said authoritatively as she and Lynn walked in the room.

"And since when did you become my mother? I can do what I want," I responded as I struck a match to light the joint. Beth glared and went to grab it from my mouth but I lunged back and blew the smoke out into her red-face.

"You're such a little brat," she yelled, plunking herself down in the squeaky wicker chair. I remember thinking I wanted the chair to break and her to fall on her hip-hugging elephant-pant ass. I didn't know why she was acting all goody two shoes. Maybe it was because they were smoking oregano.

"Relax, Beth. Leave Doorknob alone," Lynn said.

Weekends jumbled together with party after party. Now that I'd started smoking pot, it was the focus of my life. I even sported roach clip earrings, which weren't as cleverly disguised as I'd once thought, having recently found one tucked away in an old jewelry box.

Gina and I wandered around, slanty-eyed and giggly, stumbling through the woods of Forest Park, singing made-up songs.

I vaguely remember the night Mom crashed into the back room where we'd been partying. About fifteen of us were crammed in the room. I was sitting on a small radiator near the open window with a beer in one hand and a cigarette in the other, anxiously awaiting the return of the circulating joint when Mom threw open the door. She stood for a moment, trying to make sense of who was in the smoke-filled room before reacting.

"B-R-I-AN, come here now!" she yelled at the top of her lungs. It took a minute to sink into our collective inebriated minds before we scattered out the window like Charlie's cockroaches, some jumping right from the roof to the yard below while those of us who had many times climbed down the trellis by my old bedroom window took that route instead. I don't recall if there was snow on the ground, or who jumped, or who got hurt—if anyone. I just remember being confused and praying Mom didn't spot me.

I got my answer when I returned later that night. I was sneaking up the front staircase to go to my room. I stumbled on the stairs and fell on the landing, and as I was getting up, I saw Mom standing before me on the next landing with her arms folded over her red silk bathrobe.

"And just where have you been?" she asked sternly.

"Nowhere, Ma. I was just out in the yard," I slurred.

"Probably necking with some Circle boy. Were you smoking in that back room earlier?"

"No, Ma. I don't even know what you're talking about. I'm just going to bed," I said as I tried to push past her. The next thing I knew I was greeted with a sound slap across the face.

"You are grounded for a week, do ya hear me? There will be no boys coming over and no other friends," Mom said as she stormed back to her room. I wondered who she was and where she'd come from as I held my stinging face, this sudden discipline being entirely new to me.

Mom would try on occasion to be a disciplinarian, and we were blessed with these glimpses of days gone by. I would always hold tight to them when they came, praying they would not slip away like a thief in the night, but somehow they always did.

I'd been riding shotgun with Mom for so long, I could barely tell where she ended and I began. I felt as though I was drowning in her drink right along with her. I found myself in a semi-catatonic state after a few drinks one evening. I watched from the pouf in the center hall as Mom pounded down a drink with Beverly in the dining room. Then she sauntered out the door with her crazy hair, probably off to the Plush Poodle or the Little Cafe. I lost myself in the blur of her faux leopard coat as she passed me on her way out the door. I hated that coat and her stupid salad face. Did she even see me?

I felt lost like she was—maybe not for the same reasons—but I was abandoned too. Only I was abandoned by both of my parents. I stumbled out into the yard. It was dark out, but I didn't care. I needed to make sense of my life. *Who the hell am I? I'm tired of being an outcast, tired of feeling eyes on me always. Am I crazy, or are they really watching? Can they really see me?*

I clutched the bottle of blackberry brandy that Carole and I scored earlier down at the packy. Anita said brandy is good when it's cold out. I saw the fog of my breath in front of my face as I tripped on a mound of hay out in the ravine. I hoped I would die out there and never wake up. Then Mom would be sorry. Then she'd know sadness. Maybe then she'd wake up. *My silent screams haven't worked, but maybe this will,* I thought as I got up. I polished off the rest of the bottle, chucked it into the bushes, and headed out to the street. The streetlights were bright and glaring in my eyes, so I shaded them to see where I was going. I remembered when Wendy got me to dance out in the street a while back by doing the same halfway down Cherryvale Avenue where none of the people driving by could see her, and I felt the burn of being made to look the fool all over again. I stumbled near the pillars, trying to get up the courage to make my move, when Ray pulled into the street in his green Oldsmobile.

"Dorth, what are you doing out here in this cold?" he said. *He must know, he has to know,* I thought as he jumped out and grabbed me. "Come on, come back to the house with me and get warm," he coaxed. His soothing voice lulled me, and I fell into his arms sobbing like a ragdoll. He gently guided me into the back seat and drove down to the house.

"I can't go in there," I said. I didn't want to go in. I knew I wasn't making any sense, and I resisted as he tried to pick me up, but I gave in, and he carried me into the house across his arms like a child and laid me on the couch. He grabbed the purple velour coat with the white fur that had been carelessly tossed on a nearby chair and threw it over me.

"What were you doing out there, Dorothy?" Ray asked again.

"I hate everything, Ray. I hate my mother, and I hate my life. I just want it to be over," I said.

"That's ridiculous, and you know it. Life is a precious gift, and your mother loves you kids more than you know. Believe me. Nothing is worth feeling like that. You've just had too much to drink."

Just then Carole breezed into the room. "Doit, where the hell have you been? I've been looking all over for you," she said as she knelt on the floor beside Ray. "Are you okay? What's goin' on?"

I wondered when I turned into Drama Mama, full of angst. And what role was I playing now that Mom was heading toward her Joan Crawford role?

[top left] Carole is trying to sober me up, while poor Yardley doesn't want any part of it.

[top right] Beth stands on the veranda in her Howard Johnson's uniform. Mom's car "The Bomb" is in the background.

[bottom] Hanging out at our friendly ice cream truck with Tim the ice cream man. Front: Ray and I; back: Jon Fitt and Terri.

CHAPTER NINE

Mad Dog 20/20

It was Thanksgiving, and Harold was visiting for the holiday. We had moved the television set into the living room so we could all watch *Chitty-Chitty Bang-Bang* after dinner. I was already engrossed in the movie when I heard our front door slam.

"I'm looking for Michael Preston."

I looked up and saw a gangly man with scraggly dark hair and a scrappy beard that reminded me of Shaggy from *Scooby-Doo*. He stumbled into our living room holding a Budweiser can in his hand.

"Who are you?" Harold asked suspiciously.

"My name's Jon Fitt," he slurred, exaggerating the "T." "Where's Michael Preston?"

Just then Michael walked in.

"Jon, paesan! What are you doing here?" Michael hung out with all the Italians down in the south end, so he liked to pretend he was one of them.

"Michael, my bruddah. I came down to Buena Vista to visit you. You got another beer? What's your name?" Jon added with a furrowed brow as he sat on the chair next to me, leaning his face too close to mine. I did not feel like chatting with a drunk, so I glared at Jon and turned back to the television set just in time to see Dick Van Dyke fly through the sky.

I was sitting in the furry chair whose once fluffy nap had seen better days and was now matted down with sticky crud mashed deeply into its fabric. It had burn holes on both its arms, and after the loss of one back leg, was held up by books on that side. The other leg finally broke one evening when some drunk sat down. Thinking it was funny, he pulled out the dented and mangled leather-bound books from the other side and leaned back as though it were a recliner. At first we thought it was pretty cool, but eventually the furry chair found a new home in a dumpster.

"That's my baby sister, Dorothy, but I like to call her Dot because she hates it," Michael said with a guffaw as he yanked the piece of hair that was hanging in front of my face.

"Where's Toto, Dor-tee? Hey, did you know there's no place like home?"

Jon said as he slapped his knee and tilted his head back exposing his wide-gapped teeth.

"Oh yeah, witty. I've never heard that one before," I quipped.

"Hand me that ting," Jon said as he started to light up a cigarette.

"What 'ting' is that?" I asked, thinking this guy was some kind of jerk.

"You know, the goddam over there," he said, pointing to the grimy ashtray loaded with cigarette butts. We later learned that everything was a "goddam" to Jon—it was his version of "thingy." Just then Beth walked into the room wearing black pants and a tight-knit turtleneck that accentuated her sleek figure. Her long blonde hair was parted in the middle and her eye makeup was heavier than it was before she met Lynn Yarkey. I noticed Jon's eyes light up.

"Hey, Mike, is dat anudder one of your sisters? You didn't tell me you had such pretty sisters," Jon said with the unlit cigarette still dangling from his mouth as he leered lecherously at Beth.

At first I thought Jon's behavior was despicable and he grated on my every nerve, but he eventually grew on me, and before long he joined our happy household of renters. He was either a happy drunk or an obnoxious drunk, but somehow he was always lovable, which is probably why none of us were shocked when Beth started to date him.

In the spring of 1975, I was sitting in the living room with Beth, Jon, Lynn, and Gina. "You guys want to listen to Dave Mason or Deep Purple?" I asked, as I got up to change the record. Just then Ray burst through the front door with a huge grin on his face.

"You guys, come outside, I have a surprise!" Ray could barely contain himself. I figured he wanted to introduce us to his new flavor of the month.

He might as well have been blowing a flute as he skipped out the door waving his arm for us to follow. And there in the driveway was a black stretch limo.

"Did somebody die?" Lynn asked.

"It's my new ride! Come see," he said as he ran to the car, flung open the back door, and jumped in. "Look, it has a partition window," he said and hit the button to roll it up. Jon was already in the front seat flipping the visor and checking all the dashboard gadgets.

"You didn't get rid of your motorcycle, did you?" Jon asked.

"Of course not, this is just so we can cruise around in style!" he said.

"Wow, that's pretty cool! How 'bout you take us to McDonald's?" Gina suggested.

McDonald's was to Gina and me the equivalent of a steak dinner. We'd even memorized the McDonald's slogan—but then, who didn't back then. *Two all-beef patties, special sauce, lettuce, cheese, pickles, onions on a sesame seed bun.*

Gina and I jumped in the limo just as Brian was coming out the front door.

"Hey, where're you guys going? Is that Lynn with you?" He grinned as he blocked the sun from his eyes. "And what is that thing doing in our driveway, Ray?" he asked,

"It's my new car," Ray said. "Come check it out!"

"Yeah, maybe later," Brian said. "Lynn, why don't you stay here with me?" He added provocatively.

"I'll catch up with you later. Is that okay, Beth?" Lynn asked. Beth made a face but nodded okay. We knew Brian and Lynn had been fooling around. Even though Beth had Jon, I think it still bothered her. She climbed into the limo with Gina and me, Jon staying happily up front with Ray.

"Onward, James," Gina said just before closing the partition. "Look how everyone is looking at us! They probably think there's some big-wig in the car," Gina added as we drove down the street.

I made an arrangement with Ray to pick me up from school every day at 11:07. I figured as long as I made homeroom where attendance was taken, I could pretty much skip whatever class I didn't like, which was all but English class that let out at 11:07.

Ray would be stationed on the side street next to the door I escaped from outside my classroom. I could see the limo from my seat in class as I patiently waited for class to let out. I could practically smell the pot smoke billowing from the driver's side window beckoning me.

"Preston, I see you finally made it to class," the boy in front of me said. "What's with you never coming to school?" I shrugged, not knowing what to say. I thought he was cute, and I could feel my face burning. I knew his name was Chris and that he had just moved here from Seattle. His west coast air was evident from his preppy clothes and casual attitude. I wanted to ask him to run out the door with me and join me in my limo. I wanted to kiss his full red lips and run my fingers through his thick, shiny brown hair, but I was too shy to say anything to him, so I'd dash from my escape hatch alone day after day and hurl myself into Ray's limo.

I ended up stalking the new guy, Chris, for months with Gina. We'd alter our usual route to the Li'l Peach where we got our cigarettes just to walk by Chris's house on Randolph Street. Then we hung out at the Pink Church and smoked them, which was conveniently positioned so I could see Chris's house. It took a while, but Chris finally asked me out after I got over my bout of chicken pox that year.

When I got my report card at the end of my eighth and ninth grade school years, I was marked absent for about ninety-six of the required 185 days. With the help of summer school, I somehow managed to pass both years.

Arthur kept a cot in the room off the kitchen for when he was home, which thankfully was not that often lately since his Merchant Marine job usually had him somewhere up in Canada. Mom never did give Arthur an answer

to his marriage proposal, and he took up with a woman named Wanda who was the perfect match for him. Arthur never missed an opportunity to throw the fact that Mom owed him money into her face and would always add the caveat "with dividends."

Bill was the new renter that had taken over Harold's old room on the third floor. He was almost as obnoxious as Arthur and always the smartest one in the room—or so he thought. It was my cue to dash from a room when I could smell the stinky, nasty patchouli oil that preceded him.

Bill would sit and rub his dark wiry beard arrogantly as he laughed in disdain at everything I said. He'd roll his head back to reveal his gnarly teeth and tell me how stupid I was. His condescension made me want to punch him every time I laid eyes on him.

Bill struck a deal with Mom to take the trash out every week in lieu of paying rent. Of course, he never took the trash out nor paid his rent. So with no trash being taken out and nobody caring about the state of the house, the cockroach epidemic got worse. I dreaded having to go to the kitchen now. They'd click and scatter as soon as I entered. I took to stomping on the floor every time I approached in order to scare them off. Nobody wanted to be the first to have to come in when the lights were off, so most of the time we just left them on.

Dinnertime was a free-for-all. With Mom drunk all the time, she rarely had time for such menial tasks as preparing meals, even though she wasn't working. In fact, the only job I ever remember Mom holding was the one at Papa Luca's, which was clearly not a real job.

Beth and I would root around in the kitchen for whatever we could find, which was usually cereal or TV dinners that often had to be chipped out of the frozen tundra that our freezer had become. The red linoleum floor was worn and ragged with dings and several large holes in front of the freezer where we propped a mop handle up against the door to keep it closed, this having given rise to the ice problem in the first place. It could take days to defrost the freezer as it sat unplugged with pans lining the inside to catch the dripping water.

The once lovely jack-o-lantern light in the kitchen was covered with a thick coat of grease and dust. Flypaper with dead flies attached hung from it even when it wasn't summertime.

There was one closet in the kitchen that the roaches gravitated to, so Mom called it the "critter closet." I began having recurring nightmares of giant cockroaches trapping me in the bathroom where I would shrink and hide behind the toilet like one of them.

Once, as I was putting on my new brown leather lace-up boots, I couldn't quite get my foot in, so I pulled the boot off and shoved my hand inside. Something cold moved by the toe. I ripped my arm out only to see a three-inch cockroach scamper out and skid across the floor like a Matchbox car with a turbo engine. This horror led to my annoying habit of pounding on my shoes every time I put them on. The memory of that cold hard feeling still lingers on the tip of my finger, sending shivers up my spine.

Gary was a guy who worked at the car wash next door to the Plush Poodle and happened to meet Mom one afternoon after his shift. As fate would have it, he was looking for a place to stay, and he became our next stray, renting one of the back rooms. He was a tall, gangly man with shoulder-length greasy hair and horn-rimmed glasses. He wore a green army jacket and had a habit of roaming around the house with glazed red eyes that were usually half-closed, a lazy smile, and a bottle of Mad Dog 20/20 protruding from a brown paper bag—a perfect fit for our house.

One day Gary came home with a friend from the car wash.

"Hey, Mrs. P, this is Tom. He needs a place to stay. Can he take the empty room next to mine?" Of course there was no question, no vetting. Mom let just about any stray into our home.

"Hey Dorth, who is that HONG-U-NONG-KONG with the leather jacket?" Gina said the first time she spotted Tom. HONG-U-NONG-KONG was code for hunk. Gina wasn't the only one that liked Tom. Rhonda's sister Resa and I also had crushes on him, and we'd often sit in the upstairs center hall vying for his attention. In the end, it was my sister Ann who caught his eye on one of her trips home.

Ann had already graduated from her two-year college and was living in Worcester with two roommates. Now Ann was coming home more often.

One day Gina and I decided to skip school and hole up in Gary's room after he'd left for work.

"I got the munchies, Dorth. You guys got any of them sour cream and onion potato chips downstairs?" Gina asked as we were lazily draped over the two chairs in Gary's room. I wasn't going anywhere near Gary's bed, which was in a crumpled-up state of disarray, looking like he'd had a wrestling match with the bedsheets. I could barely stand the stench of the room, but anything was better than going to school.

After my covert munchie mission to the kitchen, I was sneaking up the back hall stairway when I heard the phone ring. My new school rarely called when I was absent since my absences were so prevalent, so I wasn't concerned. A bit later, I heard a knock on Gary's door. I looked at Gina in surprise. I was mid-crunch on my potato chip as I pointed to the closet that adjoined Tom's room next door, indicating we should go hide. We quietly closed the closet door as Mom began to knock on Tom's door.

"Tom, have you seen Dorothy today? The school called and said she's absent again."

"Nope, I haven't seen her all day... unless she's hiding in my closet," we heard him say with a laugh as he opened the closet door. His closet door was behind the main door so we were concealed from Mom's view. The surprised look on Tom's face told me all I needed to know. Gina and I were huddled on the floor with our fingers to our lips as we pleaded with our eyes. He briefly hesitated and then shut the door. "Nope, not in there."

After Mom went away, he opened the door back up. "Next time you want to skip school, hide in someone else's closet," he said with a hint of amusement as he slammed the door shut.

Tim Harp worked at the car wash with Gary and Tom, but he also drove his father's ice cream truck in the summer. Tim would often meander down Buena Vista, "Turkey in the Straw" blaring from the speakers as he drove down the hill. But instead of a bunch of little children clamoring for ice cream as they tugged on their mother's aprons, it was a bunch of potheads that wanted a munchie fix as we ran for the ice cream truck.

Tim was the oldest of thirteen in his family. That is how we met his brother Jay, who eventually ended up stealing my virginity.

I think it was Jay who decided it would be fun to slide down our laundry shoot, located at the base of the back hall stairs on the second floor.

Jon Fitt went down first as we all huddled in the hallway listening to him hoot and holler his way down the narrow slide.

"I guess youse guys never use that ting for laundry—I'm pretty sure I cleared the way of all the cobwebs," Jon yelled up. I imagined him down there sputtering and wiping the cobwebs from his face.

"I think I can fit," Jay said, looking down into the hole.

"I don't know, Jay, you aren't quite as small as Jon," Beth warned.

"Oh hell, I'm goin' for it," he said as he tucked up his legs and climbed in. But as he began to slip down and out of our sight, we didn't hear the same sounds we had heard from Jon a few seconds before.

"Uh, guys, I think I'm stuck. I'm a little squished up in here, and I can't move!" Jay said from the depths of the shoot. His voice had a strange echo.

We all looked at each other and shrugged. "I don't know what we can do," Beth said as she called down the hole.

"I can't move," he said beginning to sound alarmed.

"How far down are you? Maybe someone can pull you from below," Beth yelled.

"I don't know, I seem to be getting more scrunched. I'm thinking this wasn't such a good idea after all," he said in a muffled voice.

At that point, the buffoonery overtook us all as we broke out into a unanimous roar of laughter. It didn't help that we were all stoned. I could picture him inside rolled up like a snail and every time his increasingly tightened voice called up for help it became more hilarious. We were no help whatsoever to him as the lot of us were rendered helpless through our howls.

"I think I just got my foot loose..." we heard him holler. "Yup... I am wriggling the other out now. Wait, I might be... Whoa...," and out he came. Jon was the only one at the bottom to greet him.

Jay was pretty shaken up afterward, but he still saw the ridiculous humor in the situation. Jay, who always liked a good self-deprecating chuckle, was a master storyteller. He could hold court for hours relaying all manner of tales.

Although I never liked it when Mom hung around us, I knew my friends and the renters did. Drunk or not drunk, she was often the life of the party at the Preston Manor. So when Jay began telling the story, it was hard for Mom to be mad. And she ultimately ended up curled over in laughter along with the rest of us.

Later that year, Beth's friend Terri needed a place to stay after she ran away from home. Although Mom did not like the idea of harboring a runaway, it didn't take long to convince her to let Terri stay since Beth told Mom it was only temporary—it truth turned into thirty-seven years. That's how Terri joined the Preston ward for wayward lost souls.

Since all the other rooms were rented, Terri ended up on the other twin bed in my room.

I was not happy about having to share my room with a stranger, but when Terri moved her stereo and the two massive speakers into my room and cranked up "Low Spark of High Heeled Boys," I was hooked. Whenever I hear any song by Traffic, I am transported back to that time.

Terri came with a posse of new friends, three of whom I'd wind up smooching or sleeping with.

It was like someone stuck a hot stake in the coals and everything was ablaze that summer. I was fifteen and still a virgin, but every fiber of my insides was igniting.

We were all on fire—every one of us—it was as though we were connected through some invisible thread. This was different from the days of the Circle Boys; this stirred me in ways I'd never felt before, like Frankenstein coming alive.

Ray would always buy for us, and we'd either drive around and drink in his limo or hang at the Manor and party. One weekend Ray bought a giant family-sized tent and pitched it in the side yard. We brought blankets and pillows out and gathered them inside the tent, not knowing exactly who would end up sleeping there; I just knew I wanted to be one of them. And Gina and I were the first to stake our spots. I remember hoping that one of Terri's friends might join us, like Brett or Danny, and that I would end up smooching with one of them. Of course, I didn't believe either one of them would look at me.

We partied until the wee hours of the morning. I was always a diehard and wanted to stay up all night partying. That night I was up until the birds started chirping and the dark sky morphed into the amber beauty of the dawn light. I remember, in the haze of my drunkenness, being dumbfounded that the sky was getting light. Why can't it just stay dark so I can keep on partying?

I knew I wasn't making much sense and that I was slurring, but I just slipped into the comfort of the oblivion—and of not caring. I think Jon Fitt and Ray were the only other ones up at that point, and one of them said something funny. That was when I laughed my way right off the cobbled flowerbed wall on the veranda and into the yard five feet below. Probably the alcohol saved me; otherwise, I might have been deemed paralyzed from such a fall. After that, I don't remember much, but I either woke up in the tent with a large aching headache or in my bed—either way, it didn't much matter.

To my surprise, Brett Crawford actually did look my way, or more aptly, looked through me. One day he just started staring at me, which made me super self-conscious. I wondered if he could see my wet pit stains that were almost always there and always made worse by my worrying over them. Why do I sweat so much?

Brett's staring was so intense I thought his eyes might burn a hole right through me. I wanted to squirm right out of my skin, but I was intrigued, petrified, and exhilarated all at once. I tried to look back at him and smile lightly but could never hold his stare. I could feel my eyes flit about the room and then back to him where his gaze never wavered.

Finally, one day we were alone and sitting on the bent glider in the party room. It was the same glider that used to be in the screened-in porch and had somehow found its way to the third floor to co-mingle with the rest of the trash-picked furniture. Only now the glider no longer glided, and the one bent leg made the glide seem more like a thunker.

Brett began talking about his recent girlfriend whom he'd just broken up with. He told me how she used to trace her finger over his freckled arms and make shapes. I could tell he was in a deep state of fond reminiscence that had nothing to do with me, yet I listened with rapt attention, or as much attention as my pot-infused brain could muster.

Those were the days when pot was my best friend, and I was almost always in some mind-numbing state. It was as though I was looking at my brain in a glass jar that stood in the middle of a locked room that I had no access to.

Sitting there on the glider that day may have been the first time Brett kissed me. He'd been working up to that moment with his stare sessions that had been going on for about a week.

One night Brett came with me on a babysitting job. I had just put the baby down for the evening. He moved over and started to run his fingers lightly over my arm, sending shivers up my spine. His shoulder-length dirty-blonde hair was tied back in a ponytail to keep the curls away from his freckled face. He pulled my head close to his and probed my lips with his soft tongue, staring directly into my eyes with that same penetrating intensity. I gazed back and wanted to dive into his crystal blue pools, only this time I held it, intoxicated by his seduction. I wanted to stick my tongue into his mouth, but he kept licking my lips slowly and sensuously. He smelled so good, a musky, earthy scent that set me on fire with desire. With no alcohol in my system to spur my confidence, I was intimidated by his brazenness. He was so different from the other boys I'd smooched with so far. I kissed him back with as much passion as I could muster and allowed him to thrust his hand under my shirt. I felt him unsnap my bra and move his hand over my naked breast as he lightly turned my nipple while rolling his tongue in my mouth. I thought I might melt. I felt a tingling between my legs as he gently leaned me back and climbed on top of me on the couch. I wrapped my legs around him as he ground his pelvis into mine. I wanted him so badly, but I knew I was not ready yet, so I stopped him. I just can't. My pants were already unbuttoned and I wondered vaguely when he'd done that.

"Are you still a virgin?" he asked. I nodded, feeling ashamed of my inexperience with this man whom I thought so worldly. The mood changed as quickly as it began when he stood up.

"Why did you even invite me here tonight? I mean, what did you think was going to happen?" he said as he buckled his belt.

"I guess I thought we would just enjoy each other's company," I said.

I don't remember what happened next, but in my mind, I've sketched it out to be like some old Cary Grant movie where he glanced back with a sneer and walked out the door leaving me sitting there dumbfounded.

He seemed so fixated on his old girlfriend who he'd talked about numerous times. I figured I was just a Band-Aid for him, but I never expected him to be so mean. I felt like a fool.

Terri told me later that he told her I was a blank tape on which you could write anything. Those words punctured me deeply, and I began questioning my self-worth again, which set me spinning out of control. Am I stupid? Blank tape . . . blank tape . . . I played it over and over in my head until I was dizzy.

I wasn't even sure why I stopped him, but his rejection went deep into my soul, probably awakening some long lost Dad thing I had stuffed away. I'd already been to all the other bases with other boys, including Brett, but Mom's voice always echoed in my head about the sanctity of marriage and of being pure. I certainly didn't feel pure, but this last vestige of saving myself was how I justified the conflict in my head.

I hated Brett for making me feel worthless, which is probably why I slept with the next man who tried. I would prove I was no empty tape.

I later reasoned that Brett's simple act of rejection was the catalyst that set the stage for all of my future toxic relationships. But then it's easy to blame anyone but myself.

Barry was coming around more often, and at some point he and Brian started hanging out. So it was no surprise when he started renting a room from us. His wayward ways had not changed much, except they hardened him. Many things went missing from Mom's house during his tenure, including a beautiful old Westminster chime box clock that rang on the hour from the wall outside the powder room, and Mom's tall brass candlesticks, to name a few.

We assumed that Barry fenced all the stuff when we were away. Most of us were furious over it and urged Mom to throw him out. Brian didn't say much, since Barry was his friend.

"Judge not, lest ye be judged. We've known Barry forever; it had to be someone else," Mom would say, the ultimate optimist who wanted to believe Barry would never steal from us.

"Mom, that's bullshit," Ann said. "Kick his ass out of here before he steals everything of any value. I'm so tired of you letting these assholes walk all over you."

"Oh, AnnMaria, stop quibbling," Mom said, believing all people were inherently good.

Even though I joked with Barry, he still scared me. There was something ominous and creepy about him.

One day a bunch of us were out by the plaza leaning on Ray's limo; we were most likely passing around a joint, or sharing a beer or cigarette. It was the summer when some of our games included squishing each other's noses (promoted by the baby picture of me with my face mashed to the glass door), messing up someone's hair, or kicking someone in the butt just for fun. So it wasn't strange that I'd brazenly approached Barry and kicked him in the butt. What was strange was the chokehold I found myself in so fast that I barely remember it happening.

"Don't ever touch me," Barry said. His stubby form loomed over me with beady brown eyes that seared through me, his Fu Manchu mustache dangerously close to my face.

"Barry, stop!" I could hear Ray's voice off in the distance as he tried to pry me from Barry's tightening grip. Once free, I stumbled and grabbed my swollen neck and backed away. Shocked and terrified at what had just happened, I ran crying into the house to find Mom, who, despite her usual state of drunkenness, was still my savior and the one I always ran to for support when I needed it. She was shocked when I told her what happened, and she looked a little scared too.

I don't remember what happened next, but it wasn't long before Barry moved out.

I never understood why Mom rented to him, but then, we'd already had our fair share of weirdos, perverts, and about every other walk of life living in the house. Michael told me about the renter that came into his room in the middle of the night and stood leering at him. His bags were put out on the veranda the next day. Carol said she woke up with hickies once when she was passed out drunk; we never did know who the perpetrator was. So Barry's admittance as a renter was no surprise.

On December 19, 1979, four years later, it was reported in the paper that Barry, then age thirty-one, had attended a Christmas party at a local bar, from which he was asked to leave after arguing with and shoving an employee. As he was leaving the bar, a former employee, who had witnessed the earlier incident, assisted in ejecting Barry and pushed him to the ground. Barry left the area and returned later that evening with a gun. He exchanged words with the man who pushed him, and they stepped outside, at which point Barry shot the other man in the knee. A number of people chased after Barry, including the unarmed brother of the man who had just been shot and who happened to know Barry. He asked Barry to put down the gun, and Barry shot him in the chest and killed him. Barry was on the run for more than nine months until the Massachusetts State Police, following an anonymous tip, arrested him. He was sentenced to life in prison with a concurrent sentence of eight to ten years and the possibility of parole after fifteen years.

Barry was denied parole all three times that he went before the board. The parole board cited many reasons for its decision, including Barry's lack of participation in prison programs and disciplinary issues, including an escape, possession of a shank, and possession of homebrew and cocaine in prison. He was up for review again in 2017. It is my sincere hope that I never lay eyes on him again.

Barry reported to the board that he quit ninth grade at age sixteen to hang on the streets drinking. I'm pretty sure he didn't mention how he, Ray, and Michael "borrowed" cars and took them for joy rides.

Needless to say, I do not feel privileged to have known Barry. None of us were shocked, since he always lived on the edge.

Gina and I were rummaging around the moth-ridden shelves in the kitchen pantry, looking for a snack. Mom always insisted that they were "Mrs. Napolitan's moths," although I never quite understood why. Maybe her moths wanted to hang out with Charlie's cockroaches.

"Hey, Dorth, wanna go steal some food stamps again so we can get some munchies?" Gina asked. I remembered our last covert escapade when Gina distracted Mom, and I stole the food stamps from her purse so we could buy hot dogs and Lipton Onion Soup Mix at Crown Market. We always managed to find interesting treats when we shopped there. My favorite was the colorful gummy candy bar with the white stripe down the middle that was covered in sugar.

"Ooooh, maybe we can get some of them frozen fried clams," Gina said with a glint in her glazed red eyes.

"Hey, if it isn't the 'Giggly Guinea,'" Michael said fondly as he walked into the kitchen. "What are you two brats up to?"

"Nothin', Michael. We're just looking for food," Gina replied.

"Good luck with that one. Maybe you can get Mom to make you some 'pooie'," he said, mimicking Mom's voice. "Hey, either of you brats seen Terri around?" he asked.

All of my siblings seemed to be hooking up with renters, and Michael was no exception. Michael moved to the south end after he and Joanne split up, and he and Terri had been sneaking around together behind Mom's back for some time. I shivered to think that the only eligible renter left was the patchouli-soaked Bill, but I think our friend Nancy may have already snagged that prize.

Mom found out later that summer that Michael was dating Terri.

"She's still a child, Michael Joseph Anthony, and your sister Beth's age, no less. You should be begging Joanne to take you back and honor your marriage vows," Mom said. "I knew I never should have taken that runaway spoiled brat into my house."

Terri ended up moving out of the house and in with Michael later that month. I'm sure she was happy to be away from Mom, and I was happy to have my room back.

During the 70s, the Springfield Civic Center had a great concert line-up, and I'd become a concert-going fool. At age fifteen, I'd been to more concerts than most attend in a lifetime. I saw Crosby, Stills, Nash & Young; Aerosmith; Dylan; Marshall Tucker; Jefferson Starship; Fleetwood Mac; Deep Purple; Grateful Dead; and Moody Blues; just to name a few. I'd stumble in and out of these. Strobe lights, booze, and pot smoke mingled with my senses, making most of them a vague dull memory.

We had tickets to go see the Eagles later that August when Ann rolled up in her pink Cadillac to pick us up. Mom had just been brawling with Brian and was on a rampage, so when she saw Ann, her eagle eye honed in on her next victim. We were out on the veranda, and Ray was handing Ann her concert ticket, when out of nowhere, Mom swooped in and grabbed the ticket.

"And just where do you think you all are going?" Mom shouted. I could smell the vodka on her as I stood beside her. I could see that Joan was coming out to play, and I quickly checked my pocket to make sure my ticket was safe and then slowly backed away.

"What do you think you're doing, Mom? Give me back my ticket!" Ann demanded, perplexed at what had prompted the sudden attack.

"I will not!" Mom said as she stood tall and folded her arms over her chest. "You all think you are so much better than me. You think you are so mattchure," she slurred.

"This is ridiculous, Mom. Give me back my ticket—now! I don't know what your problem is," Ann said as she tried to pry the ticket from Mom's hand.

Mom quickly backed away and jammed the ticket into her bra. "There. I dare you to try and get it," Mom said, grimacing strangely.

"Yikes, Salad Face is at it again," Beth whispered to me.

"Mom, don't be stupid. Just give her the ticket. We're going to be late for the concert," Beth said.

"I don't give a goldarn about your stinkin' concert," Mom spat back.

Ann went to grab Mom to try and pull the ticket from her bra, but Mom grabbed her hair and pulled her into a headlock as Ann squirmed to get away.

"What the fuck, Mom—cut the shit! Have you lost your mind? Give me my goddam ticket, you lunatic!"

"How dare you take the Lord's name in vain!" Mom said. "I will not have you speaking to me like that. I did not raise you to speak to me like that," she said as she pushed herself away. "You all hate me. Why don't you all just go and leave me like your father did!"

"Yeah, Ma, why don't you go eat worms," Ann yelled.

"I'm going to take some pills, and then you'll be rid of me once and for all! Here! Take your goldarn ticket and leave," she slurred as she threw down the ticket in disgust, her hair a tangled mess as she stormed back into the house.

"Come on, let's get outta here before she comes back," Ann whispered to us as she scooped up the ticket.

At the concert we sat on the floor in front of the stage. "Witchy Woman" roaring in my ear. Ray selling joints faster than I could roll them. I tried to forget the nagging feeling of Mom at home trying to kill herself and hated that tiny part of me that almost wished she would put us all out of our misery.

Two months later Ann announced that she and Tom were going to get an apartment together, which sparked World War III.

"I forbid you! I will not have my daughter living in sin. I absolutely forbid it," Mom said as she stomped her foot on the floor and set her fists on her hips.

"Mom, I'm twenty-two years old. You can't tell me what I can and cannot do anymore. Sorry," Ann said.

"Then I will forbid Beth and Dorothy from ever going to your den of iniquity," Mom replied with a smug satisfied look.

"Because you're so 'holier than Thou,' Mom?" Ann said. "You sure do throw a lot of stones for someone living in a glass house."

"How dare you compare your amoral behavior to me. I am not the one who has forsaken God as you children have. Maybe with any luck Beth and Dorothy can still be salvaged," Mom said as she stormed out of the room.

Ann and Tom's apartment was right down the street from my school, so it became a convenient getaway for me on the days that Ray didn't pick me up at 11:07. Forbidden or not, I was not going to stay away.

[top] Dad in his Army uniform.

[bottom] Our last Christmas with Dad—1963—and he's looking none too thrilled.

CHAPTER TEN

Step Nine

> Step Eight: Make a list of all persons we had harmed, and become willing to make amends to them all.
>
> Step Nine: Make direct amends to such people wherever possible, except when to do so would injure them or others.

Ann called and asked Beth and me to come over to her place one rainy day in April of 1976.

"Dad reached out to Paula and John," Ann said abruptly as she sat us down.

"What?" Beth said in disbelief. "What the hell. Are you serious? He just shows up after twelve years, and we're supposed to forgive and forget?"

"He wants to meet with us. Something about one of his AA steps and making amends or some shit like that," Ann said. "Oh, and there's one more thing you need to know. Apparently, he married some black lady after he left us, and they had a daughter together."

"He has what?" I said. I have a half-sister? I didn't like that suddenly I was not the baby anymore. But I knew I would always be Mom's baby, and that was all that mattered.

"You know how I feel about it," Tom chimed in from the other room. "He's a piece of shit, Ann. He doesn't deserve to see any of you after what he did. Fucker never gave your mother a goddam dime all these years, and now he wants to be forgiven?"

"I know, Tom, just let me handle this. John thinks it will be best if we keep it from Mom and meet in Maryland at his house," Ann said. "I refuse to go see the piece of shit. But you two deserve to have the choice. If you decide to go, we'll make up some story, and you can drive out with Michael and Brian," she added.

My head was swimming, and I couldn't think straight. Who was this person who I'm now supposed to call "Dad"? I couldn't even fathom what I'd say to him or how I would act. But I was curious.

"I'll go meet him," I said as I looked down at my hands. I could feel my lower lip trembling, and I tried hard not to show it. Ann saw and came over to hug me, and the floodgates burst. I wept on her shoulder uncontrollably as she patted my hair and consoled me like a child. An old familiar feeling of how Mom used to do the same—brushing away all my hurts—crashed over me like a wave and pulled me helplessly into a deep pool of buried emotions.

I don't remember anything about the trip to John's house. Scotty could have beamed us all there for all I know. I remember wanting a cigarette so I had something to do with my hands, but I knew I couldn't smoke in this situation. I was conflicted with a plethora of feelings. I was curious, angry, sad, and ambivalent all bundled together.

We were in the finished basement at John and Phyllis's house when Dad walked in with his new daughter, Lisa—the myth of my father brought to life. I could tell he was uncomfortable, too, but despite that, he approached, looming over me as he bent to give me a warm embrace. I stiffened as he took me into his arms. I noticed his graying and thinning hair was swept back and tied into a ponytail. I knew Mom would grimace with disgust if she saw it, thinking he was grasping too tightly to his youth. I couldn't help but feel like I was somehow betraying Mom; we'd told her this was just a sibling visit. She bought it, but somewhere deep inside myself, I felt horrible. I could see her sitting on that radiator, year after year at Christmas as she yearned for Dad, swizzling around the pieces of her heart in her drink. I wanted to lash out at him and tell him how I hated him for hurting her so deeply. I wanted to tell him how I hated him for hurting each of us, and how dare he think he could just waltz back in after so long as if nothing had happened.

John was the glue that held us all together during this visit. He played host and tried to make things light, but none of us was comfortable, including Dad, who tried desperately to make us at least like him.

We stayed for two grueling nights. I colored with Lisa on the floor. It was a good distraction and helped to lighten the heaviness that permeated the atmosphere. Her innocence was the icebreaker for all of us. Lisa was only six. She was sweet and innocent and happy to discover she had seven new brothers and sisters. I'm sure it didn't occur to her that all of us were conflicted over our new reality.

Beth was sitting in a far corner. I tried to make eye contact with her, but she remained sullen and withdrawn. Paula did not make the trip since she and John and Brian had already met with Dad on Martha's Vineyard. Ann was conspicuously absent.

When I asked Brian years later, he could only remember meeting Dad on the Vineyard.

Although I was mostly consumed with my own thoughts, I knew each of my siblings struggled with their own demons with regard to Dad. It was as though we were all moving in slow motion and bouncing about the room contained within our own bubble. We didn't talk much about it after that visit.

I can only assume that the long ride home was mostly silent, or maybe we were beamed back home too.

I heard from Paula that Dad kept in touch with her after our visit, but I did not hear from him at all. Mom always said that Paula was his favorite. I was angry and envious and crushed that I wasn't the chosen one. I wanted to be "Daddy's little girl." I was always jealous when I saw shows depicting strong father-daughter relationships. I dreamed of my father being someone I could confide in, someone who would soothe my fears and be my champion, someone who rendered loving but strict discipline and set me on a straight and narrow path, someone who cheered me on at school sporting events and encouraged me to do well in school, who shed tears of pride and joy at my graduations, and who walked me down the aisle and kissed my cheek as he passed my arm to my knight in shining armor. I longed for that idyllic storybook life with a strong father figure like Ward Cleaver or Mike Brady, or even like some of my friends' fathers, like Gina and Stevie the paperboy, whose father I adored.

I didn't see or hear from Dad again until I turned thirty-one. He'd made his Step Nine and that seemed to be all that mattered to him. Sincerity was not a requirement, apparently. I fought for years with a conflicting inner dialogue over his rejection, but I just couldn't come to terms with it, so I shoved it way up on a dusty old shelf so I wouldn't have to face it.

Lisa and I never became close sisters, and I only saw her a handful of times over the years. She went on to become a successful lawyer, married with two children and living somewhere in Chicago.

I don't know how or when Mom found out about our visit with Dad, but when she did, I was the only one home. "You betrayed me," she viciously spewed as she burst into my room. "You are a Judas!"

"What are you talking about? What's wrong with you?" I said as I cringed away from her. She looked like the spawn of Satan, and all I could think was that she was about to lance me with her pitchfork.

"You know perfectly well," she said as she went to grab me. I quickly escaped her clutching hands and ran into Beth's room. I thought about dashing under the bed again, but I knew it wouldn't get me anywhere.

"You dared to go see your lying, cheating father, and you didn't tell me? I bore you! How could you have betrayed me? I, who stood by you all these years!"

"Are you kidding, Mom? He's my father. Did you ever even think I might be the least bit curious and want to meet him? I'm sorry we didn't tell you, but that wasn't my idea, so go talk to Paula or John or something and leave me out of it. I did nothing to 'betray' you, and if anything, you betrayed us by always drowning yourself in your stupid vodka bottles. You weren't the only one the jerk left behind, ya know. And besides, I didn't even like him."

Evidently, she didn't hear anything I said as she continued on a screeching tirade that ended with her storming out and slamming the door. "So that's where Beth learned it," I thought.

Mom sulked and would not speak to any of us for about a week.

[top] John sits in his sporty, bright orange Porsche he called "Punkin." He was thirty-six in this picture.

[bottom left] Tom, Brian, Ann, and Yardley pose on the veranda.

[bottom right] "Please drive us to McDonald's so we can get two all-beef patties, special sauce, lettuce, cheese, pickles, onions on a sesame seed bun." Gina and Yardley and I sit in the back of Ray's limo.

Part IV

SOBERING TRUTH

(The Dark Years)

[top left] Bouncer the stuffed monkey that Gina and I gave Ray.

[top right] Story time with Ray as he read Where Did I Come From to Rhonda, Carole, and me the night we slept in the bathroom; 1974.

[bottom] Mom's wedding when she married Harold in 1977. Boys: Michael, Brian, and Harold; girls: Paula, me, Beth, Ann, and Mom. None of us could get it together to look at the camera!

CHAPTER ELEVEN

Desertion

"Dorothy, wake up, I have some news."

I opened my eyes to find Jon Fitt standing over me. It was the morning of July 9, 1976.

Jon was choking back tears. "Ray died in a motorcycle accident last night," he said.

I thought I was dreaming. I sat up and shook my head. "No! That can't be true!"

He was only twenty-eight years old. Aside from my grandfather, this was my first experience with the death of a loved one. Only this time it was Ray. Ray was like a brother; he was our playmate and our friend.

Suddenly Beth came running from her room in her blue silk bathrobe with a tear-streaked face.

"No, no, no," she cried hysterically shaking her head.

"Beth," Jon said and let go of my hand to go after Beth. I looked up and saw Mom coming from Beth's room. She swooped down on my bed, and we sobbed in each other's arms. From the corner of my eye, I saw Bouncer the stuffed monkey Gina and I had given Ray because we thought it looked like him. We would make Bouncer jump on Ray's shoulder and say "joint-joint" in a gravelly voice to let him know that we wanted him to light one up. Bouncer would not be bouncing today.

The days that followed were all a blur. I vaguely remember the plaza still littered with firework debris from the Bicentennial Fourth of July bash. My brother Michael loved putting on firework displays, and that year he'd made the best production ever. Sadly, our celebrating ended with a crash that changed our lives. I could still hear the fireworks popping in my head as I tried to accept that Ray was gone. It just couldn't be true. I could still see his face beaming as he helped Michael set up. I could not fathom what life would be like without him.

On the day of the funeral, I pulled out a small rope bracelet that Ray had given me when he came back from California, and I put it around my wrist. I looked up at my empty birdcage and remembered when I asked Ray to care for my bird, Herkimer, while I was on the Vineyard. I had written him a silly lengthy note with illustrations to instruct him how to feed the bird and keep it from the clutches of Diablo, the cat, who ultimately got him in the end—but not on Ray's watch. I stood waiting for Ray's reaction when I handed him the note. His eyes danced with delight, and he laughed and told me I was tapped in the head as he mussed up my hair, provoking me to kick him in the butt. We loved to wrassle. I could almost hear his playful laugh ringing in my ears. I looked over at my autographed shade. Ray had been the first to sign the pink shade in my bedroom. I thought it was a good idea, so I asked everyone I knew to sign it when they came over. I scanned over Lynn's, who was an Aerosmith groupie—"Stay cool, Doorknob, Aerosmith." Then I honed in on Ray's signature at the very bottom, and there, elegantly scripted in big letters was simply "Born to raise hell. Love ya, Ray." I collapsed to the ground as tears blurred my vision, and I started to hyperventilate. Raise hell he did, I thought. Ray was the life of every party, and the instigator of almost all our crazy adventures.

I knew I had to get control of myself, so I stood up, smoothed my black skirt, and went downstairs.

After Ray died, his vibrant energy was drained from the Preston Manor as though someone had pulled a plug and the lights went off. He was the life of every party. He launched many of our adventures and so much more. All of us were profoundly affected by our sudden loss, and somehow it led to darker times ahead.

I lost my virginity to Tim's brother, Jay, that summer after Ray died. It seemed as though everything was moving in slow motion after the funeral, and we all needed each other more than ever.

Jay was poetic and deep. We lay under a blanket of stars on the Peterson's grassy hill night after night as crickets serenaded us. We talked about missing Ray and the fun we all had. We talked about the constellations and gazed into a faraway place—sometimes crying, sometimes laughing.

One moonlit night, Jay rolled toward me. His eyes were as clear as water.

"Would it be all right if I kissed you?" he asked. Nobody had ever asked me before, so I was taken aback.

Jay was several years older than me, but somehow that didn't matter. He had become a permanent fixture at our house even though he wasn't renting a room—yet. I felt I knew him well enough at that point, not that it ever mattered to me before. Our kiss was filled with a passion I had never felt before, not even with Brett.

I felt like we were kindred spirits, as if the tragedy of losing Ray united us.

"Let's go to my car so we have more privacy," he suggested.

Jay's car was a white Chevy with red seats. It was parked far enough away from the plaza that Mom couldn't see us if she looked out her window. He opened the back door and extended his hand for me to get in. We continued kissing, and before long the windows were fogged up and we were naked. I remember feeling self-conscious since I'd never been completely naked in front of anyone before. I'd held onto my virginity through all the necking and petting I'd done with other boys with a sense of anticipation, like a child waiting for the Easter Bunny. But this was nothing like I'd expected, and I didn't feel any kind of intense pleasure. Having grown up in a Catholic home, masturbation was an unknown commodity, so I had no idea about anything. It felt more like a duty to make the man happy, a feeling I'd carry with me for longer than I care to admit.

Because of our age difference, Jay and I tried to keep our relationship secret, but that was short-lived. He showered me with red roses and wrote countless poems, almost one a day. We professed our undying love, and "Wouldn't It Be Nice" by the Beach Boys became our theme song. We just wanted to be older so we could get married yesterday.

Jay took me horseback riding, to fancy dinners and autumn fairs. He loved Bruce Springsteen and managed to score floor seats, third row center, for his *Darkness* tour. I didn't know what a mosh pit was, but when Bruce jumped into the audience and stood on the chair directly in front on me, I quickly found out.

I was absurdly jealous if Jay so much as looked at another girl. Sometimes he let me skip school and hang out at Soda City Citgo where he worked. I would sit on a plastic soda crate eating burgers with ketchup and relish from the deli across the street, watching him sell soda and pump gas.

Jay was my first love, and I was completely enthralled. I walked around on a cloud most of the time. Mom said I was twitterpated—again.

Like John and Ann, Beth was able to get scholarship money for college and was preparing to go to Southern Vermont College in Bennington, Vermont, that fall. She couldn't wait to leave.

I remember asking Ann one day when she was visiting why Mom was so upset that Beth wanted to go to college.

"Dorth, don't you see? We define her—us, and this stupid house, that is. She doesn't know anything else. I think she thinks we are abandoning her like Dad did."

How could she not see that she abandoned us too? I knew she hated that her nest was emptying out one by one, but I couldn't understand why she wasn't happy that her kids wanted to go to college to better themselves. Instead, she dove deeper and deeper into the bottle.

I withdrew into my corner and watched from afar as Mom and Beth got into physical fight after physical fight, knowing my time was coming.

One night before Beth left, Mom wasn't feeling well, and she asked

Beth to run and get some milk at the store. We knew Mom was already pretty drunk and was in no shape to drive, so we figured we'd go out for a joy ride while we were out on her errand.

"She won't even notice. She'll probably be passed out by the time we get back," Beth said as we drove around. When we finally got back there was a sloppily scratched note written on a torn envelope on the kitchen table:

> Thanks a lot for bringing the milk right back. The garlic I ate made me sick. Well I hear you're planning on pulling a "Terri" on me so natch Dorothy will be next. None of you love me. One by one you save up money on the sneak and leave me. Well, now it's my turn. I've taken an overdose. May God keep you. I love you! Good night, Mom

Mom hated that she allowed Terri to move in after she ran away from home, and she always threw it in our faces.

We were used to Mom's melodrama and threats of suicide, but nevertheless I was always scared that she might actually do it. I lay in bed tormenting myself that night. I rolled over and scrunched my eyes closed, fighting the scene that kept playing in my head like the shower scene in *Psycho* that tormented me for months after Anita convinced us to watch it at her sleepover party, driving me to Mom's bed countless nights afterward. It was too much. I couldn't stand it. I threw off my blankets and sprinted to Mom's door. It was locked. I jiggled and jiggled the knob and pounded on the door. Adrenaline pumping. My every nerve like razors. It was like an out-of-body experience as I hovered over myself. That was when I saw myself kick the wood panels of Mom's door and reach in to unlock it. I rushed to her bed and violently shook her awake. Usually a light sleeper, I was convinced she was dead, but then she groaned and opened her eyes with a glazed and confused look on her face. I didn't know whether to hug her or punch her.

I did neither.

Everything was swirling like a cartoon character that had just gotten knocked out, birds and stars circling overhead. I must have yelled something at her, but all I remember is storming out and slamming the shattered door. I wondered if she played it up and wasn't responding just to scare me. She got the attention she wanted.

I was going into tenth grade at a new school. With Ray gone, and now Beth away at school, it was as though my entire world had turned upside down. Regardless of our squabbles, Beth and I were everything to each other, and we did everything together. And to top it all off, Anita, Rachel, and Wendy also left for college, and Ann and Tom were moving out to the central part of Massachusetts, so I could no longer run to them for escape. I was alone with Mom. Brian still lived at the house, but he was mostly never around.

I got a job as a cashier at the Big Y at the foot of Longhill Street and worked as many extra hours as I could after school and Saturdays just to be away from the house. I began visiting Ray's mother, Angie, who I deemed a second mother since my own was seemingly absent. I became friends with Ray's brother, Teddy, who would often come to the house and play all-night card games with Jay, his sister, and me. We all became master Pitch and Cribbage players and sometimes played until four in the morning.

Mom seemed to always be away at the Plush Poodle or holed up in her dark room.

Gina and I were going to the same high school now, so she drove us there every day. Gina got me to join the field hockey team as a goalie. I didn't care much about sports, but I wanted to at least try to fit in, so I agreed. I think I only made it to one practice.

I got good grades the first term of my tenth-grade year, but by the time I turned sixteen in February, I wound up quitting school regardless. Mom didn't put up much of a fuss. She probably thought if I wasn't in school, I would stay home longer and not go off to college.

I spent my time painting the walls at Mom's house, and it became cathartic for me. I painted all of the woodwork in the three front rooms and took pride in doing a fastidious job with all the intricate dentil work and wainscoting. Mom praised me for the good job I was doing, and some days I got glimmers of days past when she would cook me breakfast.

"Hey, Cha, how 'bout you come grocery shopping with me today, and then you can help me make a rhubarb pie?" I loved those afternoons.

When Kevin came home to visit, Mom told him I quit school. He read me the riot act and made me promise to go back.

"Dorothy, you don't want to end up like some loser on the street, do you?"

Kevin always had a way of convincing me to do things; it all started when I was a little girl "renovating" rooms and putting up Christmas lights with him. So I promised him I would go back. I probably didn't have any intention of doing so at the time, since I was enjoying my free time, but I wanted him to stop nagging at me. I did make good on my promise though and returned to school that September.

I had to repeat the tenth grade, but that was the year I actually learned something in school besides how to cut class, and it was the first time I ever made the honor roll. That was the year I learned that 2 Acetyl Coenzyme A were the central molecules involved in metabolism. I learned how to type after A-semi, S–L, D–K, F–J, G–H were pounded into my head by a drill sergeant typing teacher by the name of Dorothy Porter. I learned how to say "I live on Torledo Street" in Spanish because "*Vivo en la calle Torledo*" sounded much cooler than my real street name. I learned that my name was *Dorotea* in Spanish. I learned to recite an entire passage from Macbeth in my honors English class and was introduced to Charles Dickens when we were assigned to read *A Tale of Two Cities*. It was as though Dickens were doing a dance with the words themselves as they waltzed off the pages and twirled into my head. Yes, that was the year I learned more than any other year until I went off to college, and I found I actually liked learning.

Gina started dating David, the Zamboni driver from the ice rink at Forest Park, whom she had been ogling ever since she started skating there on Wednesday nights. David was several years older, so at first she had to keep it a secret from her parents. One day, she asked if he could rent out one of the rooms at our house, and by the following week David had moved into John's old room on the third floor.

At first I thought it was great because I would see more of Gina, but then I realized the direct opposite was true since she was now coming over only to see David instead of me.

The first time I saw Gina with a black eye, I didn't know what to do. Sometimes I would hear David yelling at her upstairs, but I never expected him to hit her. I tried to ask her about the abuse gently, but she would only say nervously that she "ran into a door." I felt powerless over the situation since Gina wouldn't talk to me.

It was sad to see Gina's spirit draining away. I loved her parents, and I wanted to run to them and tell them, but I knew they couldn't change things either.

None of us were able to persuade Gina not to marry David a few years later. I could see the pained look in Gina's mother's eyes every time the subject of David came up.

It wasn't *Bob & Carol & Ted & Alice*, but it was Beth and Jon, Mom and Harold, Ann and Tom, and Michael and Terri. All four happy couples were married within seven months of each other.

I was happy that Mom finally chose someone, and I was especially happy that it was Harold and not Barden.

Beth and Jon were the first to marry, in October of 1977. I was maid of honor at Beth's and then Mom's wedding two months later. Mom and Harold were married by a Catholic priest at the Preston Manor because Mom would have no less. Brian gave her away, and Paula and I both stood up for her.

Harold beamed as he took his vows. We knew he loved Mom. He told us later that it was the best day of his life.

Although Harold's work was still based in Pennsylvania, he and Mom began to make plans for him to move back permanently. Mom was finally released from Arthur's avaricious clutches, and Harold paid off the second mortgage on the house—dividends and all.

For reasons Mom and Harold did not disclose, they kept separate bedrooms. Harold took the room off the nursery hall that was mine as a baby and later Ann's room. On some level, Mom may have been happy to not share the marriage bed with him, but on another level, I knew she was frustrated and would have liked to. Theirs was a marriage of convenience, but also of companionship. Despite the fact that Mom loved Harold, I knew she would never love anyone the way she'd loved our father. But regardless of that, they grew to develop a special bond. Mom would holler out requests to Harold from her "eagle's nest" in the den, her favorite spot from where she could both watch T.V. and see out the window to the plaza below.

"Hey Hafey, it's time for my ice cream. Will you bring it to me?"

"Of course, Lovey. I'll be right up." Harold would yell back. Mom feigned frustration at Harold for minor things like when he rested his arm on top of his head.

"You look like a moron with your arm draped over your head like that. I wish you'd stop," she'd sputter with a disgusted look on her face. But Harold always laughed and was a good sport. "She's always nagging at me," he'd say with a wink and a laugh.

I'd been dating Jay for over a year by the time Mom and Harold got married. I don't know exactly when it happened, but things were beginning to be too syrupy for me. This was too easy! I began to lose patience with him and started looking at other boys, so I knew it was time to break up with him. Somehow I had to move on to something more dangerous and challenging. My "perfect man" image being extremely twisted, I always gravitated toward bad boys like Timmy.

Was it my selfish nature, or was I just seeking the only thing that made me feel good about myself? New relationships were like a salve to my wounded ego. I loved the feeling I got every time I was smooching with a new boy, feeling needed and loved. I knew it was empty and never lasted, but I kept searching as though somehow it would finally make me whole.

Brian started going to Alcoholics Anonymous meetings and got sober on December 3, 1977. Sometime in July of 1978, when I was seventeen, he sat me down with a contrite look in his eyes and told me he was moving to California.

"I want to start by telling you how sorry I am that I've been so awful to you girls," he said as he hung his head. We were sitting on the edge of the tattered couch in the living room, and he was fiddling with a stray spoon he'd picked up from the table. It brought back memories of when he would wait for his toast to pop in the kitchen when we were younger; he would tappity-tap his knife on the counter to some tune in his head, or maybe he was just practicing the Morse code that he studied profusely up in his room—dit dat, dit dat, tappity tap. Brian always did march to the beat of his own drum, or piano, or knife, or fork . . .

"I want to finish school eventually," he said. "I really need to get away from a lot of the old people I've been drinking with, and I have a feeling I will not stay sober if I stay here. I hate leaving you here alone, but I have to straighten my life out. And getting sober . . . you can't just . . . it's like a big storm . . . you don't look out of the storm cellar after a tornado goes by and say 'thank God the wind's not blowing' when the house is wrecked. You know what I mean?" he said.

I didn't, but I nodded nonetheless.

"My life is all screwed up, and I have to straighten it out so the only thing I can do is get out of the area. Do you understand?"

"I do, but why California? Are you going there because of Dad?"

"Are you kidding? I couldn't care less about that duplicitous piece of shit. I have no intention of even looking him up. I just want to go somewhere warm and far away."

It was hard to let go of all the anger that had built up over so many years. I loved Brian's tender side, which he randomly displayed, and I could see he was in pain and that he truly cared for and loved us all. I knew he needed to be away from the temptations of home, and that he needed to escape to a normal life away from Mom, just like everyone else.

Mom and I stood outside watching Brian pack his forest green van later that month. Mom was holding a tissue to her mouth, trying to hold back her sobs.

"Do you really have to go?" she asked.

"Mom, we've been through this a million times. You know it's the best thing for me. And if you know what's best, you'll go to one of those meetings and reclaim your life too."

Mom continued to hold her Kleenex as though clinging to a life raft. Brian hugged Mom and me tightly before jumping into his van. He waved his muscular arm out the window as he pulled out of the driveway. Brian has never moved back to New England and has never fallen off the wagon.

I felt like I had just been punched in the gut as I watched the van pull away. I was surprised to discover how much I would miss him. With all of Brian's faults and crazy temper, his presence was so oddly alive. We'd never been close but it occurred to me that he was fighting his own battle—that we all were fighting battles, not just me. I'd been so busy feeling sorry for myself that I never bothered to check in, or even try to care about anyone else. I'd miss the sounds of Brian banging on the piano that had become regular background noise, and I'd come to find that the silence was much more deafening. If I thought the lights had gone out when Beth left, now I was truly in the dark.

[top left] Ray's mom Angie sits in Mom's Queen Chair. Angie was my rock when I needed one most.

[top right] Bob Bopp rented a room from us. Here he poses with a fire log in front of the fireplace in Mom's living room, looking ever the lumberjack.

[bottom] Beverly Brown cooks in Mom's kitchen. Note the crazy wallpaper and the patched walls.

CHAPTER TWELVE

Reckless Abandon

Harold was on the road quite a bit and was still living in Harrisburg most of the time, so Mom's drunken stare was focused on me. Her crying threats echoed in my head every night as I went to sleep, and her drinking was worse than ever. She knew she had only one baby left and I would inevitably abandon her—I couldn't wait until it was my turn. Then poor Yardley would have to deal with Mom on his own.

Michael still lived nearby. Although Michael rarely exhibited his true feelings, his marshmallow insides couldn't help but seep out, and he will always and forevermore be my hero for what he did during those dark years of my life.

One day Michael decided it would be a good idea to gather up all of Mom's hidden vodka bottles. That was when I found a huge stash in the forbidden closet in her dressing room. I found others in the bathroom closet, and Michael gathered a bunch from God knows what corners of the house. Some were empty and others had a little in them. We dumped those and left the big heap of bottles on the floor in the middle of her bedroom, hoping it would shame her. It did not. In fact, it only fueled her flame and got her angrier than a raging bull.

I was angry too—all the time. The house was always dark and quiet with everyone gone. Even the renters had abandoned us. Where did they all go?

One Saturday afternoon Mom came home with Beverly, whom Michael had taken to calling Beaver Lips. It was one of the rare occasions when both my mother and Beverly were sober.

"Hey, Cha, we're going to pick up Angie and go to lunch. Do you want to join us?" Mom asked. With nothing else to do, I decided to go. I knew if nothing else it would be an adventure seeing Mom and Beverly out in their element. As long as Angie was there, I knew I had an ally.

Mom was driving, Beverly by her side, and I got stuck in the back seat.

"Elizabeth, stop driving so fahst," Beverly scolded. Her affected English accent grated on my ears.

We pulled up to Angie's two-family house tucked into a neat neighborhood with fences between the homes. Angie was nervously pacing out in front.

"Hi, hon," Angie said brightly as she slid into the seat beside me and affectionately patted my knee. "Hey, Liz, do you mind if I have a cigarette in the car?" she asked as she dug through her purse, not waiting for an answer. I could see her hand shaking as she lit up and inhaled deeply. It was her one vice, aside from the Valium that was helping her sleep ever since Ray's death. "Thanks for inviting me along. I needed to get out of the house. So where are we chicks going to eat?" she asked.

"What say we give that new place in West Springfield a whi-rul?" Beverly suggested. There was a gurgling sound in her throat, the same burp swallowing habit she always had. This gassy habit annoyed me even more than her fake accent. "I don't know about you ahl, but I'm positively stahved."

Beverly ordered lunch like she was the Queen of England, although her Goodwill clothing belied that notion. "Waitah, can you please bring me a dry martini with ah twist," Beverly said and then shooed the poor guy away with her hand. "Oh, and make sure you use yowah cheapest vodka," she yelled as he walked away.

I wanted to crawl under the table. But the best was when they asked for the check and the three of them were cackling over how to split the bill.

"I only got the Rueben and a salad, so mine should be less," Beverly claimed.

"Yeah, and the three martinis don't count, I guess," Angie said.

As I watched them battle out the bill, I wondered if Beverly's fake pearls made her feel more important.

With no parties at the house anymore, I wasn't drinking like I had been, and with Kevin's encouragement, I discovered Al-Anon meetings, which were basically geared toward the families of alcoholics. I wanted to learn to cope with Mom's drinking and to try and face the effects it had on me.

David brought a friend in to rent one of the back rooms, so there were two renters in the house who were actually paying rent for a change.

One evening Mom came home in a drunken rage and picked a fight with me for no apparent reason. I tried to ignore her but she wanted me to fight back. I knew it could potentially escalate into a hair-pulling scene like some of the brawls she had with Beth and Ann, and I wanted no part of that.

Instead, I ran upstairs into her bathroom. Not knowing how to channel my rage, I kicked the mirror on the door, shattering it to pieces. It felt good. It was sheer adrenaline. I felt I would burst if I didn't release it all. I hated Mom for who she was now. And I hated myself for hating her. She tried frantically to win me back with disgusting displays of drunken affection that only made me recoil more. She was like Dr. Jekyll and Mr. Hyde. I tried not to yell and scream as my older siblings did, but maybe that would have helped me to release it.

The mirror was only the beginning. I discovered that breaking glass was a great stress reliever. Shortly after I broke the mirror, I went out on my balcony where the old storm window still lay, reminding me of the day we climbed to the roof with Ray. I stomped on each of the four panes of glass with my dirty worn-out sneakers. With every broken shard, I was exhuming my deepest angst. My anger at Dad for leaving in the first place, my anger at

Mom for caring more about the house than for us kids, my anger at each of my siblings for leaving me all alone with Mom, who could not even care for herself anymore, let alone me. Every time I was mad I would go out and stomp on that old broken window on the balcony.

The first time I was faced with a physical attack from Mom was after I brought home a new dog. Someone at my work was giving away a one-year-old Samoyed puppy. I had always wanted one, so without asking Mom, I brought him home, hoping she would fall in love with him. Unfortunately, it wasn't Mom I had to worry about as much as Yardley, who was not keen on the idea of sharing his space and family with this newcomer.

"You're going to have to return him," Mom said to me one day after we had just finished pulling the two fighting dogs apart.

I pleaded with her, telling her I'd keep them apart. Anything.

Mom was always a softie when it came to animals, so I was confident that I would win the argument eventually. She let me keep the dog for a week after that, until I came home one day to hear her ranting drunkenly on the phone. It didn't take me long to figure out that she had called my work and was complaining about the dog. Horrified, I went to grab the phone from her to avoid further embarrassment, but I only made the situation worse. She began to slap me, and I pushed her back.

"How dare you push me," she yelled, over-dramatizing the situation so it sounded like I was attacking her to the person on the other end of the phone. After I was able to grab the phone from her, I apologized to my boss. Mom was still pushing me and trying to wrest the phone from my hands as I hung up.

"Cut the shit, Mom!" I yelled. I could feel my heart hammering in my chest. I wanted to punch her, and I tried with all my might to contain myself. Years of pent-up anger was bursting at the seams. I might have looked like Speedy Gonzales after he took a bite of a hot pepper.

"Oh, now you are going to start swearing at me?" she said. "You're just like your sisters. How dare you!" she said as she shoved me and grabbed my hair. Always the hair with her! I guess it didn't help that we all kept our hair long. Then she grabbed at the gold lariat necklace that Beth had given me before she left and yanked it from my neck. That was when I saw red. Unlike Beth, who never hit back, I could not control myself. I started to fight back. I had never been pushed to this level, and I felt like my head was going to explode. Even though Mom was raving drunk, she was still stronger than me. Once I could pull away, I ran out the door and didn't stop until I was at Angie's house.

After that scene, I gave the dog back and had to apologize at work for my mother's drunken behavior. It occurred to me later that maybe Mom was fighting for Yardley's rights—an odd thought—but maybe she was identifying with him in that he was being replaced, and she couldn't bear to stand by and watch. I knew if it had been one of us kids she would have fought just as hard—and did. Though thwarted, her loyalty was fierce.

Several weeks after Brian left, one of the renters who had lived with us when I was ten showed up for a visit. Brian was fourteen years older than me, and I'm guessing Bob was around the same age. I was always intrigued by him, but at the same time, daunted by his "esoteric" nature. Maybe it was his round, wire-rimmed glasses that made me think he was smarter than everyone else, or the way he tilted his head before he spoke as though he was communing with some all-powerful wisdom from above.

Bob Bopp lived in the house at the same time as Jim, or as he liked to call him, Stone Man. Jim was the one who took me to my first concert when I was eleven years old. He had an extra ticket to see Jethro Tull, and his date canceled at the last minute. I remember he asked Beth first, but she preferred staying home to watch *Kung-Fu,* a choice I teased her about for years.

Bob and I started taking long walks and had intriguing conversations. It was the most adult relationship I'd ever had. Bob seemed impressed that I could recite Shakespeare and the entire version of Longfellow's "The Children's Hour" that I'd memorized in the third grade.

Soon Bob and I were having intriguing conversations in the bedroom. I could listen to his flowery speech for hours as he made love to me. He talked about philosophy, most of which went over my head, but I pretended to understand anyway. Sometimes he saw that and would explain. I loved how patient he was.

I knew he was moving down south, but he insisted I would hear from him and that he would be back. I refused to let myself think our getting close would amount to anything since he was a drifter and lover of life.

At seventeen, I thought I was so mature, but I knew I was no match for this man. I felt like a doe-eyed little girl with no confidence, and compared to Bob, so naive. I protected myself with an outer veneer, its scab just beginning to form.

Bob did eventually write to me many months later, but Mom got the letter first and opened it.

I was lying on the Victorian bed from the back room that replaced my old twin bed in my pink bedroom. The snow was blustering outside my naked window where my autographed shade once hung.

"How could you?" Mom raged as she burst into my room. "You got a nice letter from Bob Bopp," she said, waving the letter as though it were a missive from Satan himself.

I bolted upright at the mention of Bob and could feel my heart race.

"How could you give away your sacred flower to him who would . . . willingly forsake Eden? That heathen! You're supposed to save yourself for the sanctity of marriage! I'm so ashamed of you!" I thought Mom was having what she liked to call an apoplectic fit—tears dripping down her blotched face, arms flying in the air like Medusa. But this was nothing new to me. I was simply delighted that Bob contacted me. I didn't care that Mom had just come face-to-face with the fact that I was no longer a virgin.

My newfound bravery developed after our fight over the dog, and I didn't hold back. I screamed at her for opening my mail, grabbed the letter, and slammed my door in her face. I no longer cared. I could hear her muffled rants, but I was more intrigued by the seventeen-page letter I held in my shaking hands, and I sat down with the glee of a five-year-old on Christmas morning to read it.

Mom was not the only one shocked by its contents. Bob's flowery and seductive letter left no room for guessing.

> Dorothy Preston! Would you label me a chauvinist if the first thing I said to you is that I think you're pretty? I know I've said that already. I seem to have developed this strange new habit of closing my eyes to be with this pretty lady with golden hair, holding her close and tasting her sweet kisses. In my dream she leans her elbow casually against my chest, and somehow, I find that almost unbearably erotic (while at the same time, paradoxically, I get a feeling from this gesture that she is truly my friend, and worthy of trust.)... Yeah, I know it's strange. I've known you for several years and yet never really tried to get close. It wouldn't have been appropriate back then—I knew it and you would have known it. But the affection was there, and so was the attraction. Stone and your brother Brian can testify to that, as they both knew I was impressed with you. I used to say that you were a real thoroughbred filly. I likened you to a beautiful young bud, and predicted that when that bud flowered, a few male hearts were due to be broken—little suspecting then that one of them might be mine.
>
> And now? Well you certainly have flowered, and I think you may have gotten the message by now that I would love to tend your garden. Would you tear up this letter in disgust if I was so bold as to say that between your delicious thighs lies a garden that I would willingly forsake Eden for? (I hope not, because then you would miss all the rest of the great stuff that's written here)...
>
> Yours, with love,
>
> Bob

So that's what Mom meant by her Eden comment, I thought. It was the most incredible letter I had ever received. But somehow, I do not remember if I ever responded to it or not. I do know that the next time I saw Bob was several years later when he showed up at Christmas with his wife. I remember I couldn't bring myself to say anything to him. There were a million things I wanted to say, a million things I should have said, but as usual I was too late.

Many years later I found an opened letter from Bob dated in early 1979 among some of Mom's old papers. He had written again after all! I was angry that Mom intervened, but I felt even worse after I read the letter that professed deep love and affection for me. Bob would never know that I didn't get that letter in a timely fashion.

But, alas, I am wrong. Many years later, Bob inadvertently found me through social media and reached out. In our ensuing email conversations, I told him I was just beginning to fight the battles that were emerging within with regard to men when I received his first letter. I then discovered, in fact, that I had never responded to his first letter, or at least he never received a response because I can't for the life of me imagine why I didn't respond.

Somewhere, maybe in some other long lost dimension, my heart broke because I wanted to reach back to my younger self and tell her to run to Virginia or to Florida where he was. Maybe I would have, if there were an invitation . . . oh, but wait . . . there was an invitation, but I was too timid to assert myself to that degree, too diffident to believe the feelings professed on paper were true. I wanted to tell that young girl to grow up and start believing in herself.

Our story could surely have been a rom-com. But as a huge fan of them, I must have a happy ending, so it would have to be altered. I'm reminded of the movie *Letters to Juliet*, in which a love letter goes missing for fifty years.

I believe we encounter the people we meet on our journey exactly when we are supposed to, and either we gratefully accept their gifts or ignore them and move on. Bob and I have been fortunate to have crossed paths three times in our lifetime. The first was when I was an impressionable eleven-year-old, and I thought he and his side-kick Jim Stone were two of the most magical and interesting people I'd ever met. The second was when I was seventeen, when he rambled back through town and through my still impressionable young life. That was when I received the best gift, and I mean much more than the sexual part. It was everything he and I shared during that time, however brief. It was a gift I've cherished forever, one that was so deeply ingrained that I barely recognized it until many years later, which might explain why, as a more seasoned woman who may still have had some impressionable tendencies, I leaped from my bed with tears in my eyes after seeing the name Robert Bopp on an email message. Yet I was the same woman who, after reading his heartfelt email, ravaged the boxes in my basement to unearth two old cherished letters from the days of yore because I had to prove to myself there was no return address; why else would I not have responded to those incredible letters? But alas, I was wrong; there were return addresses. My exact expression after reading them to myself was: "What the FUCK was wrong with me? How could I possibly not have responded to this?" I like to think I did respond and perhaps it lay unopened in some dusty postal basement among other lost letters.

This most recent communication with Bob—I believe—is our third gift to each other, one I will continue to treasure. An excerpt of the latest from Bob reads:

I really hoped that it had been a positive experience for you, and one in which you could feel and understand that the feelings directed your way from me included actual caring, and affection, and respect, and for you to come away from all of it remaining open to the recognition that love can and should be a good and worthwhile part of life . . .

Life has taught us that sometimes it's just for a little while, and sometimes that can be really painful; other times it was exactly what was needed, no more no less, and sometimes things unfold exactly as they should have.

The important thing, at least in my view, is that we had the time that we did. It was real when we were together, and I think we used our time well, including very important and significant things like being gentle and respectful with each other, as well as affectionate. We recognized both the value and the vulnerabilities of each other and followed the very human and loving doctrine of "handle with care" . . .

I'm trying to say that for all of us, there are limits to the possibilities we have for true closeness, and that we learn a valuable lesson when we realize the extent to which genuine and caring intimacy can help us with that, and with feeling good, and fortunate, about the degree of closeness that we can attain when we care enough.

Bob told me he visited the Preston Manor at Christmas time, and on one such visit, he went to the Napolitans' house to visit Christine and arrived to find Valéry Giscard d'Estaing, former President of France, sitting at their dining table:

I knocked on their door, and was escorted to a huge dining room. There were too many people to take it all in, as I stood there open-mouthed: Christine was there, and jumped up to rescue me. Her mother was making proper introductions and I heard the name "Valéry Giscard d'Estaing," which absolutely floored me.

I offer one final quote from one of Bob's original letters:

Like Walt Whitman, John Muir, and others before me, it is here that I feel close to He who provides the dictionaries of words that print cannot touch.

Print cannot touch my conflicted emotions as I write this.

[above left] Ray's brother Teddy and I are pictured here at the hairpin turn on our drive to North Adams when we drove Beth to college.

[above] This is Kevin, probably instructing me on something as we sit on Mom's couch called "The Monster."

[left] Kevin and I in Mom's front entry hallway in 1991. Mom's Persian lamp behind us is now owned by Kevin.

CHAPTER THIRTEEN

Bless Me, Father

I woke to an especially beautiful day. Red and orange streaks blazed across the early morning sky. I yawned and stretched and inclined my head toward the bare window at the foot of my bed.

The adjustable screen that kept my window open about a foot was tattered and torn and only partially did its job. A warm peaceful feeling came over me as I gazed at the branches from the oak swaying over the balcony outside. Memories whispered in my head.

I looked at the pink walls of my room and smiled when I saw the Snoopy poster Mom had given me. "I think I'm allergic to morning" was captioned over Snoopy's bedraggled image as he collapsed on top of his dog house. The poster depicted how I felt most mornings, and I remembered one morning when Michael and Terri flipped my mattress with me in it in order to get me up and out of bed.

My Big Ben alarm clock was perched on the bookcase, purposefully positioned across the room so I would have to get up to turn it off—a ploy that never worked.

As I was enjoying the morning light, I heard sounds coming from outside my window. The clanging and scraping got louder, and I jumped out of bed just in time to see a leg followed by a tuft of Jarod's thick blond hair rising over my balcony wall. We had been dating for the past few months; and he did not yet know I was incapable of being monogamous.

"What are you doing? You're out of your mind," I said as I raised the window and jammed in the stick that held it open. "You could have killed yourself."

"Shhh," he said with a sensuous smile as he climbed through and swooped me up, carrying me back to bed. My body tingled with delight. His sultry lips were begging to be kissed, and his blazing blue eyes danced with passion as he fluttered his long lashes at me.

"We can't do this. Are you crazy? My mother is in the next room," I meekly protested, knowing I was putty in his hands, as he passionately kissed me.

I tried to act like I was having an orgasm, but somehow I couldn't. I just couldn't let go and relax. It's as though my body was foreign to me.

I'm promiscuous and I don't care. I heard Mom's hollow words echoing in my ears warning me to have morals lest I burn in hell, but I defiantly ignored them. Is it retaliation? Am I behaving badly out of spite to Mom?

I thought of my dream as Jarod and I were having sex. There is always some unknown something chasing me. I run. I keep running. But I can't get away. The only time I feel any kind of normal is when I'm kissing someone because I can launch all my pent-up emotions and anger into the passion I'm pretending to feel. Only I'm numb. I can't feel a thing. I have never had an orgasm. My only solace is retreating into the arms of... anyone.

It was a Saturday morning in August, six months before my eighteenth birthday. I woke up still drunk from the night before. Al-Anon didn't seem to be working for me, so I'd taken up where I'd left off and was drinking more and more.

I'd been partying at Dave's house out in West Springfield. Dirty dishes filled the kitchen sink. Empty beer cans and cigarette packs were carelessly tossed about the room and lay forgotten next to hastily torn off T-shirts, used Q-tips, and dust balls. Dave and I had met only a few weeks back. He was mostly into cars and only drank Budweiser, but he was okay to hang out with since he liked to laugh a lot. Dave lived with his brother and his brother's wife. I vaguely remembered meeting them, along with a few of their friends before I passed out.

I looked around, not sure where I was. Dave was on top of me working himself into a lather. Wait, that's not Dave. But it looks like him. I pushed him away.

"Who are you?" I asked in horror, jumping from the bed. The man who looked like Dave got up and sauntered from the room naked just as Dave walked in, as if on cue.

"Who was that? Was that your brother?" I yelled, thinking it looked like the guy with the dirty blonde hair I'd met last night.

"Whaaaat?" Dave said with a sly grin. "He just wanted to have a little fun too—just keepin' it in the family."

Dave moved toward me, and I envisioned the wolf from Goldilocks licking his chops with his frilly bonnet concealing his devil ears. I was disgusted beyond belief.

I pushed past him draped in a bed sheet. I rummaged around the filthy room, trying to find my clothes. I couldn't find my bra. I was in a panic, suffocating. I had to get out of there. Was I just raped? I was just raped, and I did nothing!

Dave was already back in bed. He lay there naked and exposed with his arms crossed behind his head, leering at me.

"Where ya goin' so fast? Come back to bed," he said as he patted the spot next to him. I just glared and continued to gather my clothing. I had no recollection of even taking them off.

Somehow I got dressed, and I ran out the door. The sunlight sliced me like a knife. This was the epitome of the "walk of shame." Did that really just happen? The words I longed to say to Dave rolled around in my head, and I wished I had the courage to go back and say them, but I knew I never would. The humility and guilt of my Catholic upbringing always kept me from saying what I wanted to say—that and the fact that I just about never had the courage to speak my mind. Being a people-pleaser is what got me into this predicament in the first place—never being able to say no.

What a piece of shit he is. Or am I the piece of shit? I walked along, shaking my head frantically. I wondered if Dave's brother's wife knew. Maybe Dave was with her, while his brother was with me.

I began running like a crazy person. How had I gotten here? What drove me to this place of zero self-respect? I was beginning to discover the power I had over men who liked me, but I couldn't fathom that someone could genuinely like me. I'd felt undesirable my whole life, growing up in a family many thought of as the dirty ragged outcasts whose father walked out on them. But now men were paying attention to me. This isn't about sex, this is about ego, I thought as I slowed down and drew a few shaky breaths. I'd learned that in order to have control, I had to give something of myself for them to like me; I had to have sex with them. And I liked being liked. I fed off the high I got from feeling desirable. But I was also discovering that it was an unquenchable desire; I kept seeking the feeling I got when something was new and exciting. It made me feel alive.

I thought I had control, but really I had no control. I had given myself away for an empty rush. Since my father abandoned us when I was only three years old, I never had a solid male role model, it just seemed natural to keep chasing the high I got from the attention of men. But I always felt empty; I always felt like something was wrong or something was missing, and I could never put my finger on what it was.

I hadn't called Mom the night before, so I knew she was going to be furious when I got home. Even though I was almost eighteen, she insisted I check in, since I still lived under her roof. I needed to get my license. This is ridiculous, I thought, as I trudged home across the South End Bridge to Springfield.

It took almost an hour, and when I finally crept through the door of the house, Mom was gone. She'd left a nasty note on the dining table berating me for not calling. She'd scribbled how worried she was. Relieved that I didn't have to deal with her, I jumped into the shower and tried to wash the filth from my body.

It was a long, wretched day during which I napped and berated myself. I waited for Mom to come home, somehow thinking that dealing with her might be better than the thoughts in my head—until she stormed into my room.

"And just where were you last night?" she said. Her hair was a tangled mess, and her face was twisted in rage as she stood snorting at my bedside like a bull about to attack. She was wearing the blue-and-red knit shirt and baby-blue polyester pants that she always seemed to be wearing lately, and I hated it. I looked at her with disgust and defiantly lied. I told her I was at Carole's.

"You're a little liar," she slurred. "Carole called here looking for you," she said as she pounced on my bed and began swatting at me like a mad woman. I managed to push her away and roll off the bed, but just as I was getting up, I heard a loud thud.

"You hit me!" she yelled, as she got up off the floor.

"I did not hit you, Mom! Just stay the hell away from me. I don't need this shit today." And I ran from my room.

She didn't come after me, and I waited until it was quiet before I dared go back to my room. I locked my door and went to bed early. That night I dreamed I was taking a shower but couldn't seem to strip off any of my clothing. Layer upon layer of shirts, sweaters, pants, and underwear kept peeling away from my skin until I gave up and jumped in the shower fully clothed. I tried to lather off the debris of my bad behavior, but it didn't work.

The next day I woke up, and Mom was still in bed, sleeping off her hangover. I needed to go to confession. Maybe that would help. I went to church with Mom on all the holidays, but she no longer insisted we go every Sunday. Not wanting to attend my old parish, since I'd been expelled after seventh grade, I decided to go to Mount Carmel Church. I couldn't remember how long it had been since I'd been to confession.

I took the bus to the south end of Springfield and walked down a tree-lined street with branches that gently swayed and guided me toward the church. The next Mass wasn't scheduled for another hour, so there were only a few people seated or kneeling in prayer as I tentatively entered the parish doors. The old familiar smell of frankincense reminded me of my old church days when the priest would swing the thurible as he sauntered down the aisle with the altar boys at his heels. I genuflected before the crucifix, found an empty pew, and made the sign of the cross. Pushing away the feelings of hypocrisy, I pulled out the kneeler and dropped my head onto my folded hands waiting for my turn in the confessional.

"Bless me, Father, for I have sinned. It has been seven years since my last confession." I braced for some radical punishment that would hit me like lightning and fix everything. I was surprised with my light penance of three Hail Marys and ten Our Fathers—the old standard—which did nothing to alleviate the guilt of my sins, the guilt of having no morals and allowing myself to be abused, the guilt of losing control and drinking too much.

I'm meek.

I despise meek.

I have no respect for meek.

I'm angry that I ooze meekness, and I can't stop the hemorrhaging, no matter how tight I tie the tourniquet. I fake it sometimes and boost my confidence with mantra after mantra, yelling into the mirror that I love and approve of myself. I feel like the Cowardly Lion fumbling with my tail with my eyes closed so tight it makes my nose scrunch. I do believe in spooks, I do believe in spooks—I do—the spooks of my past, present, and future. But they don't haunt me in a single night like Scrooge who awakens to a miraculous new self. They haunt me always, obscured from my grasp by my obsequious outer self, which is why I'm so drawn to people who are reckless and daring. The me that I secretly want to be is hidden in their reflections. I'm spooked by my own shadow; I'm spooked by Mom's decline; and I hate her for letting herself go.

I yelled out loud as though somehow it would exorcise my demons. I convinced myself what happened with Dave was my fault. I let it happen. I let myself get so drunk I lost all self-control and dignity. I convinced myself I was the only one at fault, and I never told a soul or reported the assholes to the police as I should have. I reasoned that since it wasn't a violent act, maybe it wasn't really rape. I was haunted for days, weeks . . . still. I never heard from Dave again after that, but I found out that his brother shot himself in front of his wife a few years later.

I read somewhere that most alcoholics, if not all, suffer from an abnormally pronounced fear of abandonment, which they unwittingly pass on to their children. They also suffer from a fundamental terror of intimacy, which is disguised by the false intimacy that develops between people when they're drinking excessively. Jeez, I wonder if that's my problem, I mused, knowing full well it is. This is bullshit—I'm done!

I'd been a passenger my whole life with Mom in the driver's seat—top down, debris flying in my face as she sped along with me as her captive audience. And now there were two drunks in that car. I wanted to stop the madness and take the wheel from her at this, my utmost lowest point. I was with her on the lipstick-lined path, and her silk stockings had torn on the rutted road. I knew I couldn't do it anymore. I couldn't be her champion anymore. I needed to get out. I needed to get off the merry-go-round that was Mom.

[top] Camp Bonnie Brae counselors; 1979. I'm at the far right sitting next to the camp director.

[bottom left] I'm sitting with Beth and Jon's dog Gus on my lap and Harvey the giant rabbit on my left with Mom's radiator behind me.

[bottom right] I'm standing with Gina at the rope swing in our back yard with the Petersons' house in the background.

CHAPTER FOURTEEN

Harvey

Two months after I turned eighteen, Massachusetts changed the legal drinking age from eighteen to twenty. I was furious.

Rhonda came up for a visit later that month, and we got Gina to drop us off at a nearby bar in Connecticut where the legal drinking age was still eighteen.

When Rhonda spotted a couple guys approaching that she wasn't keen on, she pretended to be deaf and began signing. I picked up the cue and played along until I forgot the ruse and leaned over to whisper in her ear.

"What are you doing?" she said as she slapped my arm. "You dork, you just blew our cover!"

"I'm pretty sure they were on to us anyway," I laughed.

Later that night we asked the same guys for a ride home.

"I'll sit in the back," I slurred as I scooted in next to the cute guy. I caught Rhonda's glare as she was forced to sit up front.

We parked in the driveway underneath Mom's window. Me, smooching with my cutie, and Rhonda in front making small talk. Suddenly, a bellowing voice from the window above screeched "DO-RO-THY!"

"I guess that means it's time to go!" Rhonda said gleefully.

"I'm so glad your mom's screaming broke up the smooch-fest," Rhonda said later. "Why do I always get to be the wing man with your dork du jour?"

Rhonda taunted me with the sound of Mom yelling "DO-RO-THY" for many years.

Kevin knew how much I hated school, and he didn't want to see me fail, so on his advice, I tested out of high school and went straight to community college for the spring semester. I reasoned that it would have been the year I would have graduated anyway, so I actually started college a little early. The goal was to do well so I could go on to North Adams State College, where Kevin had gone, for the fall semester.

I loved college and learning. I sat up front in class, I paid attention, and I never skipped. It was a joy to finally find something I liked. Not only had I curtailed my drinking again, but I also quit smoking.

After I turned eighteen, I applied for a summer job as a Girl Scout camp counselor. I knew Mom wouldn't like it, so I put off telling her until the letter came in the mail. Mom delivered it to me one morning as I was walking toward the bathroom with my tea.

"What's this?" she asked as she handed the letter to me.

"Well, that looks like a letter." I said. "Oh, look, it's addressed to me. Why didn't you open it?"

"Don't you smart mouth me. Are you planning on leaving me, too, like your sisters? What is Camp Bonnie Brae?" I set my teacup down and tore open the letter and began to dance with joy.

"I got the job, I got the job! It's just a summer job at a Girl Scout camp. I'll only be a few towns over," I said as I reached for my cup.

"Oh, no, you won't. I forbid it. You can't leave me," she said as she pushed me, knocking the teacup from my hand to shatter at my feet.

"You've got to be kidding, Mom. I'm eighteen. You can't keep me here anymore. I think you've gone mad," I said and walked into the bathroom.

"But I thought we'd be able to enjoy our last summer together," she said through sobs. I cannot let her take my joy, I thought. But it was too late.

Mom reluctantly drove me to camp on a hot summer day in June of 1979. I was invigorated with a new sense of freedom, happy to get away from the dark house. Gnawing guilt lurked somewhere deep within, but I did my best to ignore it.

We drove with the windows down and the wind blowing our hair. Mom had her green babushka neatly tied at her neck and her "Jackie O" sunglasses covering most of her face.

Camp Bonnie Brae is nestled in the backwoods of East Otis, Massachusetts. We turned onto a rutted dirt and gravel road covered by a protective dome of pines and massive oaks. We could see a sliver of shimmering water peeking from behind the impressive log cabin at the end of the drive.

Mom pulled in and circled the patch of dirt in front of the cabin. I got out of the car and unloaded my gear while Mom stood there like a child with her head down. I knew behind her Jackie O's, pools threatened to gush from her eyes.

I knew how hard it was for her to watch the last of her seven babies tumble from the nest. Her castle walls were crumbling around her, and she could do nothing about it. I sensed the fight had finally left her, and I yearned to make it better for her, to run to her and hold her and tell her everything would be okay, like a mother to a child, but I wasn't the mother, and I had to go forward in my life. I pulled her into my arms and hugged her tightly as she sobbed on my shoulder. She didn't say a single word.

"I love you, Mom. You know we all do, right?"

She nodded, still unable to speak, and climbed into her blue Ford. She leaned her arm out the window and lowered her Jackie O's to reveal her beautiful blue eyes that were filled with tears and said, "I love you too, Cha." Then she swept her glasses back over her face and pulled away. I watched as she rolled across the drive. Smoke from the exhaust trailed behind her until it dissipated in the summer air.

Pulled from my pensiveness, I turned to look up at the big log cabin, feeling suddenly alone. The sign above the door said Big House.

"Well, hello there, and welcome!" A woman in a white uniform said as she approached.

She dug in her pocket and pulled a cigarette from a crumpled pack of Salems. I raised an eyebrow as she lit it and took a long drag.

"My name's Jan. I'm the nurse here for the summer. And what is your name?"

I told her, and she motioned with a fleshy arm for me to follow her into the log cabin.

"Well, you won't keep that name for long," she said in a sing-songy voice. I thought she might trail off into *Do-Re-Mi* as she glided through the cabin, telling me what was what. "We all take on 'camp names' around here," she added with a wink.

"This'll be the counselors' haven, and none of the campers are allowed here. You're welcome to order any supplies you like, including cigarettes," she said with a smile. "We'll just deduct it from your paycheck," she said, blowing a cloud of smoke in my face.

"I'd like to order a carton of Salems, if that's okay?" As soon as the words came out of my mouth, I wanted to recant. Wait, I quit, I can't . . . and besides, Newport was always my brand. What was I thinking? But I didn't want to look stupid—God forbid! So just like that I started smoking again. I told myself I needed something to do with my hands—a ridiculous justification, but the one I used nonetheless.

It wasn't long before I found a new boy to play with. Fred lived in the house at the top of the drive. He wasn't part of the camp, but since he lived there, he was always around. He was two years younger than me and another counselor's hand-me-down from last season, but I didn't care.

Fred reminded me of Jarod with his Nordic good looks. We romped around for a few weeks, until I started getting snide comments from one of the kitchen staff. That was when I realized I looked like an idiot dating a sixteen-year-old boy, so I broke up with him and found someone else to smooch with. We'd go out on weekends to a nearby tavern called the Cozy Café where I'd flirt and drink. I thought cigarettes and booze were my power, but they were really my kryptonite. Nothing had changed except my environment.

I was surprised to see male counselors at a Girl Scout camp, but most of them were kitchen and waterfront staff, and none had a full unit of children like the rest of us.

I met Brendan, the waterfront instructor, when we were doing our canoe tippy tests out on the lake one day.

"Hey, Nez, let me help you with your canoe," Brendan offered. Nez was my given camp name, bestowed upon me on the first day we participated in some camp games prior to the kids' arrival. One of the games was to see who could make the highest mark on the side of Big House, which was achieved by making a human pyramid. Given my size, I was on top, with one person above me. So when she fell, the rest of us tumbled down like dominoes, and my nose took the brunt of my fall—hence the name.

I was admiring Brendan's muscular legs beneath his orange shorts as he stood on the dock in his bare feet, his curly brown hair blowing in the wind. I quickly learned that he lived in North Adams, which was where I was headed to college that fall. It seemed like a good reason to start dating him.

Being a camp counselor was the most fun I had ever had in my life. Our days were spent teaching the kids various camp songs, doing arts and crafts, taking night hikes with no flashlights, and having food fights in the dining hall. My girls were twelve and thirteen, and I remained pen pals with a few of them long after the summer ended. The only camper who ever gave me trouble was Tina, who thought Skylab was going to fall on her head.

Toward the end of the summer, we counselors were getting ready to do our final show for the campers. My skit involved being fed from behind by someone else who was concealed under the poncho I was wearing to create the illusion that I was clumsily tossing food into my face. Just before I was scheduled to go on stage, I received an urgent phone call.

"Dorothy, I had to put Yardley down today," Mom said through sobs. It was the ultimate slap for her. Yardley was the last of us, and Mom was crushed. I knew she felt abandoned by Yardley the same way Dad abandoned all seven of us kids so long ago; it was the theme of her life and, ultimately, the theme of my own, and it shaped my very existence.

I wanted to skip my stage debut, but I knew I had to muster, so with a swollen red face, I puffed up my chest and allowed someone else to hoist gobs of food into my mouth, unable to resist the laughter it elicited despite my sadness.

I received a few letters from Jarod that summer, which I only randomly responded to as I dangled him, too, from my web. I learned from the best, after all.

I spent the entire summer at camp, and we were all sad when our new family had to break up for the kids to go back to school. I was somewhat consoled with the fact that I, too, was going back to school, only this time I was going away to college and would reside somewhere other than Buena Vista Plaza for the first time in my life. I had all my financial aid papers in order and was ready to go. The added plus, I thought, was that I would also have a boyfriend once I was there. What I didn't know then was that Brendan, or Grope, which was his camp name, was not who he said he was.

I brought Brendan home to meet Mom once before leaving for college.

"Grope? You call him Grope? That's the stupidest name I ever heard, and it matches his stupid personality," she said after he left.

"Thanks, Mom. That's my boyfriend you're talking about."

"Well, whoever said you had any sense when it came to boys?" she asked. "You should've stayed with Jay, who was at least smart and knew how to talk to people," she said and walked away with a disgusted look. Part of me knew she was right, and admittedly, I was a bit embarrassed that Brendan came across as a bit of a dope.

I asked Ray's brother, Teddy, if he would help me move to North Adams that September. Teddy and I had a couple brief smooching sessions after Jay and I had broken up, but it never went anywhere. I knew I could always depend on him as a lifelong friend—and still do.

I wasn't sure what was keeping me from getting my driver's license; maybe it was a combination of Ray being killed on a motorcycle and others I knew who were killed in auto crashes. I was scared to drive, and I reasoned that I didn't need a license or car since everyone else had one.

I decided I did not want to live on campus, so I arranged to share an apartment within walking distance to campus with three other women who were juniors and seniors. Once again I was sharing my room and sleeping in a twin bed. I did not like the lack of privacy, and I felt claustrophobic in the tight quarters after coming from Mom's house, so I began making plans to find another place. I ended up moving into a crappy off-campus apartment with Grope.

Later that semester Rhonda showed up with her brother and a friend, and we all took off on an excursion up to Vermont. Grope had just broken his ankle and couldn't come along, so he stood out on the back porch of our apartment, waving his crutch in the air and yelling obscenities at me as we were leaving.

"I will never understand what you see in Camp Boy. He's such a moron," Rhonda razzed as we drove away.

I had had a secret crush on Greg since I was ten years old when I first met him, so it was no surprise that we hooked up that night. We stayed in a crappy hotel that was virtually empty.

"Hey, let's go case the joint," Greg's friend Dan said.

"Case the joint? Really, Dan, what are we on *Hawaii Five-O?*" Greg laughed.

But we cased the joint nonetheless with Greg pouncing and dashing into corners like he was a spy. On our way back, we filled our ice bucket then went back to the room to party. When Dan got up to go to his room for bed, Rhonda took one look at Greg and me and could tell we wanted to be alone.

"I am not sleeping in the same room as Dan, so get that idea right out of your heads! You guys can go smooch somewhere else!"

After not getting my period the next month, I checked in with my gynecologist. When she entered the room with a blank look, I knew what she was going to tell me. I wanted to rewind, to twitch my nose like Samantha in *Bewitched* and be in another life in another time, or maybe just run from the room screaming while covering my ears. I could not bear to hear the next words she uttered. "You're pregnant."

I emerged from the doctor's office and stumbled right back into my bubble as it bounced around and ricocheted off whatever it collided with. I wasn't even sure who the father was. What if it was Greg's and not Grope's? A baby Grope—scary! How can this be happening?

I thought back to the day when Gina had told me about her abortion and how I fainted on the spot. When I came to, I was dangling upside down from my picnic bench with my hair tangled in the autumn leaves. It was the first time I ever fainted. I didn't know if I could go through with that. I grappled with the urge to vomit right there on the street. I knew people were looking at me as the stinging wind blew my hair in my face.

I had to tell someone, but who? I was petrified to tell Rhonda or Greg. Although I secretly wanted it to be Greg's, I couldn't get up the nerve to tell him since I knew he was about to go into the Air Force and was not ready for anything like a family. I was only eighteen. I didn't even know who I was. I couldn't be a mother. How would I even do that? So I made the decision to let Grope think the baby was his. And I made the reprehensible choice to have an abortion.

Grope drove me to an abortion clinic somewhere near Lenox. The first thing I saw were throngs of protesters carrying signs depicting dead fetuses designed to make a woman feel like a monster. I could feel their pious arrogance poking at me like ice picks as I crossed their lines. They might as well have spit on me. I tried desperately not to look at them or the horrific signs as Grope led me by the hand. I'm pro-choice, but what the hell kind of choice is this? Do they think this is a happy choice for a woman? How dare they judge me? How could they possibly know what I'm going through?

Grope sat by my side afterward, but I felt shrunken and despicable. After weeks of missing classes and just lying on my bed, Grope convinced me to quit school and move to Lenox with him. Feeling ever much the loser, I got a job as a cashier at the local A&P, and he went off to his mundane factory job every day.

That was when I discovered that everything Grope told me about his family and his past had been fabricated to make me think he was spectacular. He once told me he was taking me to his family's vacation home, but when we got there, he said he forgot the key so we had to break in. There was something odd about it, but I never questioned him. He told me their year-round home was a mansion, and they had a pool. He talked about their dog and how he would take him for walks on the grounds. He told me he had already graduated from high school and that the class ring he gave me was misprinted with the wrong graduation date. He talked about an old girlfriend and many other crazy stories that never sat right with me, but I just chose to ignore. I wondered why he had never introduced me to his wonderful family, but eventually I found out. I started feeling threatened and trapped by him, and his temper had grown worse, with loud angry outbursts directed at me.

On a bright afternoon sometime in January, a month before my nineteenth birthday, I decided I did not want to become a statistic. I sat listening to my Pure Prairie League album for about the millionth time. I was leaning on the giant four-foot stuffed rabbit that Mom and Harold had given me for my sixteenth birthday. I had named him Harvey, of course, after the wonderful and beloved Jimmy Stewart movie. Harvey served as my couch and my only friend in our unfurnished apartment. I'm not sure what prompted it, but I got up and grabbed the phone to call Mom and told her I was desperate to leave. She sent Michael to rescue me while Grope was away at work that afternoon. Michael dropped what he was doing and came without hesitation. When he arrived, I saw the pained look in his eyes.

"Did that asshole hurt you? Because if he did I'll kick his ass."

I assured him Grope had not touched me—yet. We did not have much to do other than to load Harvey, me, my stereo and albums, and my clothes into Michael's van. So without a word to Camp Boy and with my tail between my legs, I returned home to Mom.

Mom never asked why I quit school and was just grateful to have me home again. Harold was still away on business a lot, so it was mostly Mom and me at home.

Grope continued to pursue me after I left. He called me every night, and we would sit on the phone in silence for what seemed like hours. Mom was exasperated with it as she watched me dangle the phone from the curly cord while I rolled my eyes, just waiting for him to say something.

"Just hang up, Cha-Cha. He is not worth your time."

One evening Grope showed up at Mom's with an engagement ring. Did he think after everything that I would just jump at this opportunity? I always had a hard time saying no, even if I really didn't want something, I hated to hurt anyone's feelings. But after hemming and hawing and dancing around, I finally said no and that was the end of him.

Mom ended up renting a room to my old boyfriend Jay, who she always loved and thought of as family. It was nice to have someone responsible around. Jay loved baseball almost as much as Harold, and the two of them would sit for hours in front of the TV, cheering for their teams, Harold always with the woeful hope that just maybe the Cubs would win it this year. Sadly, that didn't happen until many years after his passing.

Many years later I drove with a dirty and tattered Harvey the rabbit by my side to deliver him to the Salvation Army. Tears flowed unchecked down my face after I let him go. Somehow I felt I was abandoning him, my only friend during a major time of crisis in my life. I'm sure the Salvation Army threw him out, but I just didn't have the heart to do it myself. I like to imagine that Harvey became the delight of some other child, or perhaps served as a couch to someone in need of a soft place to land.

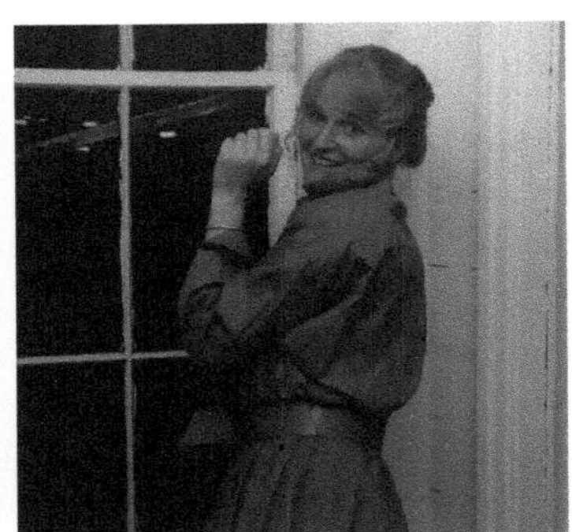

[top left] Bill and I on our wedding day.

[top right] Bill and I took a romantic trip to New Hampshire without the kids. This was the beginning of the end.

[middle left] I'm holding baby Timothy.

[middle right] This was taken when I was in labor with Heather. Timothy sits very sweetly with me while we wait to go to the hospital.

[left] Bill and I with Timothy and Heather, playing in leaves.

CHAPTER FIFTEEN

Yahooty

He had the bluest eyes I'd ever seen—like glaciers; they gazed at me from across the room. He was one of Terri's friends from the Brett days. I never thought those eyes would look my way, but they did. It was only weeks after my abortion when I bumped into Danny at a club. Carole had dragged me out, wanting to cheer me up. She was out on the dance floor, bumping up to some guy while I concentrated on my rum and coke.

"How's it goin'?" he said as he bellied up to the bar next to me.

"Not bad, I just moved back home," I said as I looked down at my drink. His silky jet-black hair was begging to be caressed. We chatted a little about "old times," which were only a few years before. He told me he was moving to Florida soon, but that he'd love to spend some time with me before he left and asked for my number.

Always the sucker for an adorable face, it was not long before I was romping in bed with him. I knew it was too soon after the abortion and my doctor even warned me to wait, but this was not someone I could say no to. We hung out for a few weeks and had some laughs.

"I'm leaving soon; let's go catch a movie Wednesday," he said one night. He arrived at my door to pick me up, sleek as ever. I had to run upstairs for a minute, and when I returned I found him perusing the dining room, taking special interest in the silver on Mom's buffet.

"Where'd you guys get all this stuff?" he asked as he looked underneath one of the heavier dishes.

"I dunno, my mother picked up a bunch of stuff at estate sales years ago, but I think the silver came from my Grandfather," I said. It struck me as odd, but only for a minute.

Later that night when he was dropping me off, I couldn't find my house keys.

"Damn, I hope I didn't lose them at the theater," I said as I continued digging in my purse. "I know I had them—shit, now I'm going to have to wake up my mother," I groaned.

I told Danny that we were going away to the Vineyard that weekend and wanted to know if I'd see him one more time before he left, but he didn't seem sure of his departure date.

"I'll call you after you're back, and we can make plans," he said, and pulled me in close for a lingering kiss. I got out of the car and drifted to the door and rang the doorbell until Mom came to let me in.

That Saturday while we were at the Vineyard visiting Paula, we got a call from Jay.

"Liz, I hate to be the bearer of bad news, but I just came home to someone robbing your house," he said. He assured Mom that he had called the cops, but the guy fled before he got a look at him.

"I'm afraid he got a few of your silver pieces from the buffet," he said. "Oh, but he did drop a spoon on his way out. I found it near the back door where he escaped. The funny thing is, it doesn't look like a forced entry," he said.

Mom was devastated. It didn't take me long to put two and two together. Needless to say, I never heard from Danny again.

Terri insisted he would never do that, but I knew we were scammed again—or I was.

I started working at a bank, and I either rode my bike to work or Mom drove me. She made me lunches every day and cooked dinner for the two of us at night. Her drinking was miraculously curtailed. I can only surmise that she cut back on her drinking because she was relieved to have a second chance with her baby. Perhaps she thought she could do things right this time; or maybe it was that she was a grandmother now with our tribe continuing to grow. Or maybe it was the fear of her own mortality. Or just maybe it was that she no longer had the financial burdens she once had now that Harold was in her life.

I always believed you had to go through the twelve-step program with Alcoholics Anonymous to banish alcohol addiction, but Mom exhibited resiliency once again and proved my theory wrong.

After Harold moved in, they renovated the kitchen—a new linoleum floor, new appliances, new wallpaper, and a lot of visits from the exterminator. It took some time, but we eventually got rid of Charlie's cockroaches.

I spent time watching the news and Johnny Carson with Mom in the evenings. She was always on top of current events and read two newspapers every day.

"People will think you're stupid if you don't pay attention to what's going on in the world," she chided when I seemed disinterested.

Mom was sixty now, but since she quit drinking, she had lost weight and was taking care of her appearance once again. She read every kind of novel and would consume several in a week. There were hundreds of books strewn all over her den. The chair that replaced Dad's old leather recliner was pushed into the far corner of the room and was Mom's "eagle's nest,"—her favorite reading spot. Sometimes I would join her and sit on the brown couch nearby with my own book. The portrait of Dad was put away into the dusty recesses of the attic, replaced by the conquistador that used to hang above the Persian lamp in the downstairs hall. He was draped in a bold red cloak with a feather in his cap. His eyes seemed to follow you wherever you went in the room and challenged you at every turn. I always averted my eyes from his unrelenting stare, but for some reason Mom loved him.

After Jay moved out, we had no more renters. The sounds from "Yahooty" grew louder now that the third floor was vacant. Maybe he too felt forsaken and neglected? We heard slamming doors and footsteps up there constantly. Mom went from saying, "there's no such thing as ghosts" and insisting it was the wind slamming the doors upstairs—even though no windows were opened—to "it's a friendly ghost." We learned to live with Yahooty, albeit reluctantly. I was still petrified to be alone in the house and was driven in fear from it on many occasions after hearing creepy sounds coming from the empty quarters above. I spent one night alone in that house during this time. I don't remember where Mom was; I just remember staying up all night with the television set on until the national anthem played and the buzzing sound started with the colorful bars as I clutched a steak knife in my hand. I'm not sure I could have warded off any ghosts with it, but it made me feel a little better.

Mom and I continued to take trips to the Vineyard to visit Paula, who now had two children, making four grandchildren total, including Michael's two from his first marriage to Joanne.

Paula asked Mom to take her springer spaniel, Tammy, because it was too much for her now that she had two children. Mom was all too happy to have another dog in the house. Sometimes I would go out drinking at night with friends and return drunk, pick up the dog, and place her on Mom's bed to be funny. I always loved seeing Mom get frustrated and discombobulated, but she would still laugh and tell me to go to bed. It was good to be forming a new relationship with Mom, a more adult version of what we had so many years earlier, before she started drinking heavily.

I signed up to go back to Springfield Technical Community College for the fall semester. I decided a business major wasn't for me, so I registered as a liberal arts student and enrolled in a theater class as well as some other basic prerequisites before I declared a major. I was able to get financial aid for school, and Mom said I could quit my job at the bank and go to school full-time since she wasn't paying for it. She assured me that Harold could afford my room and board for one semester.

That August before classes began, I visited Beth and Jon, who had just moved to New Hampshire. "Dor-tee, there's this guy I work with that you should meet," Jon announced. I was dangerously approaching my wild side again and had been dating and going out drinking more than I should have been.

"Is he cute? What's he like?"

"He's a good guy, and he's into bicycles, so you guys will get along. He said he wouldn't meet you if you were a smoker though. You haven't started up again, have you?"

I assured him I was smoke free, but I hated blind dates and wasn't interested since my last disastrous blind date.

"What's the worst thing that can happen, Dorth? I met him once and he seemed really nice," Beth chimed in.

"All right, all right. Bring it on. Why not!" I relented.

We met at Beth and Jon's house about three weeks later. They'd arranged an outing to the alpine slide park in New Hampshire near their house.

Bill and I made small talk in the back seat of Jon's beat-up Fiat on our way to the park. Bill was an engineer with a two-year degree. I heard "engineer" and my ears perked up, thinking it sounded like an impressive job compared to the jobs of most of the losers I'd dated.

Bill's loose russet curls waved in the wind as he eagerly dashed to the top of the slide and snapped up two blankets, making sure to spread mine out first as he held my arm and helped me down. His full beard looked softer than most of the scraggly beards I'd seen and felt. I couldn't stop staring at his tanned, muscular legs as he took a seat on the burlap sack beside me.

Later that evening, Beth was doling out tofu nachos onto our plates. I winced at the thought of eating tofu, but Beth assured us it was delicious. I didn't want to sound like a complainer on my first date, so I kept my mouth shut.

"I think the road from here to Springfield will be well-traveled," Bill said. Delighted that he was interested, but afraid to make too much of it, I gingerly bit into a nacho and then demurely dabbed my napkin to my mouth, hoping my lady-like manners would impress him. I knew we'd made a connection that day, and I didn't want to scare this guy off. Two weeks later Bill rode his bicycle all the way from Gardner, Massachusetts, where he lived, to Springfield to see me—a distance of about fifty-seven miles. I was impressed and so was Mom!

After Mom met Bill, she told me how nice and polite she thought he was. She even offered to give him a ride back so he didn't have to ride his bicycle home. Since it was a hilly ride, he gratefully accepted.

For the next three or four weeks we saw each other every weekend. The first time Bill met Ann and Tom, we went to their camp in Ashburnham after he picked me up at the bus station. During that visit, Bill went outside and split a half a cord of wood for them just because he felt like it. Both Ann and Tom liked him instantly—who wouldn't!

We did not waste any time before we were having a chat about exclusivity. At nineteen, I could barely stand it if any of my boyfriends even looked at another woman, so I definitely needed to know that I was the only one he was sleeping with.

We hadn't even been seeing each other a month when I found out I was pregnant. *How could I have been so stupid after my last mistake?* Only this time, I knew who the father was.

The first person I called was Ann. I sobbed on the phone with her.

"Calm down, Dorothy, he's a great guy. Just think, it could be Grope's again. You know I hated that guy!" she said.

"Ann, you aren't helping. What am going to do? I can't get another abortion."

"Just tell him. You have to tell him. And then just take it from there," she said. "Tell you what, come out here and stay with Tom and me, and you can tell him here."

I took the bus out to Central Mass that weekend and broke the news to Bill on the dock at Ann and Tom's place. I looked out at the water, afraid to make eye contact. Several ducks frolicked nearby and dipped their heads into the water, revealing the tips of their bottoms before coming back up. I wanted to jump in and bury my head with them and never emerge.

"It's just that I've been through this very recently," I began. "I was stupid and it just happened—I'm completely ashamed—but I made the choice to have an abortion. The thing is, I don't know if I can do it again . . . " I stammered and absently kicked a rock into the water. As I spilled my guts, I noticed that Bill was deep in thought. His eyes reflected the clear autumn sky as he rubbed his beard and looked out at the lake.

"Should we just get married?" he blurted out.

It felt like a ton of bricks fell off my shoulders as I slid into his arms, and we both cried. I don't really know how I wanted it all to work out, but marriage certainly wasn't out of the question for me. I thought of how one of Paula's friends had given up her baby for adoption many years ago, and how her parents had kept her holed up in the house in shame throughout her entire pregnancy. I knew I didn't want that either.

"Is that what you want?" I asked. I felt shaky inside and was petrified of rejection. "I don't want you to feel cornered by this, ya know?"

"I don't feel cornered," he said. "I knew when I met you that I was in love you. Let's just do it!"

I was now faced with the logistics of what I had to do next. Tell Mom, plan a wedding, and finish school. I was overwhelmed, but so relieved.

Mom cried when I told her I was pregnant, but as soon as I told her that Bill asked me to marry him, she drew me into her arms and hugged me without another word.

I continued with my classes and began to plan my shot-gun December wedding. Mom said we could have the reception at the house, but I had some work to do. I wanted to finish painting the walls I'd started after I quit school when I was sixteen. It was pretty difficult going to college full-time, working on a play with my theater group, planning a wedding, painting and prepping the house, and being pregnant. The first thing that happened to me physically was that my breasts were suddenly huge. But I still wasn't showing, so nobody at school knew my predicament. All of my siblings seemed happy for me. They knew I was getting reckless, so they figured marriage and a baby might settle me down.

Bill was Episcopalian, and when we suggested getting married by his priest, Mom had a complete fit.

"The Episcopal Church is Henry VIII's church. I will not have my baby married by heathens. It would be sacrilegious! I will disown you, I swear it!" Mom yelled.

After a fight that almost sent us both to a place we did not want to revisit, Mom finally won.

Having been ostracized from St. Joseph's so long ago, I did not want to be married in that church. So, we were married in Sacred Heart Catholic church where Beth had attended high school. This meant Bill and I had to go through a thing called Pre-Cana, which is essentially a crash course in marriage, as orchestrated by the Catholic Church. They told us that couples who are expecting a baby undergo extra scrutiny during marriage preparation to ensure that neither of them perceive the pregnancy as an urgent situation or a requirement for them to hurry into marriage.

Bill made a point of having me meet his parents before the wedding, and they welcomed me warmly and lovingly into their family. Bill grew up in the central Massachusetts area and had two older brothers. His mother secretly told me that she was hoping the baby was a girl since it would be the first girl in their family.

I was four months pregnant when Bill and I were married, stuffed into my white gown that grew increasingly tighter by the day. The reception was held in the three front rooms of Mom's house. Both of our families were there and many of the neighbors, including Mrs. Napolitan and Christine as well as Kevin, Anita, Rachel, Wendy, Carole, Rhonda, Gina, and David. Everyone knew I was pregnant, but that was no shocking surprise given the history of the Preston Manor.

Mom's friend Beverly offered to make our wedding cake, telling us she was a pro. It was hard to believe she was pro at anything other than making screwdrivers, but since we were tight on money, we agreed.

In anticipation of the glam shot I'd always seen of the happy couple's hands cutting the wedding cake, I had my nails done.

Aside from the late December snow that blanketed the ground that morning, I thought my shotgun wedding plans were flawless, until we went to cut the cake. Or was it a rock made to look like a cake? I wanted to cry, but then I looked at Bill and we both burst out laughing.

We honeymooned in New Hampshire after the wedding, and we were blissfully in love.

Our son Timothy was born May 29, 1981. With a baby at home and no car or license, I was beginning to feel trapped, so at twenty years old, I took driving lessons and surprised Bill. Driving was a wonderful freedom that I'd had no idea I was missing.

Our first fight was over the way I folded Bill's T-shirts.

"Are you kidding? I'm using cloth diapers and hanging all our clothes on a clothesline outside, and you're going to complain about how I fold your T-shirts? Here, fold your own," I said as I tossed one at him. But soon thereafter I complied and fastidiously folded them just as he instructed.

I became obsessed with losing all my baby weight and started working out with Richard Simmons and Jane Fonda, or as Tim eventually called her, "Jane Bomba." Sometimes I would work out twice a day.

Three years later our daughter Heather was born. I loved domestic life. The party girl had put away her dancing shoes, and while all my other friends were off at college and having fun, I was at home knitting and crafting and changing diapers.

I took a part-time job a few nights a week during my pregnancy with Heather as a front end manager at a grocery store, but before long the walking got to be too much, and they put me in the courtesy booth where I cashed out all the drawers at night. Bill would come home from work, and I would leave to go to work. My days were fun-filled with games, teaching the kids, and working out; I was a fanatic about my physical appearance. On the outside, things still appeared to be good.

[top] Mom sits with Michael and Terri's youngest child, Andrea. Jon Fitt is shown left.

[middle] Ann, Luke Napolitan, Harold, and Mom eating on the screened-in porch.

[bottom] The new generation of stair posers in the Preston family: Ann's sons, Benjamin and Christopher; Beth's son, Aaron; Paula's daughter, Pamela; a friend; and my son, Timothy, on the far right.

CHAPTER SIXTEEN

Déja Vu

A couple years later I took a full-time job at Fitchburg State College. This allowed me to take classes free of charge, and I decided it was finally time to get my degree. I kept my part-time job one night a week at the grocery store, and some nights I would go out for drinks with friends after our shift. That's when I began seeing glimmers of my old life; it was lurking in dark corners trying to lure me back, an evil force calling to me. I tried attending Adult Children of Alcoholics (ACOA) meetings, but even that didn't work.

Heather was three years old when I finally allowed my wild child to rear its ugly head, stirring up all the darkness and terror and self-annihilating impulses from the muddy depth of my being. I tried my best to stuff her away, but she kept me paralyzed in her grip. I'd made it seven years with Bill as the domestic housewife. But that seven-year-itch is real, ya know. I know because I'd been itching subconsciously through most of them.

My ego was pumped by all the flower-giving, poem- and song-writing men I'd turned away—boring, soppy. Drama—that's what fed me. I only wanted the ones that didn't want me, an old familiar theme. How fucked up is that? Like Mom, I kept them dangling as backup for when my ego needed a quick fix, the chance to toy with their affections. Either they weren't attractive enough or not confident enough, or just not bad enough to entice me. I'd let so many good men slip through my fingers. And now I was about to let the best one go—the father of my two beautiful children.

Sometimes I would dance around our living room with Heather clutched to my breast to the tune of Dan Fogelberg's "The Reach" as the music rushed into my soul and overflowed onto the floor, taking part of me with it.

This song would always sing to me of my daughter's sweet spirit, reminding me how she clung to me like I once clung to my mother whenever she was sad. Heather could never bear to see her mama cry even if she didn't know why; often her empathy would bring her to tears along with me.

"The Reach" was the song that would carry me away to a made-up world where I was the perfect mother doting on my children as they deserved to be doted on. It was the song that took away all of my despair and toxic nature. I clung to Heather with her head down on my shoulder and danced myself into oblivion, wanting the thoughts that were creeping into my head to go away, not wanting to be the kind of mother who runs away from her problems and her children. My life had become centered on knitting needles, building blocks, and *Sesame Street*—and what's so wrong with that?

"It's as though I'm driven by some pull that I don't even understand," I said to Ann one day while I was visiting.

"Dorth, you'd better be 100 percent sure before you walk out that door because once you do there's a good chance he won't let you back," Ann said. "Benjamin, you go pick that up this instant," she barked at her son who just threw a toy across the room. "If you leave, you may lose the kids, and then you won't have this," she said as she spread her arms out at our kids playing in her toy-laden living room.

"I know, but he drives me nuts sometimes," I said.

"So, welcome to life, Dorth. That's what happens. Do ya think I love Tom every day? Unh-uh! There are days I hate him! Why don't you guys go to counseling?"

"I dunno know. I'm so damn confused. The thing is, I know he's a great guy, and he's done nothing wrong. I don't even have a good reason. I'm just not happy anymore."

"I know, honey, but you have to think long and hard about this," she said. "Think about what Dad did to us and how fucked up we all are—well, maybe not so much anymore!" she corrected. "We all know what it did to Brian, and look at him now—happier 'n a pig in shit, and sober too!" she said. But I knew she still thought I was f'd up. It was her way of telling me that I needed to face my "Dad" issues.

In January of 1988, I told Bill I needed a break. "I knew this was coming. You've been acting so distant ever since you took that job at the college. I won't let you take the kids," he said as he paced around the kitchen table wringing his hands.

"Let's talk about this," I said quietly. "Maybe we can just make it a trial separation. It's probably best if we don't disrupt the kids, so I'll agree to leave them with you," I said. He just looked at me as though I had ripped his heart from him and walked out. I packed my bags and found a tiny apartment close to the college.

I wanted to punch my sociology teacher the day he asked me in class what I thought about the movie *Kramer vs. Kramer*, which had paved the way for women leaving the home instead of the man. He knew I had defied the norms of society by leaving my children. I wanted to crawl under my desk; he got the response he was looking for.

When I wasn't seeing the kids on the weekends, I was busy playing college kid. At first I thought it was great, but I quickly realized that I was crying myself to sleep every night, missing my babies and the life I left behind.

Had I fallen out of love with Bill, or was I just a horrible wretched monster? I decided it was a little of both. And in Mom, or Scarlett O'Hara fashion, I buried my head in the sand, in my studies, in my job, in running races. It was the same dilemma I always had. Bill was too available, too good. Why was I always attracted to the unavailable assholes? I knew it was my Dad complex, my fear of commitment, and my anger that had driven me to leave my own children. I hated myself more than ever.

Bill served me with divorce papers a year after I left, and Mom served me with this harsh and scorching letter, which takes the wind out of me even now when I read it:

> Fri., Dec. 30, 1988
>
> Dear Dorothy,
>
> We stopped in to visit Bill and the children Tuesday night after visiting his cousins. I know the lawyer's letters, etc., were badly timed (but won't they always be?). Bill told me he asked you out and would you try again?
>
> Yes, you say you like your freedom and we know you like your men! You have no intent of even trying to save the family you, with God, created? Not even try? Marriage is a sacred vow and motherhood—how can you NOT HURT every moment you are separated from your babies!!?
>
> Do you only feel for yourself—does what makes you happy count the most above all else? Do you see what Timothy has become since you, like your father, deserted the home? He's bitter, defiant, deeply scarred and angry—a complete change that you caused.
>
> He and Heather don't feel you "stopped loving Bill," they feel you stopped loving them too, no matter about you're around once a week lip service. You'll never find another man to love you more than Bill and can date and chase and flirt for the next 40 years—you had it all—if you'd tried, could really work at it, and find something besides the "Teen"ish Rainbows you're now hunting. You'll find Emptiness at the rate you're going.
>
> I wish you did visit a church—maybe God's grace could illuminate your soul and wrench you to your senses. Only God can. I am totally ashamed that you can do just what you hated in your father and when you were the same age! I love you and always will, but I am ashamed of you. I've done much to be ashamed, but I would die, before I didn't have loyalty to my family.

May God find you, his "little lost sheep," and reunite you with your "lost lambs"—and with a Miracle I pray you, Bill and children have a Blessed Happy New Year!

All my love,

Mother

I knew Mom was reliving her pain from what Dad had done to us. What I was doing was unconscionable to her.

I did go out with Bill again. We made a date and went out dancing. When he picked me up, he looked dashing in his mint green button-down shirt and khaki pants.

"It's amazing what depression does to you, isn't it," he said with a laugh after I commented on his weight loss.

We danced to "You Look Wonderful Tonight" by Eric Clapton. He whispered in my ear, "... you just don't realize how much I love you." Tears dripped from my eyes and smudged his new shirt. I knew he'd bought it special for this occasion.

"Go back to your ACOA meetings if it will help rid you of your demons," he said as he pulled back and gazed at me through glistening eyes.

"Let's just try and enjoy this night, Bill. Maybe then we can see where it takes us," I said. But I knew in my gut I wasn't going back. My inner demons were too powerful to fight.

One evening, I dropped the kids off at Bill's and hung around to tuck them in to bed.

"I'm not lettin' you go," Timothy said as his little arms clung tightly around my neck. It was all I could do not to collapse in his arms. How could I be doing this to my precious little boy? I could hear Mom's sanctimonious words rushing into my head: "I am totally ashamed of you!" I wanted to shout her out of my head. *Stop! Don't you know that I am totally ashamed of me too?*

I leaned in closer as Tim clung to my neck so he wouldn't know I was crying. I glanced at the blue-and-white *Sesame Street* curtains I made for his room back when I was the good domestic mom. The monkey picture I had cross-stitched for him was lovingly perched on the nightstand beside his bed.

Once I could pull away from Tim's little arms, I stood up, wiped my face, and took Heather, who was reaching for me from Bill's arms with pleading sobs not to go away. I took her to her bed and went through a similar scene. I assured her I would be back, but this was the hardest thing I had ever done. Why couldn't I just stop?

Part of me wanted to come back home and be the mother I knew I could be, but the other selfish, self-absorbed part of me wanted to go have fun with other men. My life here had become drab and dull. I was twenty-seven years old with two children.

I couldn't face my own demons. I was fiercely afraid of loving anything as much as I loved my children, and all I knew how to do was run. After so many years watching Mom run away from the reality that Dad abandoned us, here I was doing the exact same thing. I needed to run away and stop hurting. I needed to stuff my emotions into my fortress of fear and self-loathing. I dredged up some mysterious strength like a coat of armor. Otherwise, I would have fallen apart if I'd let myself feel the pain.

I went to counseling and even attended a couple weeklong sessions called Values Realization—Getting Unstuck with the hope of finding solace—or maybe myself.

I felt as if I was caught in a riptide, fighting to get my bearings and to get air into my lungs. I just couldn't pull myself from the water I was drowning in.

The next time I came to drop off the kids, I ran upstairs to look at something Tim wanted to show me in his room. Something made me enter Bill's bedroom—the room we used to share. When I spotted a gold woman's watch on the bedside table, I went ballistic and ran down the stairs to the kitchen as fast as my adrenaline-pumped legs could carry me.

"You're sleeping with someone?" I yelled, not caring that the kids were within earshot. "Whose is this?" I asked, waving the watch.

"Are you serious? First of all, stop yelling when the kids are around, and second, how dare you be upset. Whadjya think—I would become a monk once you left me?"

"How dare you have another woman in this house and around my kids," I said as I tore the watch into pieces with my hands. Bill tried to grab it from my hands but the damage was done.

"Stop . . . raising . . . your voice. You know I hate it when you do that. Just because you came from a household of screamers does not mean it's okay," he said in an annoyingly calm tone. I wanted to make him fight with me. I felt rushes of Mom's antics flowing through me as I screamed at him in the kitchen, not caring who would hear me.

"Calm down. You have no rights here anymore. You're the one who left us. Remember that?" he said as he gripped the back of a kitchen chair. I looked over and saw that Timothy was standing in the doorway, and I rushed to him.

"I'm so sorry, Bunk. It's okay. Daddy and I are just arguing. Go take care of your sister, and I'll come kiss you both goodbye in a minute," I said as I desperately fought off my unwarranted anger. I knew I had no right to be upset since I, too, was dating. He was bound to find someone else, but I just didn't expect him to start dating quite so soon, and I left feeling heartbroken over it.

I met Rob later that year. It was by far the most pernicious relationship I'd ever had. I was like a junkie, and Rob was my drug. I was completely and utterly obsessed with him and his dark menacing looks. Beth hated him and referred to him as Blob because she thought it fit his lackluster personality—and it did.

My new motto was: Try everything once—twice if you like it! And I did. Even though I was obsessed with Rob, I hooked up with college guys, dabbled in a *ménage à trois*, posed nude for an artist for fifty bucks because I was broke; I even had a fling with one of my college professors.

By the time I pulled myself away from the degradation I was wallowing in, a year and a half had gone by. I was renting a house with Beth and her son, Aaron. Beth and Jon had split up around the same time as Bill and me. With roles reversed, I had become the stereotypical "weekend dad," or mom, as it were.

I was out sunning on a private beach in Watch Hill, Rhode Island, one weekend. Rob was a contractor and had been working in a lavish mansion on the ocean, so I had the beach to myself for most of the summer. I was expecting Rob to join me, but instead, his buddy Stu showed up and informed me that Rob wouldn't be making it because he'd been arrested after starting a brawl at a wet T-shirt contest. That was the proverbial straw for me. I packed up my towel and went home.

I plunked myself down beside Beth who was lounging on the couch. "Have you ever just done something and not known why you were doing it?" I asked. "I don't even know, Beth," I sobbed. "I just don't know how I can keep doing this. What the hell is wrong with me, anyway?"

"Maybe you should try going to counseling?"

"I can't afford that," I said. "How the hell am I going to afford that on my measly salary?"

"I don't know, Dorth, but I think you should look into it and start trying to figure out your issues around men. Obviously, we both know it has something to do with Dad, but you're the only one who can fix it, and you need help. I know I have my own issues with Lou, but at least Aaron is living with me and not with Jon." Lou was the man Beth had been dating who was never fully available to her.

"Oh, thanks for that. Always a bright ray of sunshine when I need it most," I said.

"Speaking of Dad, did you know he still keeps in touch with John and Paula?" Beth asked.

"Are you kidding?" I said, lifting my head from the couch pillow. "I knew he kept in touch with them way back when, after we met him, but I guess I never asked. I don't really care," I lied. "Hmmm, guess we just don't rate, huh?" I added.

Beth was looking off in the distance. "Yup!" she said. "Asshole is living out in Carmel, California, with his new family. Guess they own some frozen yogurt shop out on the beach somewhere," she added.

"Carmel? Isn't that a real swanky place in Orange County or something?" I asked.

"Actually, it's a little north of there, I think, but swanky nonetheless—and on the ocean—'magine that! Mom would be furious!" she said. "I guess sister Lisa is thinking of law school, or going to law school . . . or whatever," she said with her pinkie waggling. "Must be nice to have someone actually pay for that crap, unlike the rest of us, paying off school loans. I heard Brian is really pissed about it," she said.

"Well, so am I. I know it's not Lisa's fault, but it's not fucking fair that we got the shit end of the stick!" I said as I got up off the couch and marched to my empty room upstairs.

Ultimately, I was finally able to extricate myself from the toxic mire I was drowning in with Rob. But the next puddle was right around the corner.

[top] Back: Beth and her husband, Jim, Ann, Tom, Terri, Mom, Michael, Harold, Vinnie (my college boyfriend I lived with in Maine); front: the youngest group of Mom's grandchildren including Timothy and Heather.

[bottom] Vinnie building a snowman with the kids outside our house on Higgins Beach, Maine.

PART V

FORGIVING HEARTS

(Healing Begins)

[top] Reunion, July 1992: "We stood in age order, all of our arms interlinked, first Michael, who stood grimacing with his hands in his pocket, then Ann, Paula, Beth, and me. I leaned into Mom's shoulder. Mom stood next to Dad with one arm behind me and the other hanging by her side while Dad carefully placed one hand on Mom's back. I wondered what was going on in her head. She looked stiff and had a forced smile, but her eyes spoke volumes in that picture: decades of anguish mixed with an undying love for a man who had been absent for so many years, years of pent-up emotions and unspoken words teetered on the brink, threatening to overflow, but they never did."

[bottom left] Dad and Mom, both looking a little uncomfortable.

[bottom right] Beth and I pose for a special photo.

CHAPTER SEVENTEEN

A Gold-Covered Rose

My communications/graphic design degree required that I do a full-time internship. I chose a print shop up in Portland, Maine, for my final semester in 1990. Since it was a non-paying internship, I also had to take on two other part-time jobs just to make rent. I was living on Higgins Beach in Scarborough, Maine, with my latest bad boy named Vinnie whom I'd met in a class called Caribbean Culture the semester before. Mom refused to come to our home since we were living in sin. Beth was the only one of my family to visit me the entire three plus years I lived in Maine.

I drove down to pick up the kids every other weekend and would either stay at Beth's with them or drive them back and return them to Bill on Sunday, which made for an awfully long weekend of driving. Those long drives were when the three of us shared our most intimate thoughts and fears with one another. They were when we sang silly songs together and laughed and played games and cried.

Driving in a car became our safe place, where they had me all to themselves with no Vinnie, or Ric, or Rob, or even Auntie Beth. But always, when I left them, I would cry all the way home.

"You've been leakin' again, haven't you," Vinnie would tease when I got home, which would make me break down all over again. "Why don't you go sit over there with my other blonde bitch and let her cheer you up!" he said, referring to his "blonde" dog Casey. I smiled, but I wasn't in the mood to laugh at his jokes.

"I just hate this, and I hate myself. I can't stand that I'm not there for them every day." But after a few days, I would go back to burying my head in the sand until the next weekend when I went to get them, and it would start all over again.

While the kids and I enjoyed our time on the beach, there was still the underlying current of abandonment that had been so prevalent throughout my life, and which I unwittingly passed along to my own kids.

I hadn't seen Dad for fifteen years, but he started sending letters, birthday cards, and trinkets at Christmas around the time of my thirtieth birthday. I was angry it took him so long to figure it out. I gave it a try back when I was fifteen, but I never understood how he'd had the audacity to disappear again. I knew I needed to forgive Dad if I ever wanted to move on and forgive myself for having done the same thing to my kids.

About this time, I read something that got me thinking about why I kept repeating my mistakes:

> The subconscious mind is the automatic mind that repeats our acquired conscious experiences lest we forget them. Without it we would have to start out everyday like babies. And yet the subconscious memory–mind may be your worst enemy, for it will stimulate your conscious mind to repeat, parrot-like, against your will, your worst habits . . .
>
> So be careful what you choose to do consciously, for unless your will is very strong, that is what you may have to do repeatedly and compellingly through the habit-influencing power of the subconscious mind.
>
> —Paramahansa Yogananda

As I gazed out the window from the floral couch of our furnished beach house, I contemplated what I'd write. Surfers bobbing up and down in the surging water reminded me of the whack-a-mole game you play at the amusement park. The heat rising from the sand emitted a wavy haze as though I were hallucinating. Surfers loved Higgins Beach, and they were out sporting the waves in droves that day. Crooning seagulls, crashing waves, and salt air besieged my senses, evoking the nostalgic feeling of how much Mom loved the beach, which enhanced my fury at Dad. That was all I needed to break the damn of pent-up emotions I'd kept for years, and I began pouring my heart out, page after page.

I told Dad exactly how I felt and how all of us were affected by his leaving in different ways. I wanted him to know that it was unfair that we all had to struggle just to go to college while his other daughter was coddled and sent to the finest schools. It felt good to get it off my chest after so many years.

Beth and her boyfriend Lou came up to visit Vinnie and me one weekend. Later that night when we were settled on the couch with a roaring fire and full glasses of wine, I told Beth about my letter to Dad.

"So I finally wrote to Richard after his lame attempts at communication," I said. I still had a hard time uttering the word "Dad."

"Dorth, it's weird that you call him that," Beth said. I ignored her and continued.

"You should see the latest thing he sent me. It's a gold-covered rose—so tacky! He thinks after no communication for, what, fifteen years now that he can just waltz back in—again! And we are all just supposed to forgive him—again! What is this, step eighteen?"

"Ha! He sent me the same stupid rose, and I think Ann and Paula got one too!" Beth said. "So what'd you say in your letter?"

"I pretty much laid it all out. I did a first vomit draft and even swore at him, but then I went back and cleaned it up. I kept a copy if you ever want to read it," I told her.

"Wow, it must have been sort of healing to write it," Beth said.

"Ya know, it was, but I still think he's a pompous ass!"

"Dorth, you have to let it go." Beth said softly. "You can't be like Ann and hold on to it forever, ya know? At some point you have to just forgive him," she said. "I've been working on forgiveness with him too. It just won't help you to hold onto it, I'm tellin' ya."

Dad's response to my letter was sending us all a thick, spiral-bound packet of his memoirs, telling us everything he'd done both before and after he left, of course skipping the real reason he left because it was too painful for him.

Twenty-seven years and thirteen grandchildren later, Mom was finally getting to see the love of her life who had abandoned us so long ago. She was like a child getting ready for prom, her nervous tension filling the room. Mom was seventy-two and Dad was sixty-eight.

Mom had been talking to Dad on the phone for months. I don't know what prompted the communication, but maybe it was that they were both getting along in years. Dad finally decided he was truly sorry this time and not just making a "step."

Harold supported Mom and encouraged her to speak to Dad since he knew she needed the closure. They made a plan for him to come out for a family reunion, but first Mom had to convince Ann, who was still harboring some anger.

"Ya know what AnnMaria?" Mom said one night when we were all visiting. "I don't think I even like him anymore. He certainly isn't the man I once knew. He's actually a little odd when I talk to him on the phone, but I think he's harmless," she said. Mom finally convinced Ann to at least meet him. Ann told me later that Mom led her to the path of true forgiveness. "If she could forgive him, how could I not?" she said.

I'm sure Mom played it over and over in her mind. What would she wear? What would she say? It was like I had returned to my childhood, watching her primp in front of the same vanity mirror in her dressing room, pursing her lips to apply her lipstick as I had seen her do a thousand times. She wore a floral cotton dress that flared at the waist and stopped just below her knees. One of Ann's friends had made it just for this occasion. Mom stood at her mirror fixing her hair and spouting about how old she looked.

"Mom, you're beautiful," I said. "And who cares what he thinks, anyway?"

"Goldarn it, now look what I've done," she stammered as she tried to wipe a lipstick stain from her dress.

Mom had never colored her hair. It was no longer white-blonde, but had grown mousy. And after years of teasing, it was frizzy and dull, but she did her best to curl it.

Nothing less than perfection was going to satisfy her. I knew how badly she wanted Dad to see her as beautiful, and my heart went out to her. In fact, she had aged quite considerably. After she stopped drinking, Mom lost a lot of weight. She was always afraid of doctors and would never go see one about her bad hip. She hated her cane, but she never let it slow her down. It was as though she was racing from the cane itself as she hobbled quickly through the house, half the time leaving the cane behind in defiance.

When she was finally ready, we made our way over to Ann's house. The meeting was tense. Ann tried to make it as pleasant as she possibly could, given the circumstances.

Tom still refused to speak to our father, but he knew that Ann needed to make amends with him since she had not seen him since 1964. So he made himself scarce that day by going over to hang out with Harold.

Dad had been calling me about once a month after I sent my letter, and we made terse small talk. But on this day, I was more concerned about Mom. This was Mom's day, and we all knew it. As Mom always said, "Judge not, lest ye be judged," and I was certainly no angel. We decided not to include the grandchildren for this first visit since it was more about us at this point. All the kids were relieved since they all thought of Harold as their true grandfather.

Ann set up her back yard with a circle of chairs for our barbeque. Mom barely spoke and was on her best behavior as she sat poised and ladylike, smiling nervously.

Although I didn't know Dad, I could tell he was nervous too. His thinning gray hair was still pulled tightly into a skimpy ponytail. And he was thinner than I remembered. He told me in one of his letters that he was trying to eat only organic food and stay healthy. He sent me countless recipes to encourage me to do the same, not knowing I already did eat healthy.

Mom told me inside how stupid she thought his ponytail was and that he looked completely ridiculous.

"Not to mention that ugly scraggly beard he's sporting—must think he's still in his thirties," she said as she grabbed the bowl of potato salad from the counter and hobbled out the door. Once she was outside she was all smiles and nice again. I knew Mom was also struggling with her inner demons.

Dad tried to make small talk with us.

"So, Dorothy, how's your bicycle-riding going?"

"It's good. I have another weeklong trip planned later this summer for the Diabetes Association. Would you like to sponsor me?" I asked.

"Why sure, sure. Just send me the info," he said. I knew I never would.

It took me many years before I could finally call Dad, "Dad," but on this day, I just avoided calling him anything at all lest it sound too disrespectful. I knew Mom wouldn't like it if she heard me call him Richard, and that was all that mattered to me.

Mom hated to have her picture taken once she started showing signs of age; we have countless pictures of her with her hand in front of her face. "Put that away. You know I don't like having my picture taken. I'm so ugly," she would sputter.

But that day she allowed pictures to be taken, and she proudly stood in line with all of us. John and Brian were not present since they lived so far away. I knew Brian had been in touch with Dad out in California, and he told me they had a rocky and tumultuous relationship at best.

Brian had a love–hate relationship with Dad his entire life. Michael never talked about his feelings at all, so none of us knew how he felt, but the perturbed look on his face in the picture we took that day told enough.

We stood in age order, all of our arms interlinked, first Michael, who stood grimacing with his hands in his pocket, then Ann, Paula, Beth, and me. I leaned into Mom's shoulder. Mom stood next to Dad with one arm behind me and the other hanging by her side while Dad carefully placed one hand on Mom's back. I wondered what was going on in her head. She looked stiff and had a forced smile, but her eyes spoke volumes in that picture: decades of anguish mixed with an undying love for a man who had been absent for so many years, years of pent-up emotions and unspoken words teetered on the brink, threatening to overflow, but they never did.

[above left] In 1993 I climbed the Kancamagus Pass in the White Mountains of New Hampshire as part of my Diabetes 500-Mile bike ride just before Mom passed.

[above right] Mom grew to hate having her picture taken as she got older and would always cover her face when a camera was aimed her way; hence, it became a "thing" for our family.

[left] Mom and Harold looking very happy in this picture taken around 1992.

CHAPTER EIGHTEEN

Panty Hose

On a hot summer day in July 1993, I rode with vigor as I raced into the final stretch of my weeklong 500-mile bicycle tour around New England for the American Diabetes Association.

A hazy glow of heat rose from the pavement as I stood on my pedals to pump up the last hill. I knew I only had five miles to go when I noticed a stream to my right. The sun danced and sparkled on the surface, beckoning me as water always did on these trips. I called to my friend Tom who was riding ahead to pull over for a final dip in the cool water.

When I remember that day, it's always warm and wonderful; the vast sky stretched out to infinity with puffy clouds gleaming overhead and tires whirring along the road for mile after mile, my heart still in one piece. A melodic chorus of birds sang off in the distance as I dipped my head into the water. But soon this would all be a fog, a distant memory that might never have happened, or was in slow motion as if I watched from another self.

Soon I would check my answering machine and hear the tremulous voice of my brother-in-law Tom, telling me to call him back at Mom's number. I knew instantly and with panic rising in me like a swelling sea. I dialed, and then I heard Mom's voice crooning the number we'd always had—RE4-5335. It seemed an eternity before I heard the words I could not bear to hear: Mom was gone.

I hung up the phone. A buzzing din of voices from some faraway place lingered. I walked—or floated—down the stairs. My friend Tom drove me to Springfield. From the passenger seat of my Mazda MX6, I stared at the triple-stitched hem of my spandex bicycle shorts through a blur of tears that flowed uncontrollably. I don't remember moving. I was transfixed in time, and time swirled around me. Nothing would ever be the same.

It was almost a year to the day after seeing Dad that Mom died peacefully in bed of congestive heart failure. Having lived so many years with a broken heart, it's no wonder it finally gave out on her.

It was the most agonizing blow of my life, but we knew she finally had the closure she had so long yearned for.

Mom was never a perfect mother—far from it. She was melodramatic, overly emotional, and the most obstinate woman I've ever known, but she always loved us with the ferocity of a lioness protecting her cubs. We criticized her constantly about forgiving too easily, thinking she always got taken advantage of, yet her lesson of forgiveness rubbed off, and none of us had any animosity toward her for the years when she was lost. She redeemed herself many times over with a heart so big and full of love. Anyone who knew her could attest to that.

Mom's pallbearers were two of Beth's exes and two of my exes, including Bill and Jay, who'd stolen my virtue so long ago, illustrating once again the forgiving nature Mom had bestowed upon the world.

Jay wrote and read the eulogy at the service:

> How do you describe in mere words what took a lifetime to achieve? The life of Elizabeth Franklin was certainly an achievement, and no words will do her justice.
>
> We all need to search inside ourselves for what she meant to us and for how she touched our lives. Wife, mother, grandmother, confidant, and friend. She was all of those and more.
>
> She had a zest for life that affected everyone who ever met her, and she lived life to the fullest. Nothing slowed her down, though many times there were trials and tribulations that to an ordinary person would have seemed insurmountable. But this was no ordinary woman. She overcame the obstacles that life sent her way. She held her family together through the good times and the bad. And what a family!
>
> Her husband, her children, and her grandchildren all a testament to the selfless, giving, loving person that she was.
>
> What Liz wanted to do, she did. Where she wanted to go, she went. It didn't matter if it was snowing, sleeting, or whatever. If she wanted to get in her car to go visit one of her kids, she did it.
>
> I remember Harold telling me more than once, "I wish she wouldn't go rushing off by herself and drive all that way, but I can't stop her."
>
> Nobody could stop her. She did what she wanted and she'd do anything within her powers to help someone in need. She gave so much of herself in everything she did.
>
> Liz was a fighter; she never gave up on anything. She saw things through to the end no matter what it took to get there. She was a joy to be with and to talk to. You could never have a dull conversation

> with her no matter what the topic. Her wit and her wisdom made any subject a lively one.
>
> As we prepare to say goodbye, we know that we'll remember her, each in our own special way. We all have our own personal memories that will stay with us always. There are stories that will be told again and again. Her legacy lives on.

We all puddled and huddled in the front pews of St. Joseph's Church as Jay read.

Father Tourigny was the pastor who conducted the service that day. He was the brother of the schoolmate I used to pass notes to about the white picket fence. After the service he came to Mom's house, and when Ann saw the footsteps pin he wore on his lapel, she broke down.

"Mom always hated shoes," she said as she gently touched his pin. I still remember the pain on her face as she stood there in Father Tourigny's loving arms sobbing her heart out.

I'm told that Dad came to the funeral, although I have no recollection of that. I mostly remember sitting in a fog of grief with my daughter, Heather, protectively by my side while people drifted in and out.

So many people from our past showed up out of the woodwork, including the Russos, the Napolitans, Kevin, some of the old Circle Gang, Teddy and Angie, and many old renters and friends, including many who were on that epic bike ride with me. The church pews were full that day. Mom was truly loved!

We never knew why, but for some reason Mom died wearing pantyhose under her nightgown. Perhaps she would have preferred her old sleek silk stockings, but the pantyhose were all she had, and Mom always went out in style.

[top] Dad married Norma in 1994 in Las Vegas. I'm on the far left, then Ann, Dad, Norma, and Brian.

[bottom left] Brian and his beautiful wife, Ruth, at their California home after Dad's wedding.

[bottom right] This photo of me was taken at the Mirage Hotel where we stayed in Las Vegas.

CHAPTER NINETEEN

Days of Yore

With Harold still living in the house, Michael took it over after Mom died. He demolished the entire third floor and stripped out the pecky cypress wood. He also tore down Mrs. Page's beautiful mural. We were all saddened and upset with him because it had been so precious to Mom. Michael's taste did not match the Victorian style of the house; he preferred new and modern. For many of us, it was a shame to see so many things destroyed in the name of "renovating," but to him, each change was an improvement. To his credit, he did improve many things and sank many dollars into the rehab with absolutely no return when he finally sold the house in 2012.

Mom's will instructed us to "draw straws" for all the pieces that remained in the house. She did not want any of us fighting over things like she did with her siblings.

We stayed in touch with Dad who got remarried nine months after Mom died to his third wife, Norma. Dad invited Ann, Brian, and me to attend his tacky Las Vegas wedding. I begrudgingly went—it was a free vacation—and Dad even sprang for two rolls of quarters so Ann and I could play the slots at the Mirage where we were staying.

The song by the Tubes, "What Do You Want from Life," comes to mind—in which they mention a Las Vegas wedding and a Mexican divorce. Dad must have heard it too.

We had another family reunion in Arizona on Dad's eightieth birthday, the first time in years all seven of us siblings were together in one place.

Dad had many patents and was plenty wealthy, living in his gated multi-million-dollar home in Sun City, Arizona. He told us he set up insurance policies as well as a trust fund from which we'd all get at least $10,000 after he died. How could Dad have known that Norma would steal it all and give it to her own daughter, Malba, who was not only not a blood relative but also not owed a lifetime of back child support? Norma even rearranged the trust so that most of us only received $4,000, and some nothing at all. There was nothing we could do to fight it, and Malba changed her phone number and conveniently disappeared after her mother died, taking Dad's hard-earned money that was rightfully ours.

I was furious, but also exhausted. Brian tried to sway Paula, who was Dad's executor, to do something about Norma's theft. To her credit, she did contact a lawyer, including our half-sister Lisa, who also got robbed, for advice, but ultimately, nothing came of it. I envision Malba living high and mighty on Dad's money, sipping a piña colada with a smug look on her face.

After Mom died, Michael began hosting Thanksgiving dinners at the house every year. I loved how hard he tried to keep us united as a family, and I know we were the reason he held onto the house as long as he did. It was for us and for Mom. Maybe the house hijacked Michael, too, since he kept it so long.

That first Thanksgiving, everyone but Brian was present. In addition to the six of us, Mom's thirteen grandchildren were there as well as Harold's and Terri's families.

Michael rented tables, chairs, dishes, and utensils for the occasion. The tables spanned from the dining room into the living room. When I entered the house, there was a palpable difference resulting from the lack of Mom's presence. The aroma from the turkey that Mom cooked through the night was conspicuously absent. Did Michael rent the turkey too? I discovered later that in fact he did have it brought in.

Somehow everything seemed foreign and out of place. I walked around the house in a daze as we waited for dinner. Some magnetic pull drew me to Mom's room where nothing had changed yet. I ran my hand across one of her pillows and drew it to me as I took in the waning scent of Mom I imagined was there. I had taken the pillow she slept on the night she died months before and slept with it every night. For the life of me, I have no recollection of when I was finally able to wash that pillowcase, drinking in her lingering scent night after night.

On the bedroom's back wall stood an antique mahogany credenza with ornate carvings of faces. I noticed the framed picture of Mom and Dad in their late thirties. Had it been there all these years? The bottom cupboard of this magical cabinet was stuffed with school papers and drawings that we kids gave Mom over the years. Ann eventually went through them and distributed them to each of us. I didn't look in my packet until I started writing this book. I found the shoe drawing with the yellow yarn-hair I had drawn while Paula and Gary smooched on the bed beside me. There were poems and countless silly notes I had written to Mom. Also, tucked beneath some of the papers, was the second letter from Bob Bopp.

The top portion of the credenza had a glass door with a key where Mom kept most of her nicer jewelry. I used to pretend I could shrink myself and go live in that cabinet with all the glamorous jewels.

I opened the door and was overwhelmed with throat clenching

nostalgia as the scent of Tabu perfume and lipstick—the same smell Mom's purse emitted in her glamor days—nearly knocked me over. And there, prominently perched in the center was the creaky ring box Beth and I named Chopper, later dubbed as a silly nickname for Mom because we thought it was cute.

My eyes could no longer hold the brimming tears, and I picked up the picture of Mom and Dad and placed it in my bag. The picture sits to this day on my own credenza, reminding me always to live with hope and deep love as Mom did—even against all odds.

Before dinner, we all sat around the living room reminiscing and telling stories about Mom. Paula talked in a stream of reverie as we listened and sometimes laughed. "Like when we went to Minnesota and Dorth got left behind. Or when Ann and I cut Dorth's bangs at Uncle Herb's house! Or the fact she left with four girls in a junk car to drive to Minnesota at all! When she slept and thought she was being attacked and bit her own arm and gave herself a huge bruise! When she brushed her teeth with Desitin and sprayed her hair with powder deodorant instead of hairspray! When every time you had to go somewhere we had to search all over for her purse, glasses, shoes."

"Oh my God, she used to drive me crazy with that! Sometimes it would take hours to find her stupid purse," Beth interjected.

"I loved it when she hummed to herself with her cute little-girl look. She loved ice cream and her one cup of coffee in the morning."

"Yeah, that we always had to make for her," I laughed. Paula looked like she was going to cry, but she kept talking as she held her daughter Melissa close.

"I loved the way I could weasel a school skip-day if I promised to bring her coffee and grapefruit in bed. I loved watching morning movies with her—the old classics. It was great! I loved to go for rides and get lost because she was never afraid and thought she or we could just bat our eyelashes at someone for help! Oh! Oh! How 'bout when she ditched the car in the ravine when she was trying to outrun the cops 'cause she didn't have an active license? Or would talk the cop to death to get outta giving him a license? When she would use the story of her seven children for help," Paula said, winding down.

Ann picked up where Paula left off. "Remember when Mom came to help each of us when we had our babies? She worked so hard to make all of our Christmases special, in spite of the pain she had from the desertion," Ann said. "Can't even imagine how hard it must have been raising seven children. My two are plenty for me!" she added.

"Yup, she came to stay and help after Pamela was born," Paula added and continued. "She even drove her to the post office so I could nurse her on my break! I loved how she loved all dogs and animals. I would catch her rubbing the cat with her foot in the middle of the night! Her clumsiness . . . her feistiness . . . her gall . . . her love of vocabulary . . . her love of a party . . . her love for us and people in general and wanting to help everyone. She never made any money renting rooms; they were just more expense! Late nights rocking on the screened-in porch were my favorite. I miss her and our family gatherings at the big house!" Paula finished, as she wiped the streaming tears from her face.

"Do you remember the movie night when our kids were little, and we broke out the home movies and watched them just before John and Jan left for Italy?" Ann said. "How wonderful that was—the kids thought they were looking at themselves."

"How 'bout the water fights we had?" Beth said.

"We were sooo bad!" Ann said. "Squirting hoses through the kitchen window and flooding her kitchen. She sputtered but never yelled. I would have killed my kids—she didn't—and we did that a lot!" she added.

"Mother and Dad used to have Kriegspeil parties in the Idaho Falls house when I was little," John said. "Bet none of you even know what that is."

"Well ya got me stumped," Ann said.

"Kriegspeil is basically a blind chess game, and you had to be pretty smart to play. Mother was certainly no dummy," he laughed. "She was one hell of a lady."

Then there was Michael's story, one I hadn't heard before since it happened only a few months before Mom died.

"I had a dumpster on the side of the house for the renovations I was doing, and one day I came home and saw something fly out from it as I pulled in to the driveway. I figured some bum was in there looking for cans or somethin', but when I went over to investigate, I saw Mom's cane leaning up against the side like in dat movie dere, ya know—*Miracle on 34th Street*—only Santa wasn't the one in the dumpster. Sure enough, I looked over the edge and there she was digging through all of her 'treasures,'" he said, mimicking her voice. "And complaining that I had the nerve to throw them out."

We all laughed, knowing it was just like her to jump into a dumpster and not care what anyone thought of her. She was like that for her whole life. She was a rebel and a nonconformist. The story brought back the memory of when she dug through the trash bag that Kevin and I had filled so many years earlier. Some things never change, I mused fondly.

Harold sat by and listened to our stories. I saw the tears welling up in his eyes, and I moved over next him and laid my head on his shoulder. He just patted my head. We didn't need words.

Afterward, I instinctively made my way to my usual seat at the dining table, but one of Terri's family members was sitting there. How could they have known it was my childhood seat? Mildly irritated, I made my way back to the kiddie table in the living room to sit with my kids and nieces and nephews. Harold was not sitting where Mom always sat at the head. Instead, Michael was there directly across from me.

There was a brief knowing look between Michael and me. For an instant I imagined I saw Mom sitting right behind him on her spot on the radiator where she emoted over Dad my entire life, only now she was smiling.

Remains of a shipwreck on Higgins Beach in Maine.

Epilogue

I was still living in Maine when Mom died. Vinnie stuck around until after the funeral and then took his leave and moved back to Boston, leaving me alone.

I picked up a part-time seasonal job with L. L. Bean in the evenings after driving eighty miles one way from my day job at Colby College. I wandered the beaches, I meditated, and I rode my bike for miles on the weekends. I dove into my Ninjutsu classes. I joined a Shaman apprentice group with the hopes of becoming more spiritual and letting go of guilt. I wrote incessantly in my journals, and they became therapy for me.

I knew I had to get back to my children, so I found a job back in Massachusetts, and eventually they moved in with me and I enjoyed their high-school years.

It wasn't building blocks and *Sesame Street*—I missed so much of that—but it was soccer games, cheerleading, gymnastics, and field hockey. And what's so wrong with that?

I ran from conflict, raised voices, relationships, circumstances that haunted me, and, yes, from my children; I learned that from Mom. But Mom wasn't running from something like I was. She was running after something: the elusive memory of what glued her together in the first place—the memory of Dad.

I've written countless letters over the years to both of my children in a lame attempt to apologize and explain. Although I can do both endlessly and forevermore, it will never remove or alleviate the pain and suffering that my actions caused. But we're all survivors, and we've all overcome and learned to forgive. And isn't that what it's all about?

[top] Ann, Michael, me, John, Paula, and Beth at Paula's son's wedding in 2005. Ann's arm is out, pretending our missing sibling, Brian, is next to her.

[bottom left] Mom at Christmas. A rare moment of her not covering her face and looking much like a gleeful child. She loved Christmas so much!

[bottom right] Beth and I sharing a close sister moment.

[top] Ski trip to Sugarloaf with Heather and Timothy and a few of their friends in the late 1990s. My daughter, Heather, is on the left.

[bottom] Timothy, Heather, and I on the day we dropped Heather off at Syracuse University.

About the Author

Dorothy Preston has a degree in communications/media and has worked in the publishing industry for over twenty years, including at Prentice Hall/Simon & Schuster, Houghton Mifflin, and Little Brown, to name a few. She has lived in Maine, New Hampshire, and New York, but is currently settled in her native state of Massachusetts in Johnny Appleseed country just outside of Boston. She and her husband recently purchased land in Downeast Maine, and are planning on settling there in the next few years.

If Preston is not hiking, cycling, running, or skiing, she's taking in the aroma of apples and tapping away on her computer at her house on the hill with her dog, Rylee. It is her hope that by sharing her journey with those who have gone through similar ordeals, others might learn that forgiveness truly is divine and along with it comes peace.

CPSIA information can be obtained
at www.ICGtesting.com
Printed in the USA
BVHW020323060921
616150BV00019B/527